ollege
D0896126

3rd Edition | Completely Revised and Updated

Patrick W. Miller, Ph.D.

GRANT WRITING

Strategies for Developing Winning Government Proposals

Grant Writing: Strategies for Developing Winning Government Proposals, Third Edition

Copyright © 2000, 2002, 2009 by Patrick W. Miller. Printed in the United States of America. No part of this book may be used or reproduced in any manner whatsoever without written permission from Patrick W. Miller and Associates except in the case of brief quotations embodied in critical articles and reviews. For additional information, please contact Patrick W. Miller and Associates at www.grantwritingpro.com.

Patrick W. Miller, all rights reserved.
Library of Congress Control Number: 2007910282
ISBN 978-0-9673279-3-8

Printed in the United States of America

10 9 8 7 6 5 4 3 2 1

Patrick W. Miller and Associates
Munster, Indiana 46321
www.grantwritingpro.com

Preface

Grant competitions are rigorous. Each day more and more organizations compete for the same external dollars. Some institutions view grants as icing on the cake, while others see grants as essential to maintain and improve programs. Many institutions, however, are not prepared to respond to grant solicitations. They often lack understanding about the government agency's rules and regulations, knowledgeable and prepared staff members with formal training in grant writing, and supportive upper administration. In these situations, the typical grant proposal seldom wins funding because it is an unorganized response to a solicitation.

Winning grant applications identify good project ideas that offer solutions to a problem, use clear writing to describe projects, and identify reasonable project expenditures. Grant writers must have a thorough understanding of the subject matter, as well as the time and commitment to develop a successful proposal.

Grant Writing: Strategies for Developing Winning Government Proposals, Third Edition is designed to introduce funding seekers to the fundamental aspects of grant writing. Chapter 1 provides a brief overview of government and non-government funding sources. Chapter 2 provides a summary of the strategies needed to prepare winning grant applications. Chapters 3–8 provide an in-depth look at the six fundamental phases of proposal development:

- Complete work before the RFP/RFA is released.
- Conduct prewriting activities after the RFP/RFA is released.
- Write, review, rewrite, and edit the proposal narrative.
- Prepare, review, and revise the proposal budget.
- Produce, assemble, and submit the grant application.
- Perform postsubmission activities.

Funding seekers should carefully review the suggested strategies presented in this book and use the information that best fits their particular situation. This book includes more than 100 examples of winning grant proposal ideas. Summaries, review questions, and exercises are presented at the end of each chapter to reinforce learning. Exercises in this book were developed to teach proposal writing and budget development skills to new and experienced grant writers. A glossary of key terms, list of resources, and comprehensive review questions and exercises are at the end of the book.

About the Author

Patrick W. Miller, Ph.D., has worked as a grant writer, grant facilitator, proposal manager and contracts administrator, and director of grants and contracts. He has served as national grant reviewer and panel leader for the U.S. Department of Education. In addition, Dr. Miller has been a grant and project consultant to school districts and a mentor to college and university faculty and staff on developing effective methods for completion and submission of government grant applications.

Dr. Miller has been a university professor and academic administrator teaching professional and technical courses, advising graduate and undergraduate students, and serving on numerous departmental, college, and university committees. He has written more than 100 articles in professional journals and authored five books.

Dr. Miller frequently speaks about grant writing at conferences for professional associations. He teaches grant writing classes to faculty and graduate students at several universities and conducts proposal development workshops throughout the United States for members of nonprofit organizations. For more information, please visit www.grantwritingpro.com.

Patrick W. Miller is listed in *Who's Who in American Education, Who's Who in America,* and *Who's Who in the World.* Dr. Miller holds a Ph.D. in Education from Ohio State University, as well as a master's certificate in Government Contracting from the George Washington University School of Business and Public Management.

Acknowledgments

Many friends have helped me formulate my methods for developing successful grant proposals that win funding. Discussions with Robert Stanton provided valuable insight into understanding the complexity of the proposal development process. Richard Kulka taught me the significance of paying attention to details. Michael Kwit gave me an appreciation for clear and accurate budgets. Cat Auer, Susan Erfurth, and Francie Margolin taught me the importance of editing for style. I thank them all for sharing their professional expertise.

A number of people read the manuscript for this book and offered encouragement and helpful suggestions. I thank Jim Skaine, Jon Duff, Marshal Chaifetz, and, especially, Pat Owens.

Many thanks to my daughters Joy and Tatum for their design work, which greatly improved the appearance of this book and my website.

Table of Contents

Chapter 4
Conduct Prewriting Activities After the RFP/RFA Is Released 71

Chapter 5

Write, Review, Rewrite, and Edit the Proposal Narrative 97

Chapter 8

List of Exhibits

Chapter 4

Conduct Prewriting Activities After the RFP/RFA Is Released 71

Chapter 5

Write, Review, Rewrite, and Edit the Proposal Narrative 97

Chapter 6
Prepare, Review, and Revise the Proposal Budget 137

Chapter 7
Produce, Assemble, and Submit the Grant Application..............................163

Chapter 8

Perform Postsubmission Activities..181

For my beloved wife and best friend, Jean—
who has always stood by me and supported my dreams

Chapter 1

Government and Non-Government Funding

With increased competition for external dollars, funding seekers are looking at both traditional and nontraditional opportunities of financial support from government (federal or state agencies) and non-government (individuals, corporations, or philanthropic foundations) sources. Government agencies awarded more than $450 billion in 2007,[1] and non-government charitable donors gave more than $295 billion in 2006.[2] Although this book is written for grant writers, funding seekers applying for other forms of government and non-government funding can use many of the same principles and strategies.

Government Funding

Government funding is provided through (1) grants, (2) cooperative agreements, and (3) procurement contracts. Grants and cooperative agreements are classified as *assistance agreements* that provide financial support to funding seekers who want to complete projects that directly relate to a government agency's mission. Procurement contracts acquire property, services, or products for government use.

Grants

Government grants transfer money, property, or services to eligible recipients in order to accomplish a public purpose where no substantial involvement is anticipated between the funding agency and recipient during the performance period. Government grants come from federal (e.g., National Institutes of Health) and state (e.g., Minnesota Department of Education) agencies where funding seekers prepare proposals in response to government solicitations.

Government grants are grouped into the two broad categories of (1) discretionary and (2) mandatory, entitlement, or formula. *Discretionary grants* are competitive grant opportunities wherein the government agency has the authority to determine the award amount and recipients. With discretionary grants, award decisions are based on how well applicants respond to solicitation criteria. Government agencies allow funding seekers the opportunity to indicate what will be done and how funds will be spent in response to specific criteria.

---

[1] DHHS. (2007). *Grants.gov/Annual Report for Fiscal Year 2007*. Washington, DC: Department of Health and Human Services.

[2] Giving USA. (2007). *2007 Yearbook of Philanthropy*. Glenview, IL: Giving USA Foundation.

Most small discretionary grants (worth less than $250,000) are for one year, while large discretionary grants (worth more than $250,000) are for multiple years. Continued funding may be awarded to recipients after the initial year of a multi-year grant if applicants meet the agency's terms and conditions specified in the grant award notification. Funding is not automatic, and agencies may impose terms and conditions that must be met before additional funding is awarded.

Mandatory, entitlement, or formula grants are general revenue or federal pass-through funds allocated by state agencies to institutions and organizations based on predetermined formulas. State agencies give awards as long as recipients meet statutory and regulatory conditions. Once these conditions are met, state agencies must make awards available. State agencies can refuse to award grant funds only if the grantee fails to comply with requirements under which the entitlement program was established. Mandatory, entitlement, and formula award recipients must develop and submit written project and budget reports periodically throughout the performance period. **See Exhibit 1-1**.

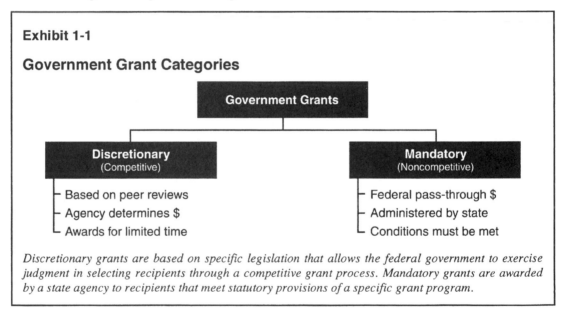

Exhibit 1-1

Government Grant Categories

Discretionary grants are based on specific legislation that allows the federal government to exercise judgment in selecting recipients through a competitive grant process. Mandatory grants are awarded by a state agency to recipients that meet statutory provisions of a specific grant program.

Cooperative Agreements

Cooperative agreements transfer money, property, or services to recipients to accomplish a public purpose where substantial involvement is anticipated between the funding agency and recipient during the performance period. A cooperative agreement is basically a grant with ongoing oversight from the government agency; it involves a partnership-type relationship between the agency staff members and the funding recipient to achieve the goals/objectives of the project. Some programs may combine a cooperative agreement and grant, depending on the complexity of the project and the recipients' ability levels. In other situations, a project may begin as a cooperative agreement and convert to a grant. Cooperative agreements are often used in large clinical research trials.

Grants and cooperative agreements are very similar—the key difference between these two assistance agreements is the concept of substantial involvement. *Substantial involvement* is when government agency staff members provide assistance, guidance, or participation in the management of the project. This participation may include such activities as:

- Assist in selecting and training project staff and/or subcontractors.

- Design, direct, or redirect project activities.

- Review and approve project phases before subsequent phases are started.

- Assist in the collection and analysis of project information.

- Participate in the presentation of results at conferences and in publications.

Grants or cooperative agreements are normally used when the government agency wants to provide assistance for such projects or activities as:

- Services to the general public.
- Training projects where the sponsored recipient selects the trainees and develops the curriculum.
- Publications or multimedia work necessary to complete a sponsored project.
- Research to add to an existing body of knowledge in a specific area and dissemination of the results to the general public.
- Evaluation services to benefit the sponsored project.[3]

The *Federal Register* is the official government publication used by funding seekers to locate information about grant and cooperative agreement solicitations. Experienced funding seekers also use the Internet, various grant newsletters, agency websites, and their university or college office of sponsored programs to locate government funding opportunities. Further details about locating funding opportunities are discussed in Chapter 3.

Procurement Contracts

Procurement contracts acquire property or services for the direct benefit of or use by the federal government. In one of the earliest procurement contracts issued on December 23, 1907, the U.S. Army Board of Ordnance and Fortification published Signal Corps Specification No. 486 for "a heavier-than-air flying machine." On February 28, 1908, the U.S. War Department signed a contract with Wilbur and Orville Wright at 1187 W. Third Street, Dayton, Ohio for $25,000 to manufacture and deliver one flying machine on or before August 28, 1908.[4]

---

[3] Slocum, J.M. (2006). Federal Research Contracts. In E.C. Kulakowski & L.U. Chronister (eds.), *Research Administration and Management* (pp. 325–353). Sudbury, MA: Jones and Bartlett Publishers.

[4] Requirements concerning this contract as well as additional information can be found at http://www.ascho.wpafb.af.mil/birthplace/PG14-1.HTM.

Procurement contracts are grouped into two broad categories: (1) fixed-price contracts and (2) cost-reimbursement contracts. *Fixed-price contracts* are used to procure commercial supplies or services (with detailed specifications) that can be based on reasonably accurate cost estimates and where invoicing is based on deliverables. *Cost-reimbursement contracts* are used to procure noncommercial items or services that cannot be based on reasonably detailed specifications and where invoicing is based on expenditures. Government agencies use cost-reimbursement contracts primarily for basic research and development efforts. Specific contract types range from *firm-fixed-price*, where the funding seeker has full responsibility for the performance costs and resulting profit or loss, to *cost-plus-fixed-fee*, where the funding seeker has minimal responsibility for performance costs and the negotiated fee (profit) is fixed.

Procurement contracts are governed by the *Federal Acquisition Regulations* (FAR). These regulations constitute a system of uniform policies and procedures governing the acquisition of all federal executive agencies. The FAR require that government agencies post all public notices about federal procurement actions greater than $25,000 at *FedBizOpps* (FBO) www.fedbizopps.gov. FBO publishes 500–1,000 synopses each business day. FBO is the single point of electronic public access to search, monitor, and retrieve government-wide procurement opportunities. Potential bidders can also sign up to receive e-mails about pre-solicitation information, notices, and procurement announcements. Questions regarding the site can be directed to support staff by e-mail at fbo.support@gsa.gov or by calling toll free at 1-877-472-3779.

Procurement contracts usually require two separate proposals: (1) a technical proposal (also called a narrative) and (2) a cost proposal. The technical proposal presents a detailed project plan and the cost proposal identifies the specific expenditures for completing the proposed work.

Procurement contracts are normally used when the government agency wants to acquire products or services for government use such as:

- the design or development of specific items;
- professional or technical services;
- training projects, where the government selects the trainers and identifies the content;
- publications or multimedia materials;
- conferences;
- research efforts (e.g., large survey research studies); or
- evaluation of a sponsored program or project.

Assistance Agreements and Procurement Contract Comparison

Assistance agreements provide financial assistance for a public purpose (e.g., funds to help underrepresented students succeed in college). In contrast, procurement contracts are awarded to secure goods or services to meet government needs. For example, the government may issue a procurement contract solicitation to acquire 10,000 widgets for the U.S. Department of Defense. Or, the U.S. Department of Justice may issue a procurement contract to obtain information regarding effective treatment for drug offenders. Assistance agreements allow funding seekers the opportunity to indicate what will be done and how funds will be spent. However, in procurement contracts, funding seekers indicate how specific tasks will be accomplished to provide products or services to the government. Assistance agreements offer multiple awards and upfront payments. Procurement contracts provide one award, and payments are made after expenditures. **See Exhibit 1-2**.

Exhibit 1-2

Analysis of Assistance Agreements and Procurement Contracts

Assistance Agreements (Grants and Cooperative Agreements)	Procurement Contracts
Information listed in the *Federal Register*	Information listed at *FedBizOpps.gov*
Project announcements	Competitive bidding announcements
Provides assistance	Procures property or services
Multiple awards	One award
Idea conceived/initiated by the funding seeker	Idea conceived/initiated by the agency
Funding seeker determines direction	Agency determines direction
Grant recipient may keep equipment	Government may keep equipment
Cost sharing may be required	Cost sharing is not required
Sample proposal sections: (Always follow the solicitation guidelines.) • Abstract • Introduction • Problem/Need • Goals/Objectives • Methods/Activities • Evaluation Plans • Budget • Appendix	Sample proposal sections: (Always follow the solicitation guidelines.) • Executive Summary • Introduction • Statement of Work • Management/Organization/Staffing • Corporate Experience • Facilities and Equipment • Budget (as a separate document) • Appendix
Award contains general conditions	Award contains detailed specifications
Payments made upfront	Payments made after expenditures

Assistance agreements provide assistance to recipients to accomplish a proposed project. Procurement contracts are used to acquire products or services for the government.

Non-Government Funding

Non-government funding is provided through private gifts or grants from individuals, corporations, or foundations. Individual donors and corporations may support global issues, while community foundations may focus on problems and concerns within a specific geographic region. The terminology and interpretation of key terms used by an institutional advancement officer is very different from that used by a sponsored programs administrator. For example, the term "grant" used by an advancement officer may imply a gift, but a sponsored programs administrator would consider a grant a contractual arrangement. According to the Council for Advancement and Support for Education (CASE), a *gift* is a voluntary transfer of property to another made gratuitously and without consideration; a gift may be either restricted or unrestricted. A restricted gift is targeted for a particular use; an unrestricted gift is donated without contingencies.[5] According to Giving USA, total charitable giving in the United States amounted to more than $295 billion in 2006. The majority of giving came from individual donations, which was approximately $223 billion and accounted for about 76% of the estimated giving.[6] Non-government funding has been used to support such initiatives as the national emergency 911 medical services program, the hospice movement, and even the children's program *Sesame Street*. **See Exhibit 1-3**.

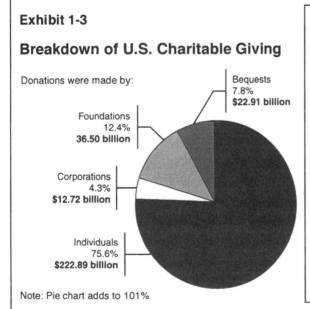

Exhibit 1-3

Breakdown of U.S. Charitable Giving

Donations were made by:

Bequests
7.8%
$22.91 billion

Foundations
12.4%
36.50 billion

Corporations
4.3%
$12.72 billion

Individuals
75.6%
$222.89 billion

Note: Pie chart adds to 101%

The $295.02 billion in donations went to:

- Religion ($96.82 billion)
- Education ($40.98 billion)
- Human services ($29.56 billion)
- Foundations ($29.50 billion)
- Unallocated ($26.08 billion)
- Public-society benefit ($21.41 billion)
- Health ($20.22 billion)
- Arts, culture, and humanities ($12.51 billion)
- International affairs ($11.34 billion)
- Environment/animals ($6.60 billion)

Giving USA (2007). *2007 Yearbook of Philanthropy*. Glenview, IL: Giving USA Foundation.

According to Giving USA 2007, individuals accounted for the majority of all giving in 2006 in the U.S.

[5] Council for the Advancement and Support of Education. (2004). *Management and Reporting Standards for Annual Giving and Campaigns in Educational Fund Raising, 3ᵈ Edition*. Washington, DC: CASE.

[6] Giving USA. (2007). *2007 Yearbook of Philanthropy*. Glenview, IL: Giving USA Foundation.

Government and Non-Government Funding Comparison

A comparison between government and non-government funding indicates considerable differences. In general, government proposals are lengthy and require specific narrative and budget components, while non-government proposals are usually brief and may not require specific components. Peer reviewers evaluate government proposals, while a board of directors reviews non-government proposals. Progress reports are usually required by both funding sources. **See Exhibit 1-4**.

Exhibit 1-4

Analysis of Government and Non-Government Funding

Government (Public) Funding (Assistance Agreements)	Non-Government (Private) Funding
Based on federal government legislation and the specific mission of the agency.	Based on the mission of the philanthropic foundation, organization, or corporation.
Focus is on solving problems.	Focus is on helping people through aid.
More likely to make large awards to support moderate to large projects.	Will provide various amounts of funding to support moderate to large projects.
More likely to pay all project costs and cover indirect costs.	More likely to pay some project costs and less likely to cover indirect costs.
Proposals may be lengthy and require narrative and budget components that follow specific formatting.	Proposals are brief and may not require specific narrative and budget components; some foundations do not accept proposals.
Funding is provided to accomplish a specific purpose explained in the solicitation—a detailed plan of work is required.	Funding may be provided for a general or specific purpose (e.g., AIDS research or adding a new wing to a building).
An agency contact person is identified.	A donor may not be identified.
Procedures are more bureaucratic.	Procedures are less bureaucratic.
Terms and conditions are required.	Terms and conditions may be required.
Proposal deadlines are firm.	Proposal deadlines are flexible.
Information on policies and procedures are relatively easy to find and use.	Information on policies and procedures must be investigated.
Peer reviewers evaluate proposals based on criteria published in the solicitation.	A board of directors may review proposals in relationship to the organization's mission.
Reasons for rejection are usually available but not always given to funding seekers.	Reasons for rejection are usually not provided to funding seekers.
Regular formal progress and expenditure reports are required.	Regular progress and expenditure reports may be required for stewardship purposes.
Funds must be spent within the project period. Unspent funds are returned to the agency.	Funds are typically irrevocable.

Government funding comes from federal and state governments. Non-government funding comes from individual donors, corporations, and philanthropic foundations.

Chapter Summary

External funding comes from government (public) and non-government (private) sources. The U.S. government provides funding in the form of grants, cooperative agreements, and procurement contracts. Non-government funding comes from individuals, corporations, or philanthropic foundations. Although similarities exist among these funding sources, each has a distinct purpose.

Government grants transfer money, property, or services to eligible recipients in order to accomplish a public purpose where no substantial involvement is anticipated between the government agency and recipient during the performance period. Grants are grouped into two broad categories: (1) discretionary grants, and (2) mandatory, entitlement, or formula grants. Discretionary grants are competitive, and funding agencies have the authority to determine the award amount and recipients. Mandatory, entitlement, or formula grants are general revenue or federal pass-through funds allocated by state agencies to institutions and organizations based on predetermined formulas.

Cooperative agreements provide money to recipients to accomplish a proposed project wherein substantial involvement is expected between funding agency staff members and recipients during the performance period. Cooperative agreements are primarily used in large clinical research trials. Government grants and cooperative agreements are classified as assistance agreements that provide financial support to funding seekers who want to complete projects that directly relate to a government agency's mission.

Procurement contracts acquire services or products for the direct benefit of or use by the federal government. Procurement contracts are grouped into two broad categories: (1) fixed-price contracts, or (2) cost-reimbursement contracts. Procurement contracts are governed by the Federal Acquisition Regulations, which provide uniform policies and procedures for governing federal procurement acquisition activity. Procurement contract solicitations are published at www.fedbizopps.gov.

Non-government funding is provided through private gifts from individuals, corporations, or philanthropic foundations. According to CASE, a gift is a voluntary transfer of property to another made gratuitously and without consideration. A gift may be either restricted or unrestricted.

Review Questions

(Answers to Review Questions are on p. 273.)

Directions: For statements 1–15, circle "T" for True or "F" for False.

T F 1. Non-government gifts come from individuals, corporations, or philanthropic foundations.

T F 2. Grants and cooperative agreements are assistance agreements.

T F 3. Government grants transfer money, property, or services to eligible recipients in order to accomplish a public purpose where there is no substantial involvement between funding agency staff members and recipients during the performance period.

T F 4. Discretionary grants are noncompetitive.

T F 5. Mandatory grants are allocated by state agencies to institutions based on predetermined formulas.

T F 6. Cooperative agreements transfer money, property, or services to recipients to accomplish a public purpose wherein substantial involvement is anticipated between the funding agency and recipient during the performance period.

T F 7. Grant and cooperative agreement solicitations are published in the *Federal Register*.

T F 8. Procurement contracts acquire services or products for the direct benefit of or use by the federal government.

T F 9. The *FAR* contain uniform policies and procedures governing federal procurement contract acquisition activity.

T F 10. Procurement contract solicitation synopses are published in the *Federal Register*.

T F 11. Procurement contracts require two separate proposals: a technical proposal (or narrative) and a cost proposal.

T F 12. Assistance agreements provide payments after expenditures.

T F 13. "Individuals" provide more than 75 percent of charitable giving.

T F 14. Peer reviewers evaluate government proposals.

T F 15. Non-government funding foundations and organizations are less likely to cover indirect costs.

Exercise 1-1

Describe Government and Non-Government Funding Sources

(Answers to Exercise 1-1 are on p. 276.)

Directions: Describe the major characteristics of government and non-government funding sources.

Grants

Cooperative Agreements

Procurement Contracts

Gifts

Chapter 2

Proposal Development Process—An Overview

As mentioned in Chapter 1, the United States government appropriates more than $450 billion in grants on an annual basis to support projects and programs at state and local governments, academic institutions, not-for-profits, and other organizations. Federal agencies start the process by issuing a request for proposal (RFP) or request for application (RFA) that announces funding opportunities on a wide variety of topics stemming from government legislation. Some federal programs offer one-time funding opportunities, while other programs provide financial support year after year, with little or no change to solicitation requirements. Each year, the competition for these grants becomes more rigorous with more institutions seeking external funds. It is not how many grant applications you write, but how many you win that is important.

Funding seekers develop grant applications or proposals that provide strategies for solving or improving problems related to a government agency's needs. Being successful in a highly competitive environment requires that funding seekers use extensive planning before developing grant applications. Government agency reviewers evaluate grant applications according to criteria published in the RFP/RFA. After the application review, government agency representatives may hold discussion and/or negotiation sessions with funding seekers before a final award decision is determined. Grant winners receive a notice of award or contract that must be signed before the project begins. **See Exhibit 2-1**.

To win government funding, grant writing must be a planned priority. The proposal development process consists of a series of six phases, each of which must be completed if funding seekers plan to win consistently:

1. Complete work before the RFP/RFA is released.

2. Conduct prewriting activities after the RFP/RFA is released.

3. Write, review, rewrite, and edit the proposal narrative.

4. Prepare, review, and revise the proposal budget.

5. Produce, assemble, and submit the grant application.

6. Perform postsubmission activities. **See Exhibit 2-2**.

Exhibit 2-1

Grant Process: From Legislation and Acquisition to Award

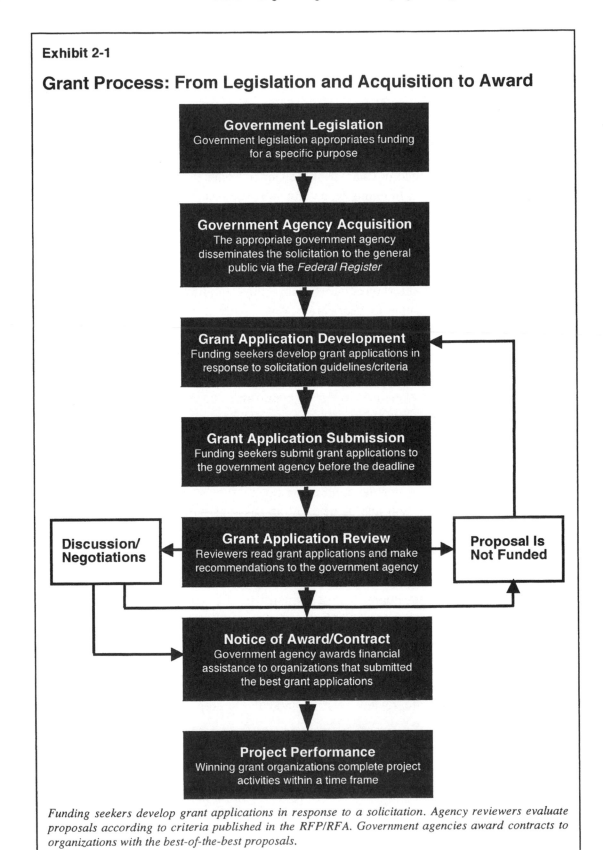

Funding seekers develop grant applications in response to a solicitation. Agency reviewers evaluate proposals according to criteria published in the RFP/RFA. Government agencies award contracts to organizations with the best-of-the-best proposals.

Exhibit 2-2

Proposal Development Process

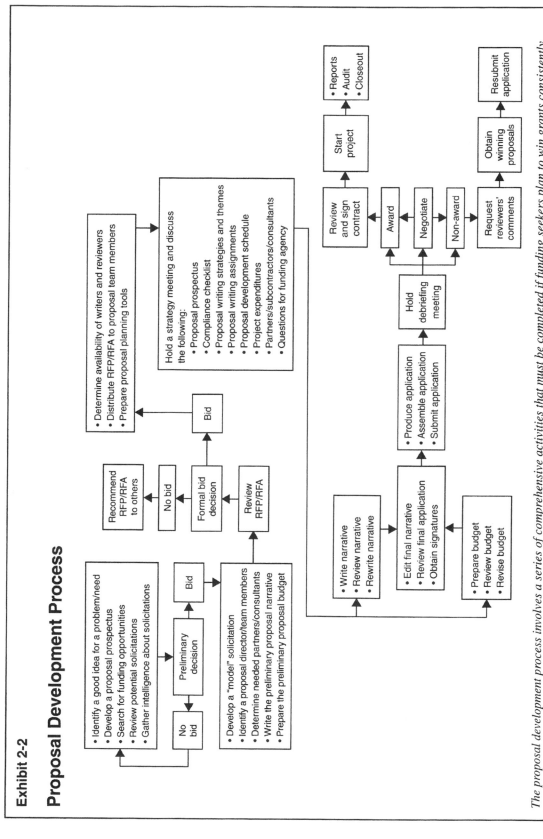

The proposal development process involves a series of comprehensive activities that must be completed if funding seekers plan to win grants consistently.

Complete Work Before the RFP/RFA Is Released

Many grant seekers fail to receive funding because they wait until the RFP/RFA is released before developing a proposal. Waiting until the RFP/RFA is publicly announced is a critical mistake made by inexperienced funding seekers. Developing winning grant proposals is based on the ability to (1) identify a "good" project idea that addresses a problem/need, (2) develop a proposal prospectus, (3) search for funding opportunities, (4) review potential solicitations, (5) gather intelligence about solicitations, and (6) make a preliminary bid/no-bid decision. If the decision is to bid or develop a grant application, then the funding seeker should (1) develop a "model" solicitation, (2) identify a proposal director and key team members, (3) determine needed partners, subcontractors, and consultants, (4) write the preliminary proposal narrative, and (5) prepare the preliminary proposal budget. Details about activities before the RFP/RFA is released are discussed in Chapter 3.

Conduct Prewriting Activities After the RFP/RFA Is Released

After the RFP/RFA is released, funding seekers normally have 30 days to submit a grant application. Many funding seekers lose grants because they fail to plan winning strategies before developing a proposal in response to a solicitation. The adage "plan your work and work your plan" is the theme for this phase of the proposal development process.

Prewriting activities after the RFP/RFA is released involve three days of preparation and planning before attempting to develop the narrative and budget required for a grant application.

The first day after the release of a solicitation is spent reviewing the RFP/RFA, estimating the probability of winning, and making a formal decision (with upper administration) to bid or not bid.

If the decision is to bid, then the second day after the release of the RFP/RFA is spent determining the availability of writers and reviewers and developing proposal planning tools (e.g., compliance checklist, proposal outline, and schedule) that will be used to help writers prepare the grant application.

The third day after the release of the RFP/RFA is used to hold a strategy meeting with all proposal writers and reviewers. Discussion should focus on writing strategies and proposal themes, adhering to a proposal schedule, formulating budget assumptions, identifying the roles to be completed by needed partners, subcontractors, and consultants, and identifying questions about unclear segments of the RFP/RFA. Details about prewriting activities after the RFP/RFA is released are discussed in Chapter 4.

Write, Review, Rewrite, and Edit the Proposal Narrative

Armed with the necessary proposal planning tools, successful writers prepare, review, rewrite, and edit two to three drafts of the proposal narrative.

Most grant proposals include the following narrative components:

- Abstract—Comprehensive and clear summary of the proposed project that must be written in such a way that reviewers quickly understand the merits of the grant application.

- Problem/Need—Persuasive statement that convinces proposal reviewers that a problem needs to be resolved or a situation improved and demonstrates a rationale for funding. Use facts, statistical data, and research results to support the claims made in this section.

- Goals/Objectives—Direction statements that identify project outcomes. Goals are broad outcomes and objectives are smaller "stepping-stones" to each goal. Goals and objectives must be measurable and must state what will be done, under what conditions, and how the target population will be affected.

- Methods/Activities—Specific activities and events that will be completed to meet each goal/objective. Activities should describe the "how," "who," "where," and "when" of the project. A timetable is often used to present a schedule of activities and events for the project duration.

- Evaluation Plans—Assessment procedures and criteria used to determine project success. This section identifies what information will be measured and how data will be collected and analyzed. Evaluation plans should also describe what would be included in reports to the government agency.

Experienced proposal teams prepare two or three drafts of narrative. After each proposal draft, in-house reviewers should provide detailed feedback to writers about the strengths and weaknesses of each narrative section. Reviewers should provide constructive criticism that can be used to improve the proposal. The final proposal draft (including all tables and figures) should be checked for compliance by proposal team leaders and edited for content and style.

All assurance and certification forms must be carefully completed and signed by an appropriate administrator as part of the grant application. Details about writing, reviewing, rewriting, and editing the proposal narrative and completing assurance and certification forms are discussed in Chapter 5.

Prepare, Review, and Revise the Proposal Budget

Based on RFP/RFA specifications, prior budget assumptions, and actual cost figures, several budget drafts are prepared, reviewed, and revised to account for cost items discussed in the project narrative. Proposal budgets should include a breakdown of all direct and indirect costs (unless indirect costs are not allowed).

Direct costs are specific expenditures required to complete the proposed project and generally include (1) personnel salaries and fringe benefits, (2) travel and per diem, (3) equipment and expendable supplies, (4) contractual services, and (5) other direct costs.

Indirect costs are shared expenditures for organizational facilities and general administration. Indirect costs are incurred for common organizational objectives and therefore cannot be identified specifically with a sponsored project. (See Office of Management and Budget Circular A-21.) Indirect costs are calculated as a percentage of the *Total Direct Costs* (TDC) or *Modified Total Direct Costs* (MTDC).

State and federal government agencies may also require cost sharing by the grantee to indicate project commitment. *Cost sharing* obligates the grant-seeking institution to make financial and/or resource contributions toward the completion of a proposed grant project. Cost sharing contributions are grouped into two categories: (1) in-kind, and (2) matching funds. *In-kind* contributions include internal donations (from the grant-seeking institution and partners) and external donations (from local business and industry) and may include direct costs and indirect costs (donated personnel time, equipment, supplies, furniture, printing, lodging, etc.). *Matching funds* are monies that may come from the institution's general operating funds, private donations, or foundation funds. Most government agencies require grant seekers to complete standard budget forms as part of the grant application.

Grant applications should include budget detail and narrative to provide a thorough explanation and justification of unusual or complex cost expenditures. Final budgets must reflect realistic costs sufficient to complete the proposed project within the government agency's funding ranges specified in the solicitation. Details about preparing proposal budgets are discussed in Chapter 6.

Produce, Assemble, and Submit the Grant Application

The most important rule in grant writing is to be compliant. Grant seekers must follow agency directions (provide exactly what is requested—no more and no less) and meet deadlines. A grant application is only a winner if it is produced and submitted to the government agency on or before the deadline.

Grant application production involves verifying that all proposal sections identified in the RFP/RFA are included in the grant application. Grant applications with missing or out-of-order sections or components are usually considered noncompliant and are not considered for funding. Quality control checks before and after the grant application is produced are vital to ensure a complete and error-free submission.

Most federal agencies require electronic submission of grant applications. Agencies may also require funding seekers to submit paper copies of the grant application. Details about how to produce, assemble, and submit grant applications are covered in Chapter 7.

Perform Postsubmission Activities

Immediately after proposal submission, a debriefing meeting should be scheduled with all writers and reviewers to discuss the grant application's strengths and weaknesses in anticipation of questions from the government agency. Proposal team members should determine application deficiencies and be prepared to defend project decisions.

Grant applications that meet the government agency's requirements are evaluated and scored by peer reviewers. Reviewers evaluate each grant application on the basis of how well applicants responded to criteria in the RFP/RFA and on the quality of the proposed project idea. Reviewers provide ratings and written recommendations to the government agency. The government agency uses these ratings and written comments as a basis for funding the best-of-the-best proposals. If your project is not chosen for funding, the proposal director should contact the agency program officer in an effort to ascertain the strengths and weaknesses of the grant application. The proposal director should also obtain the reviewer's comments and request copies of grant applications that were funded. In some cases, a funding agency may want additional information about the application prior to making a funding decision. Government agencies may ask questions that require funding seekers to revise project objectives, clarify points, correct errors, or respond to suggestions made by reviewers. A funding agency may also believe your project can be done for a lower budget. Funding seekers should respond positively to such requests and only make necessary budget reductions. If your grant application was selected to receive funding, the proposal director and upper administration should carefully review the notice of award before signing.

Grant award terms and conditions are binding and must be followed by the grantee. The project should only start after the government agency and all parties involved in the grant have signed the contract. The principal investigator (PI) or project director (PD) must prepare accurate financial records and reports for all grant activities. Details about postsubmission activities are discussed in Chapter 8. **See Exhibit 2-3**.

Exhibit 2-3
Sample Proposal Development Schedule

Day-to-Day Schedule

Scheduling varies for each proposal. Scheduling of activities depends on the number of participants involved in the proposal team and the complexity of the proposed project.

Work Before the RFP/RFA Is Released
- Identify a good idea that addresses a problem/need
- Develop a proposal prospectus
- Search for funding opportunities
- Review potential solicitations
- Gather intelligence about solicitations
- Make a preliminary bid/no-bid decision
  (Continue with this list if the decision is to bid.)
- Develop a "model" solicitation
- Identify a proposal director and key team members
- Determine needed partners, subcontractors, and consultants
- Write the preliminary proposal narrative
- Prepare the preliminary proposal budget

Activity	1	2	3	4	5	6	7	8	9	10	11	12	13	14	15	16	17	18	19	20	21	22	23	24	25	26	27	28	29	30
Conduct Prewriting Activities After the RFP/RFA Is Released																														
- Review the RFP/RFA and make a formal bid/no-bid decision	X	X																												
- Determine the availability of writers and reviewers	X	X																												
- Distribute the RFP/RFA to proposal team members		X																												
- Develop a compliance checklist		X	X																											
- Prepare a proposal outline and schedule		X	X																											
- Hold a strategy meeting			X																											
- Discuss writing strategies/proposal themes			X																											
- Discuss writing assignments and schedule			X																											
- Determine project expenditures			X																											
- Formulate questions to ask the funding agency			X																											
Write the Proposal Narrative and Prepare the Budget*				X	X	X	X	X	X	X	X	X	X	X	X	X	X	X	X	X	X	X	X							
- Prepare the first draft of proposal narrative and budget				X	X	X	X	X																						
- Review the first draft of proposal narrative and budget									X	X																				
- Prepare the second draft of proposal narrative and budget											X	X	X	X																
- Review the second draft of proposal narrative and budget															X	X														
- Prepare the final draft of proposal narrative and budget																	X	X	X	X	X	X	X							
- Review the final draft of proposal narrative and budget																								X	X					
- Edit the final proposal narrative																										X	X			
- Obtain signatures from upper administration																												X		
Produce, Assemble, and Submit the Grant Application																												X	X	
Perform Postsubmission Activities																														X

*Note: The two proposal development phases "write the proposal narrative" and "prepare the proposal budget" are completed concurrently.

The proposal development process includes activities before and after the release of the RFP/RFA. After the solicitation is released, funding seekers have 30 days to submit a grant application.

Chapter Summary

Successful grant applications are developed by funding seekers who (1) identify a "good" project idea that addresses a problem/need, (2) use clear narrative techniques to describe the project, and (3) identify project expenditures that are reasonable.

The proposal development process consists of a series of comprehensive activities, each of which must be completed if funding seekers plan to win consistently. Most winning grant applications require the completion of six distinct proposal development phases:

1. *Complete Work Before the RFP/RFA Is Released.* The funding seeker must identify a "good" project idea that addresses a problem/need, develop a proposal prospectus, search for funding opportunities, review potential solicitations, gather intelligence about solicitations, and make a preliminary bid/no-bid decision. If the decision is to develop a proposal, then the funding seeker should develop a "model" solicitation; identify a proposal director and key team members; determine needed partners, subcontractors, and consultants; write the preliminary proposal narrative; and prepare the preliminary proposal budget.

2. *Conduct Prewriting Activities After the RFP/RFA Is Released.* The adage "plan your work and work your plan" describes this phase of the proposal development process. Prewriting activities after the solicitation is released involve three days of preparation and planning. The first day should be spent carefully reviewing the RFP/RFA, clearing up any solicitation ambiguities, calculating the probability of winning, and making a formal decision to bid or not bid. If the decision is to bid, then the second day is spent developing proposal planning tools to assist writers and reviewers prepare the narrative and budget. The third day involves holding a strategy meeting with all writers, reviewers, and other internal and external staff members to discuss writing strategies and proposal themes, adhering to a proposal schedule, and formulating budget assumptions.

3. *Write, Review, Rewrite, and Edit the Proposal Narrative.* This phase of the proposal development process takes approximately 21 of the 30 days allowed by most government agencies. During this time, funding seekers prepare two or three drafts of the proposal narrative and have in-house readers review each draft carefully in an effort to ensure compliance and improve the proposal content. The final proposal draft (including all tables and figures) is checked for compliance by proposal team leaders and edited for content and style.

4. *Prepare, Review, and Revise the Proposal Budget.* The proposal budget should include a breakdown of direct and indirect costs necessary to complete the proposed project. Direct costs must account for cost items discussed in the project narrative. Indirect costs include facilities and administrative expenditures associated with the project. Cost sharing may also be a government agency requirement. Cost sharing requires the funding seeker to provide in-kind (non-financial contributions) or matching funds (financial contributions) to the project. Most government agencies require standard budget forms as part of the grant application.

Grant applications should include budget detail and narrative to provide a thorough explanation of unusual or complex cost expenditures. Final budgets must reflect realistic costs sufficient to complete the proposed project within the funding ranges specified in the solicitation.

5. *Produce, Assemble, and Submit the Grant Application.* Grant applications must be produced and organized according to RFP/RFA guidelines. Quality-control checks should be made prior to submitting the grant application to the government agency. Most government agencies require that grant applications be submitted electronically through Grants.gov. Government agencies may also require funding seekers to submit paper copies of grant applications by mail, commercial carrier, or hand delivery.

6. *Perform Postsubmission Activities.* Immediately following the submission, the proposal director should meet with all proposal writers and reviewers to discuss the grant application's strengths and weaknesses. In anticipation of questions about the application from government agency representatives, proposal team members should determine proposal deficiencies and be prepared to defend project activities and costs.

Grant applications that meet the government agency's requirements are evaluated and scored by at least three peer reviewers. Reviewers evaluate each grant application on the basis of how well applicants responded to criteria in the RFP/RFA and the quality of the proposed project idea.

If the grant application was not chosen for funding, the proposal director should obtain the reviewers' comments and copies of several winning proposals and consider resubmitting a revised application.

If the grant application was selected to receive funding, the proposal director and upper administration should carefully review the grant award terms and conditions before signing the contract and starting the project. A grant is a promise to deliver what is proposed in the application.

Review Questions

(Answers to Review Questions are on p. 273.)

Directions: For statements 1–15, circle "T" for True or "F" for False.

T F 1. The U.S. government awards more than $450 billion in grants on an annual basis.

T F 2. Grant solicitations are disseminated to the general public via the *Federal Register*.

T F 3. A "good" project idea that addresses a problem/need is the first activity to be completed before the RFP/RFA is released.

T F 4. A proposal director and key staff members should be identified before the RFP/RFA is released.

T F 5. Funding seekers should gather intelligence about potential solicitations before the RFP/RFA is released.

T F 6. The normal time allocated to respond to a solicitation is 60 days.

T F 7. Many organizations fail to receive awards from government agencies because they wait until the RFP/RFA is released before starting to develop a proposal.

T F 8. A compliance checklist, schedule, and outline are proposal organizational and planning tools used to guide writers and reviewers in developing the grant application.

T F 9. Proposal organizational and planning tools are developed the first day after the RFP/RFA is released.

T F 10. A strategy meeting is where proposal writers and reviewers meet and discuss writing assignments, budget assumptions, and scheduling.

T F 11. Experienced proposal teams prepare two or three drafts of the narrative before the final grant application is edited.

T F 12. Final budgets reflect the cost to complete the proposed project within the government agency's funding range.

T F 13. Grant applications with missing or out-of-order components are considered noncompliant.

T F 14. Most federal agencies require that grant applications be submitted electronically.

T F 15. A postsubmission debriefing meeting gives writers and reviewers the opportunity to discuss the grant proposal's strengths and weaknesses.

Exercise 2-1

Determine Winning Grant Proposal Characteristics

(Answers to Exercise 2-1 are on pp. 277–278.)

Directions: Most successful grant proposals share common attributes. Develop a list of 10 winning proposal characteristics based on your background in preparing grant applications. Rank each characteristic from most important (1) to least important (10). *

1.

2.

3.

4.

5.

6.

7.

8.

9.

10.

*Note: Exercise 2-1 was intentionally placed here to cause readers to think about the characteristics of winning grant proposals in preparation for what will be discussed in the next chapters. This exercise is most effective as a group discussion activity with three to four participants per group. After 20–30 minutes of discussion, one member of each group should provide a brief summary of their group's responses.

Chapter 3

Complete Work Before the RFP/RFA Is Released

Grant seekers often fail to receive funding because they wait until the RFP/RFA is released before developing a proposal. Waiting until the RFP/RFA is publicly announced is a critical mistake made by inexperienced funding seekers. Most institutions lack proper planning and, as such, they are neither prepared nor organized to write grant applications. By the time a funding seeker sees a solicitation in the *Federal Register* or Grants.gov, it is generally too late to prepare a winning grant application in the time allotted by government agencies. Background work about the government agency, solicitation, and competition is a prerequisite to winning grants. Proposal planning and writing must also be done before the RFP/RFA is released if a winning application is going to be prepared.

Experienced funding seekers complete the following activities prior to release of the solicitation in an effort to be better prepared than their competition.

- Identify a "good" project idea that addresses a problem/need.
- Develop a proposal prospectus.
- Search for funding opportunities.
- Review potential solicitations.
- Gather intelligence about solicitations.
- Make a preliminary bid/no-bid decision.
  (Continue with this list, if the decision is to bid.)
- Develop a "model" solicitation.
- Identify a proposal director and key team members.
- Determine needed partners, subcontractors, and consultants.
- Write the preliminary proposal narrative.
- Prepare the preliminary proposal budget. **See Exhibit 3-1**.

Identify a "Good" Project Idea that Addresses a Problem/Need

Before searching for grant opportunities, funding seekers must identify a project idea that requires external funding to solve or improve a problematic situation. A well-defined "good" project idea is a prerequisite to looking for grant opportunities. Funding seekers should look for gaps in the literature and talk with colleagues, other grant seekers, administrators, and staff members from the office of sponsored programs about possible project ideas.

Exhibit 3-1

Complete Work Before the RFP/RFA Is Released

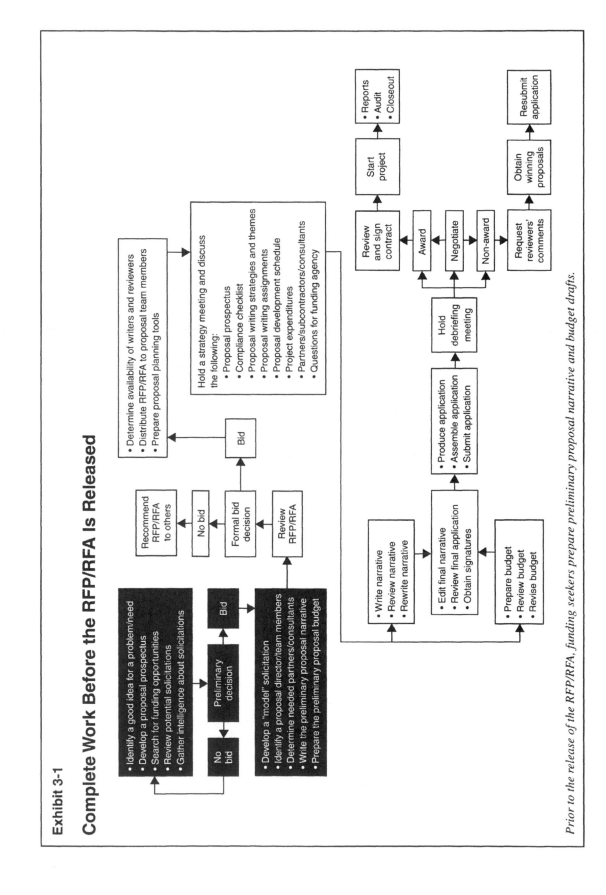

Prior to the release of the RFP/RFA, funding seekers prepare preliminary proposal narrative and budget drafts.

A good project idea is worthwhile, realistic, original, compelling, feasible, and well planned. A good project idea goes beyond personal interest and must persuade agency reviewers that the idea is exciting, new, and interesting. Thus, a good project idea is an innovative solution to a problem—presented in a clear format—that agency reviewers will easily understand and passionately support. Good project ideas must answer the following questions:

- Does the project idea address an important problem?

- If implemented, will the project idea make a difference?

- Is the project idea clear and understandable?

Government agencies receive many "good" project ideas that are not funded because they are difficult to understand and follow. Funding seekers must write for the audience and consider the reviewers' background and expertise—are they generalists or experts in the field? If reviewers are generalists, the funding seeker must make sure that all technical jargon is thoroughly explained. The "average" reviewer must be able to comprehend the most technical project idea. Government agencies will not fund poor ideas, duplicated ideas, or unclear ideas. Grant writing is an "essay contest." Funding seekers must be knowledgeable and creative people who have a comprehensive understanding of their topic and are able to present their ideas in a logical manner. **See Exhibit 3-2**.

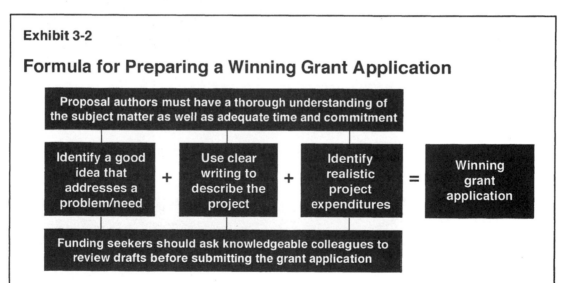

Exhibit 3-2

Formula for Preparing a Winning Grant Application

Proposal authors must have a thorough understanding of the subject matter as well as adequate time and commitment

| Identify a good idea that addresses a problem/need | + | Use clear writing to describe the project | + | Identify realistic project expenditures | = | Winning grant application |

Funding seekers should ask knowledgeable colleagues to review drafts before submitting the grant application

Winning grant applications are developed by funding seekers who (1) identify a "good" project idea that serves as a solution to a problem, (2) use clear proposal writing to describe the project, and (3) identify realistic and reasonable project expenditures. Proposal authors must have a thorough understanding of the subject matter as well as adequate time and commitment to prepare a winning application. Knowledgeable colleagues should be used as critical proposal reviewers prior to submitting the grant application to the funding agency. Funding seekers should ask colleagues who are good readers to commit to review the proposal in advance. Funding seekers must allow colleagues sufficient time to read the grant application and provide feedback prior to the submission deadline.

Develop a Proposal Prospectus

To communicate a good idea to others, funding seekers should develop a 1–2 page proposal prospectus (brief concept paper) that provides details about the project. Funding seekers should share this prospectus with knowledgeable colleagues for constructive feedback. The prospectus is used to communicate the project idea to upper management, proposal team members, and potential government agency representatives. Based on the proposal prospectus, funding seekers should develop a list of keywords to be used to search for potential solicitations. **See Exhibit 3-3**.

Exhibit 3-3

Proposal Prospectus Form

Note: The questions below serve only as a guide; always provide the exact content specified in the RFP/RFA when preparing the grant application.

Directions: Answer the questions below as they relate to the proposed project. Share your prospectus with colleagues and ask for feedback.

Project Title. What is a brief, descriptive title of the proposed project?

Problem/Need. What is the problem? How will the project idea correct, reduce, or improve the problem? What evidence (data, reports, or trends) is available to support the need for this project?

Goals/Objectives. What is the overall purpose of this project? Are the goals and objectives specific and measurable? Can the goals/objectives be evaluated?

Exhibit 3-3 continues on the next page.

Exhibit 3-3 (Continued)

Proposal Prospectus Form

Methods/Activities. What is the plan of work for the proposed project? What are the qualifications, responsibilities, and time commitments for key personnel? What is the management structure of the project? When will activities be completed?

Evaluation Plans. What formative and summative evaluation strategies will be used to assess the project? Who will be responsible for conducting the project evaluation?

Estimated Cost. How much will the project cost? Are indirect costs applicable? Is cost sharing required? Do project costs fit within the agency's funding range?

A proposal prospectus is a brief concept paper that provides an overview of the proposed project. The prospectus communicates project plans to internal administrators, team members, and government agency representatives in an effort to describe project concepts and locate potential funding sources.

Search for Funding Opportunities

Armed with a comprehensive proposal prospectus of a cutting-edge idea and keywords that describe your project, the funding seeker uses the Internet to locate external funding opportunities. Federal government programs are not solicited for funds, but rather provide funds to organizations that have project ideas similar to what they want to fund. Funding sources will often shift priorities and time frames. Funding seekers should involve staff members from the office of sponsored programs to assist in locating potential funding opportunities.

Checking funding source databases (e.g., Grants.gov) and determining the right funding program for a project idea can be a laborious and time-consuming undertaking. Funding seekers have the difficult task of trying to locate a government agency with a mission that supports the proposed project idea. A match between what the funding seeker wants to do and what a government agency will fund may not exist today, but it may exist sometime in the future. **See Exhibit 3-4**.

Exhibit 3-4

Selected Government Agency Mission Statements

Agency	Mission Statement
USDE www.ed.gov	The U.S. Department of Education (USDE) "promotes student achievement and preparation for global competitiveness by fostering educational excellence and ensuring equal access." The USDE is dedicated to: • establishing policies on federal financial aid for education and distributing as well as monitoring those funds, • collecting data on American schools and disseminating research, • focusing national attention on key educational issues, and • prohibiting discrimination and ensuring equal access to education.
NSF www.nsf.gov	The National Science Foundation (NSF) is an independent federal agency created by Congress in 1950 "to promote the progress of science; to advance the national health, prosperity, and welfare; [and] to secure the national defense." In many fields such as mathematics, computer science, and the social sciences, the NSF is the major source of federal backing. Another essential element in the NSF's mission is support for science and engineering education, from prekindergarten through graduate school and beyond.
NIH www.nih.gov	The National Institutes of Health (NIH) "is the steward of medical and behavioral research for the Nation. Its mission is science in pursuit of fundamental knowledge about the nature and behavior of living systems and the application of that knowledge to extend healthy life and reduce the burdens of illness and disability."

A proposed project idea must fall clearly under a government agency's mission. For example, if your project idea is concerned with student achievement and educational excellence, it will probably fall under the USDE's mission; if your project idea is concerned with science or engineering, it will probably fall under the NSF's mission; and if your project idea is in epidemiology, human growth and development, or mental or physical disorders, it will probably fall under the NIH's mission.

Federal funding priorities are constantly changing and often depend on the goals of national leadership. Consequently, the grant-seeking process is not a one-time effort, but rather a continuous process where funding seekers regularly use the Internet to search for funding opportunities that match project ideas. In addition, the funding seeker's project schedule may not follow the government agency's timeline. Consequently, if funding seekers do not have the time to develop a winning proposal when the agency offers the funding opportunity, they must look for funding opportunities at a later date. Savvy funding seekers use a variety of sources to locate funding opportunities. Locating appropriate funding sources takes time and patience. **See Exhibit 3-5**.

Exhibit 3-5

Grant Funding Sources

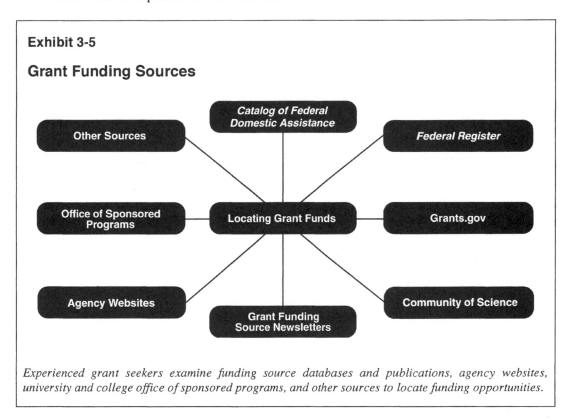

Experienced grant seekers examine funding source databases and publications, agency websites, university and college office of sponsored programs, and other sources to locate funding opportunities.

Catalog of Federal Domestic Assistance. The *Catalog of Federal Domestic Assistance (CFDA)* is a government-wide summary of federal projects, services, and activities that provide financial and nonfinancial assistance or benefits to the public. The *CFDA*'s primary purpose is to assist users in identifying programs that match the needs of potential applicants. The *CFDA* is issued annually (in two editions) and is available at most public libraries or online at www.cfda.gov. The *CFDA* is a good starting point for funding seekers to locate information about grant opportunities offered by federal government agencies. *CFDA* also offers an excellent user's guide, *Developing and Writing Grant Proposals,* as well as a very informative series of frequently asked questions.

CFDA's website allows grant seekers the opportunity to search for assistance programs that provide a wide range of benefits and services available to state and local governments; U.S. territories; domestic public, quasi-public, and private profit and nonprofit organizations and institutions; specialized groups; and individuals. *CFDA* offers assistance information about both discretionary and mandatory, entitlement, or formula grants. Assistance programs have been grouped into 20 basic grant categories and 175 subcategories that identify specific areas of interest. **See Exhibit 3-6**.

Exhibit 3-6

Catalog of Federal Domestic Assistance Program Categories

- Agriculture (7)
- Business and Commerce (9)
- Community Development (11)
- Consumer Protection (3)
- Cultural Affairs (2)
- Disaster Prevention and Relief (4)
- Education (23)
- Employment, Labor/Training (11)
- Energy (6)
- Environmental Quality (6)

- Food and Nutrition (4)
- Health (21)
- Housing (12)
- Income Security and Social Services (19)
- Information and Statistics (4)
- Law, Justice, and Legal Services (9)
- Natural Resources (7)
- Regional Development (9)
- Science and Technology (3)
- Transportation (5)

Note: The number of subcategories for each program is indicated in parentheses.

CFDA programs provide benefits and services in 20 grant categories and 175 subcategories.

Each *CFDA* assistance category provides a list of grant programs, which in turn identify subcategory programs that include the following information:

- name of federal agency overseeing the funding program,
- legislative act that authorized the program,
- goals and/or objectives of the program,
- type of assistance offered (financial or nonfinancial),
- uses and restrictions placed on a program,
- eligibility requirements,
- application and award process,
- assistance considerations,
- post-assistance requirements,

- financial information,

- regulations, guidelines, and literature relevant to a program,

- information contacts at the headquarters, regional, and local offices,

- related programs,

- examples of funded projects, and

- criteria for selecting proposals.

Funding seekers should use six steps in searching the *CFDA* for federal assistance:

1. Browse the *CFDA* using the index or keyword search to locate assistance for your specific needs. A review of the *CFDA* may or may not identify programs that provide funding for a specific project idea. Both the applicant and government agency must have similar interests, intentions, and needs, if a funding seeker is going to win.

2. Read potential funding solicitations' eligibility requirements, objectives, assistance type, restrictions, and application procedures.

3. Consider the reality of preparing a proposal in relationship to the deadline date. Deadlines for submitting grant applications are not negotiable and are usually associated with strict timetables for agency reviews. Some programs have more than one application deadline during the fiscal year.

4. Review the "Information Contacts" section of the program description and identify the government agency's *Point of Contact* (POC), phone number, and e-mail address. Develop a list of specific questions about the possibility of funding assistance for your project idea.

5. Contact the POC or program officer and ask first if your proposed project matches the government agency's intent. If there is a positive response, ask specific questions not addressed in the RFP/RFA.

6. Based on responses from the POC, decide to apply or not apply to the government agency. If feedback from the POC is encouraging, the funding seeker must consider the proposal requirements and deadline date before deciding to submit a grant application. Funding seekers must also consider the reality of implementing the project in terms of the starting date and period of performance.

Federal Register. The *Federal Register* (*FR*) is the official federal government publication used by funding seekers to locate information about grant opportunities. The *FR* is a legal document published every business day (except federal holidays) by the National Archives and Records Administration (NARA) that lists all federal agency regulations and legal notices, including details about all federal grant competitions. The *FR* publishes a wide range of federal funding opportunities and is available in most major libraries that house government documents. Each issue of the *FR* has a table of contents organized alphabetically by agency that lists each document and span of pages. *FR* announcements include full grant application notices (including necessary forms) or provide information about how to obtain these forms online or as an application package from the government agency that is responsible for the particular funding program. Grant application packages usually include (1) program rules and regulations, (2) guidelines for proposal development, (3) application forms (coversheet, certification, assurance, and budget forms), and (4) application submission instructions.

Funding seekers can search and download *FR* notices and other documents at no charge. The *FR* online edition has the same table of contents as the paper edition with hypertext links that take users directly to each document in the current issue. Funding seekers can search past issues of the *FR* by subject, agency, category, issue date, and other parameters to retrieve documents from 1994 through the present day. The *FR* online is available at www.gpoaccess.gov/fr/index.html. *FR* documents are available in abbreviated text, full text (with graphics omitted), and Adobe Portable Document Format (PDF).

Grants.gov. Grants.gov is a free online service that helps funding seekers find, apply, and manage grants from federal agencies as well as some state and local governments. Funding seekers can use Grants.gov to search by agency, project idea, *CFDA* number, or other parameters. To find grant opportunities, funding seekers should:

- Go to http://www.grants.gov.
- Click "find grant opportunities."
- Click "basic search," "browse by category," "browse by agency," or "advanced search."
- Complete the information requested (keywords, funding opportunity number, or *CFDA* number) on the "grant opportunities" screen and click the "search" button to provide a display of applicable grant titles. (Note: A link is available from the title to the synopsis or full-grant announcement.)

Funding seekers can also use Grants.gov to receive automatic e-mail notifications about newly posted solicitations based on specific parameters. To receive notices about new grant opportunities, funding seekers should:

- Go to http://www.grants.gov.

- Go to "find grant opportunities."

- Click on "e-mail subscription." Funding seekers can select "all grant notices," "notices based on advanced criteria," "notices based on funding opportunity number," or "unsubscribe from grant notices."

- Complete the necessary fields on the subscription services screen.

Grants.gov also offers helpful resources, user guides, and a glossary of terms and definitions. If you have problems using Grants.gov, you can contact support services by e-mail at support@grants.gov or by phone at 1-800-518-4726. Grants.gov/apply is discussed in Chapter 7. **See Exhibit 3-7**.

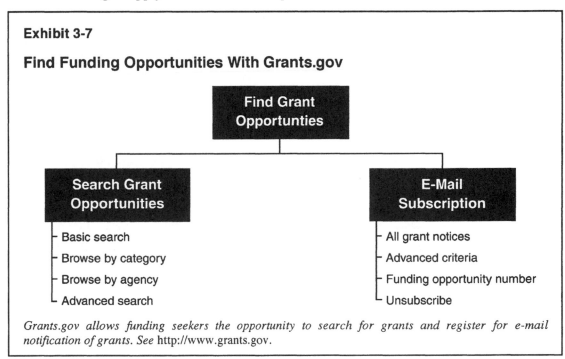

Exhibit 3-7

Find Funding Opportunities With Grants.gov

Grants.gov allows funding seekers the opportunity to search for grants and register for e-mail notification of grants. See http://www.grants.gov.

Community of Science. Community of Science (COS) (http://www.cos.com/) is the largest single storehouse of grant information on the web. COS offers three databases that are valuable resources to funding seekers:

- *COS Funding Opportunities* is a searchable database of public and private funding opportunities in all academic disciplines and beyond.

- *COS Funding Alert* provides funding seekers with weekly e-mail updates of funding opportunities in specific areas of interest.

- *COS Expertise* provides funding seekers with an opportunity to create expertise profiles, which can be viewed by potential grant collaborators.

Other searchable databases that use keywords to locate government and non-government funding opportunities include the Sponsored Program Information Network (SPIN) and the Illinois Researcher Information Service (IRIS).

Grant funding source newsletters. Numerous funding source newsletters are available that identify potential funding opportunities and provide specific guidance for developing grant applications. These paper and/or electronic reports disclose information about upcoming grant solicitations in terms of purpose, deadline, eligibility requirements, project areas, contact person, funding range, and number of awards. **See Exhibit 3-8**.

Exhibit 3-8

Selected Grant Funding Source Newsletters

Newsletter	Description
Aid for Education http://www.cdpublications.com	Provides funding information for education professionals K–16.
Federal Assistance Monitor http://www.cdpublications.com	Provides information about government and non-government funding opportunities.
Federal Grants and Contracts Weekly http://www.shoplrp.com	Provides early alerts about solicitations being developed by government agencies.
Education Grants Alert http://www.shoplrp.com	Provides information about grant opportunities for K–12 funding seekers.

Numerous newsletters provide paper and online summary information about grant funding opportunities.

Agency websites. Most federal and state agencies have websites that serve as sources for learning about funding opportunities as well as providing proposal development guidelines, agency award abstracts, and appropriate forms necessary to submit a grant application. Some government agencies also offer weekly e-mail alerts about funding opportunities (e.g., "National Science Foundation Update"). Comprehensive resource lists also exist on the Internet and provide links to other websites that are extremely useful to funding seekers. Funding seekers should bookmark specific grant funding databases and websites that are used on a regular basis. See pp. 255–260 for additional funding resources.

Office of Sponsored Programs. The office of sponsored programs at most colleges and universities offers assistance locating funding opportunities. In addition, this office usually has staff members who are very experienced in helping grant seekers develop the proposal narrative and prepare grant budgets.

Other Sources. Other grant funding sources include (1) past and present solicitations such as Program Announcements (PA), Broad Agency Announcements (BAA), and Funding Opportunity Announcements (FOA); (2) past and present grant agreements and contracts; (3) government agency–published information; (4) government agency reports in the public domain; and (5) government agency meeting minutes. Funding seekers can also use Google and/or Yahoo as a good starting point to locate funding sources.

Review Potential Solicitations

Funding seekers should carefully review potential solicitations that seem to support a project idea or concept. When reviewing solicitations, funding seekers should pay special attention to the eligibility requirements, program purpose or mission, selection criteria, funds available, and deadline. Highlight action verbs that indicate compliance issues (e.g., "shall," "will," and "must") and note proposal development guidelines (e.g., format and length requirements). Funding seekers must decide if a winning proposal can be developed within the limited time frame imposed by the government. **See Exhibits 3-9 and 3-10**.

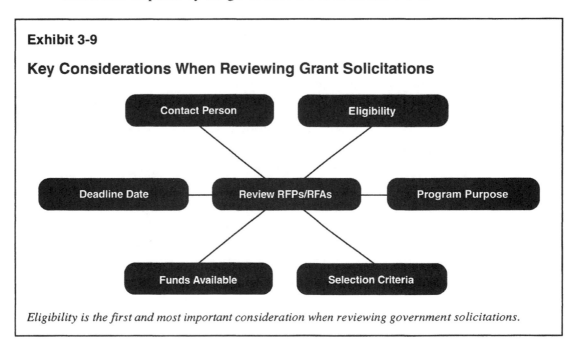

Exhibit 3-9

Key Considerations When Reviewing Grant Solicitations

Contact Person   Eligibility

Deadline Date   Review RFPs/RFAs   Program Purpose

Funds Available   Selection Criteria

Eligibility is the first and most important consideration when reviewing government solicitations.

Exhibit 3-10

Sample RFP/RFA Summary

Title: Higher Education Challenge Grants

Eligibility: U.S. colleges and universities offering a baccalaureate degree or first professional degree in agricultural sciences.

Purpose: To strengthen the nation's agricultural professional workforce.

Selection: Projects should have the potential for high impact, innovation, multidisciplinary effort, and generation of products and results. Projects must address curricula design, faculty preparation, instructional delivery systems, or student experiential learning.

Funds: $4,000,000 total for grants of up to $100,000 for regular projects and up to $250,000 for joint projects. Awards are for one year.

Deadline: February 14, 20XX; 4:00 p.m. EST

Contact: Jeffrey Smith, 987/654-XXXX; e-mail: jsmith@reeusda.gov

RFP/RFA summaries provide specific information about upcoming agency funding opportunities.

Gather Intelligence About Solicitations

Intelligence-gathering activities conducted prior to the release of the solicitation are vital to preparing a winning grant proposal and are used to help verify information, build bridges, and establish credibility. Whether you are an individual or part of a large organization, information-gathering activities are essential to successful grant seeking. Funding seekers should start by studying the government agency's website and examine past award recipients' abstracts and proposals as well as the background of successful principal investigators.

Funding seekers must understand both the government agency's "needs" (basic requirements included in the RFP/RFA) and "wants" (what the government agency would ideally like to see mentioned in a winning proposal) in order to win grants on a consistent basis. Understanding the government agency's needs and wants goes beyond the information included in an RFP/RFA. Government agency needs are proposal requirements that may not be disclosed until release of the RFP/RFA or may be readily available in previous solicitations or reports. These needs reflect the government agency's mission, goals, and institutional environment. Government agencies assume that grant seekers will fulfill these requirements. Government agency wants reflect the government agency staff members' interpretation of RFP/RFA guidelines and requirements. Knowing these wants could make the difference between a winning or losing proposal.

To fully understand the government agency's needs and wants, the funding seeker should obtain information from three sources: (1) the POC, (2) past award winners, and (3) government agency reviewers. **See Exhibit 3-11**.

Exhibit 3-11

Intelligence-Gathering Activities

Documents to Read/Review	Personnel to Contact
• Read the eligibility criteria, program requirements (purpose, instructions, due date, budget limits, cost sharing, etc.), and evaluation criteria in past agency solicitations to ensure an understanding of the agency's needs and wants. Determine if your proposed project idea fits within the agency's mission.	• E-mail the agency's Point of Contact (POC) about your project idea and ask if it relates to a specific solicitation. Ask other questions about the RFP/RFA for clarification purposes.
• Review government agency web page(s) for information related to the solicitation.	• Contact past award recipients in an effort to obtain insight from individuals who have been awarded funding. Ask for a copy of their winning proposal.
• Read funded project abstracts to learn about the project ideas that the agency has funded in the past.	• Contact peer reviewers (field readers) and ask them about the review process.
• Read several winning proposals from past recipients to understand what the government is interested in funding.	• Contact staff members from your office of sponsored programs to clarify institutional policies and procedures and to assist you in preparing the narrative, budget, and standard forms.
• Obtain and read other government agency documents, reports, and publications to have a complete understanding of the government agency and its goals.	• Talk to colleagues with successful grant writing experience and seek their advice.
	• Contact business and industry representatives from your local community about being partners.

Experienced grant seekers review relevant government documents and talk to numerous personnel in an effort to gather intelligence about specific funding opportunities.

Point of Contact

Pre-knowledge about grant competition is imperative to winning. According to David Bauer (2003), your chances for success go up 300% when you contact the POC before the proposal is written.[1] Funding seekers must understand the:

- government agency's priorities and agenda,

- proposal guidelines and application materials,

- proposal themes to be emphasized (as well as points to be avoided), and

- proposal review process and procedures.

[1] Bauer, D. G. (2003). *The "How To" Grants Manual: Successful Grantseeking Techniques for Obtaining Public and Private Grants.* Westport, CT: Praeger Publishers.

Funding seekers should direct all inquiries about the RFP/RFA to the POC identified in the solicitation. The POC is the single most important contact you can cultivate in seeking grant funds. The POC is an excellent resource to provide you with recent grant information and guidance. If the RFP/RFA has not been released, the proposal director should contact the government agency and ask for the name, address, and contact information (e.g., phone number and e-mail address) of the POC for upcoming grant competitions.

The initial contact should be a brief e-mail to the POC asking if there is a good day and time when you could talk with the program officer about a solicitation. Always include the specific RFP/RFA or *CFDA* number and complete solicitation title in the subject heading of your e-mail message. Attach your proposal prospectus and include your name, title, and contact information.

Before calling the POC, the funding seeker should formulate questions to direct the conversation. Write specific questions that require specific answers—vague questions will invite vague answers. Remember, you don't get a second chance to make a first impression. The phone conversation with the POC should be well prepared and brief (no more than 10–20 minutes). Face-to-face visits with the POC can also be very beneficial and productive. **See Exhibit 3-12.**

Stress your project objectives and ask the following questions:

- Does the proposed project fall within the agency's funding priorities?

- What is the total funding available? What is the average award?

- Will awards be made on the basis of special criteria?

- What is the anticipated application/award ratio?

- What common mistakes have prevented funding seekers from winning?

- What should be in a proposal that other applicants may have overlooked?

- Should the proposal be written for reviewers with non-technical backgrounds?

- How are proposals reviewed? How many grant applications are reviewers expected to read? How long do reviewers have to read the applications?

- Would you send me a copy of the evaluation form used by reviewers to assess proposals?

- Is a compliance checklist available for funding seekers to follow when preparing a grant application to ensure submission of all requirements?

- Would you review a two- to three-page prospectus and/or proposal draft?

- Are you aware of other funding opportunities to support this project initiative?

Exhibit 3-12

Interviews With the Point of Contact

Direct inquiry is one of the most effective ways of acquiring information from government agencies. Since time is a precious commodity, the POC may not give face-to-face interviews with potential applicants. If a personal meeting is not possible, try to talk with a POC about your project over the phone or through e-mail. (Note: Some government agencies may not allow the POC to conduct one-on-one meetings with prospective applicants.)

Before Talking with the POC

- Know the name of the POC with whom you would like to speak.

- Send a brief e-mail to the POC and ask for a date and time when you could discuss your project idea in relation to a specific solicitation. Attach your proposal prospectus.

- Prepare a list of questions about the suitability of your project and clarify information about the solicitation. Do not ask questions answered in the RFP/RFA.

The Phone Conversation

- Introduce yourself and describe succinctly what your responsibilities are within your organization. State the reason(s) for contacting the POC. If you contacted the agency previously, ask for the same individual for follow-up conversations.

- Ask the POC specific questions about your project.

- Do not ask vague questions about the fundability of a project or use the interview time for brainstorming. Rather, briefly outline the benefits of your project and cite statistics to support it. State how project methods will address current needs.

- While you should have conducted research in advance to determine whether or not the project falls within the activities of the funding source, confirm whether the project coincides with the funding source's priorities. If needed, ask for further clarification about the criteria used to evaluate proposals.

- Be sure to take notes of recommended changes to your plan and/or issues clarified by the POC during your discussion.

The Follow-up

- Make follow-up contacts with the same POC for any future questions. Keep follow-up contacts to a minimum since the POC has duties other than answering questions about the RFP/RFA and proposal submissions.

- Upon contacting a prospective funding source, you may receive a negative response regarding a project idea. React positively. A "no" can lead to as much useful information as a "yes." If the response is negative, ask the POC to explain why the project does not meet funding priorities; whether there are any recommended proposal changes to increase the fundability of the proposed project; and whether other areas within the organization might be more appropriate for your project.

Grant seekers should formulate questions before contacting government agency representatives.

At the conclusion of your conversation with the POC, request a list of past award winners and ask for copies of winning grant proposals from prior years. You may be required to pay for postage, duplication cost, and clerical time to reproduce proposal copies; however, these documents may prove invaluable in preparing your grant application. Send a letter that references the *Freedom of Information Act* (FOIA) when requesting copies of winning proposals from non-responsive agency representatives. The FOIA is part of the *Administrative Procedures Act* that allows the public to have access to agency records maintained by government agencies, except for privileged information or proprietary material that is exempt from disclosure by law. Note that some agencies post winning grant application abstracts and/or proposals online for funding seekers to review. **See Exhibit 3-13**.

Exhibit 3-13

Sample Letter to Request Winning Proposals

JOHN W.
JONES
& ASSOCIATES

April 3, 20XX

Mr. Todd Henson
U.S. Department of Housing and Urban Development
451 Seventh Street, SW
Washington, DC 20410   ⟵ **Include *CFDA* Number and Title**

Subject: *CFDA* #14.511–The Community Outreach Partnership Centers Program

Dear Mr. Henson: ⟵ **Cite FOIA, if Necessary**

In compliance with the Freedom of Information Act, John W. Jones and Associates requests examples of winning proposals for the above-referenced grant. Please invoice John W. Jones and Associates for any costs incurred and send copies to:

⟵ **Where to Send Winning Proposals**

    Evelyn Lesniak
    John W. Jones and Associates
    596 W. Jackson Blvd.
    Chicago, IL 60606

Thank you for your assistance in this matter.

Sincerely,   ⟵ **Contact Person and Phone Number**

Evelyn Lesniak
Evelyn Lesniak
Director of Grants and Contracts
312-567-1234

Funding seekers should reference the FOIA when requesting copies of winning grant proposals from non-responsive government agency representatives.

Past Award Winners

Funding seekers should review potential agency websites and read funded project abstracts, grant proposal guidelines, and other reports and special publications related to the solicitation. In addition, funding seekers should contact several past grant award winners (principal investigators or project directors) with similar projects to gather relevant information that may not be available elsewhere. A list of award winners is public information and is available from government agencies. Before contacting past winners, prepare questions relevant to the proposal development process and grant submission criteria. Specific questions for past award winners might include:

- Did you contact the POC before preparing the grant application?

- Whom did you find most helpful on the government agency's staff?

- Did the government agency's POC review a concept paper or proposal draft prior to final submission?

- What materials did you find most helpful in developing your grant proposal?

- What was your problem/need statement and what approach did you use to improve the situation?

- How close was your initial budget to the awarded amount? What budget items, if any, were cut?

- What would you do differently next time?

- Would you be willing to send us a copy of your winning grant application?

Government Agency Reviewers

Names and contact information of agency reviewers are usually not available to the general public. If a list of reviewers is not available, ask the POC to provide general information about the agency reviewers' background, training, and selection process. In addition, ask the POC to describe the grant application review process and how points will be allocated to proposals. Prepare specific questions before contacting reviewers, such as:

- How did you become a grant application reviewer?

- How many grant applications were you given to read? How much time were you given to read each application?

- Did you follow a particular scoring system?

- What were you told to look for in grant applications?

- What were the most common mistakes you saw in grant applications?

- How would you write a grant application differently now that you have been a proposal reviewer?

Make a Preliminary Bid/No-Bid Decision

After gathering intelligence from various sources, funding seekers should weigh the risk/reward ratio and make a preliminary decision to develop a grant proposal or to terminate all activity. Funding seekers must decide if a match exists between what you want to do and what the government agency wants to support. In addition, the funding seeker must determine if the timeline for completing the proposed project agrees with the government agency's period of performance. If you do not have adequate time to complete the project within the government agency's time frame, it is probably better to wait for a later funding opportunity. If a poor match exists between your proposed project goals and timeline and the government's mission and the solicitation's purpose and period of performance, the funding seeker should continue to search for RFPs/RFAs and/or revise the project idea and search for other potential solicitations. A decision to not bid is correct if you (1) are not prepared to write a winning proposal, (2) do not have adequate support from your administration, or (3) cannot complete the proposed grant activities within the agency's time frame. A decision should be based on first-hand information obtained from intelligence-gathering activities. If a good match exists between the project idea and the agency's mission, the funding seeker should (1) develop a "model" solicitation, (2) identify a proposal director and key team members, (3) determine needed partners, subcontractors, and consultants, (4) prepare the preliminary proposal narrative, and (5) prepare the preliminary budget. **See Exhibit 3-14**.

Exhibit 3-14

Preliminary Decision about Developing a Grant Application

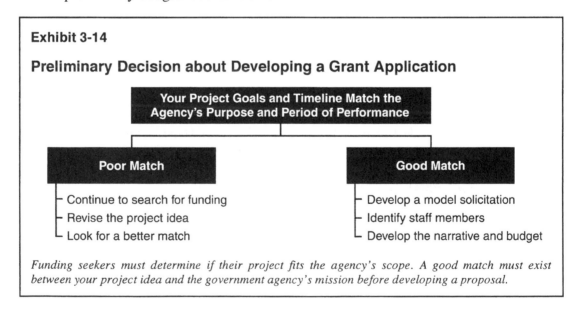

Funding seekers must determine if their project fits the agency's scope. A good match must exist between your project idea and the government agency's mission before developing a proposal.

Preliminary bid/no-bid decisions should be based on whether proposal development team members are able to prepare a winning grant application within the limited time allotted by the government agency. To make the best decision, funding seekers should consider the following questions:

- Is there time to gather information from the POC, past award recipients, and government agency reviewers prior to release of the solicitation?

- Is there time to formulate a quality project design?

- Is there time to complete "in-house" grant application reviews?

- Is there time to complete grant application draft revisions?

In making a decision to proceed one should consider answers to the following questions:

- Is your organization eligible to apply for this funding? Can your organization meet or exceed the solicitation requirements?

- Why is this proposed project important to your organization? Does the proposed project fit within your organization's strategic plan? What will change as a result of receiving funding for this project? How does the project represent an improvement over current practices? What is innovative about this project?

- What will it cost to develop a winning grant application? Does your organization have the necessary intellectual workforce available to prepare a proposal within the time limits?

- What are your chances of winning? How many applications are expected from peer institutions and how many awards will be made by the government agency? Why should the government agency award your organization the funding?

- Can your organization do the work within the budget range? Are adequate staff members available to complete the proposed grant activities and submit reports to the government agency in a timely fashion? Can the project sustain itself after the grant-funding period?

Ultimately, the decision to go forward with developing a grant proposal is based on knowledge about:

- the government agency and their needs and wants,

- your organization's odds against the competition, and

- your proposed project's strengths and weaknesses.

A preliminary bid/no-bid decision should also consider whether your organization has a competitive advantage. If the competition can do similar grant work for the same cost, your organization has no competitive advantage. A competitive advantage is determined by identifying features that distinguish you from the competition, identifying benefits derived from these features, and using these benefits in themes throughout the grant proposal.

Government agencies will often host pre-application workshops in different locations throughout the United States that provide learning opportunities and a chance for funding seekers to ask agency representatives specific questions about the solicitation. Pre-application workshops will vary in length and value—some workshops offer a vast amount of information while others repeat information from the RFP/RFA. Funding seekers should create a list of questions prior to attending the pre-application workshops.

Develop a "Model" Solicitation

A *"model" solicitation* is a "mock-up" RFP/RFA that funding seekers develop from information obtained from an analysis of similar solicitations from the government agency. In some instances, very few if any changes are made from year-to-year to the RFP/RFA. If this is the case, last year's solicitation will serve as an accurate guide to developing a proposal draft prior to release of the RFP/RFA. Funding seekers should never wait until the RFP/RFA is released to prepare a proposal draft. Sound intelligence-gathering practices will provide sufficient information that can be used to prepare a preliminary grant proposal.

Identify a Proposal Director and Key Team Members

Proposal directors should be identified as soon as a decision to prepare a grant proposal has been made. Proposal directors must have the experience, knowledge, leadership ability, and time available to guide the grant proposal development effort. In addition, proposal directors should be emerging or demonstrated leaders, who are committed to—and believe in—the proposed topic. The proposal director should brief all team members on major points of the RFP/RFA and provide a rationale for the proposed project. After the proposal director is identified, key staff members must be selected to work on the grant proposal. Always identify and organize a good working team. Distribute duties and develop a firm schedule of activities needed to prepare the proposal in a timely manner. Roles assigned to these team members include writing the narrative, preparing the budget, and/or reviewing the proposal at various stages of development.

Proposal writers and "in-house" reviewers are content experts who are innovators in their discipline. Financial/budget staff members must be cognizant of contemporary costs associated with the proposed project. Other grant preparation team members may include an editor, graphic designer, statistician, and other support staff members. From the onset, proposal directors at universities should work closely with staff members from the office of sponsored programs. These staff members can assist in (1) reviewing RFP/RFA guidelines, (2) preparing internal and agency documents and forms, (3) establishing teaming agreements with partners, (4) developing the budget, (5) reviewing the final grant application, (6) obtaining appropriate signatures, and (7) submitting the grant application. A cohesive team with a common mission and support from upper administration will lead to a well-developed grant application. **See Exhibit 3-15**.

Exhibit 3-15

Proposal Development Team Members

Team Members*	Responsibilities
Upper Administration/ Management	• Read the RFP/RFA and make a formal bid decision • Provide release time for staff members to work on the proposal • Provide the necessary resources for proposal development • Serve as a final in-house reviewer of the grant application • Sign the cover sheet and assurance and certification forms
Proposal Director (Note: The proposal director will often assume the role of the principal investigator (PI) or project director (PD) after the grant is awarded.)	• Read the RFP/RFA and make a formal bid decision • Develop a proposal prospectus and a compliance checklist • Develop a proposal outline and schedule • Identify the necessary staff members to develop the proposal • Chair the strategy meeting • Work with financial staff members to secure cost-sharing commitments • Work with administration to complete assurance and certification forms • Serve as the contact with government agency representatives • Serve as the contact with partners, subcontractors, and consultants • Chair the proposal review meetings with writers and reviewers • Serve as a final in-house reviewer of the grant application • Oversee the proposal quality control prior to submission • Chair the debriefing meeting after proposal submission • Respond to questions from the government agency about the proposal
Writer(s)	• Read the RFP/RFA • Write the proposal narrative • Rewrite the proposal narrative based on feedback from reviewers
Financial/Budget Staff Member(s)	• Read the RFP/RFA • Work with the proposal director to prepare a budget • Review cost-sharing commitments • Check partner, subcontractor, and/or consultant budgets • Revise the budget based on feedback from reviewers
Reviewer(s)	• Read the RFP/RFA • Review the proposal narrative and budget • Provide feedback to writers and budget staff members
Editor(s)	• Read the RFP/RFA • Develop a proposal style sheet • Review the proposal narrative for style and consistency • Edit/rewrite the proposal narrative and budget justification • Serve as a final in-house reviewer of the grant application
Graphic Designer(s)	• Develop proposal tables, figures, charts, and illustrations • Review the overall design and layout of the grant application
Partner(s), Subcontractor(s), and Consultant(s)	• Provide necessary proposal narrative and budget expenditures • Provide support documents (e.g., résumés, biographical sketches)
Staff Members from the Office of Sponsored Programs	• Locate funding opportunities and review solicitations • Review narrative drafts and assist in the preparation of the budget • Submit the grant application to the government agency

*Teams often have members who play multiple roles. In some cases, only a few people develop a grant application. Project ideas that address complex problems may require collaboration with staff members from other institutions.

Proposal development members must have expertise and time to prepare winning grant applications.

Determine Needed Partners, Subcontractors, and Consultants

Administration must understand their organization's capabilities and deficiencies when responding to solicitations. If you are planning to respond to a solicitation and your organization has specific deficiencies, you should identify partners, subcontractors, consultants, and/or external grant writers who can fill those voids.

Partners, Subcontractors, and Consultants

Partners, subcontractors, and consultants should be included only when it will enhance your project or when it is a requirement indicated in the RFP/RFA. Partners, subcontractors, and consultants must be able to demonstrate successful past performance with similar work and be able to meet deadlines. Formal written teaming agreements should be established with partners, subcontractors, and consultants before the grant application is submitted to the government agency. Within the teaming agreements you should identify the work to be completed by partners, subcontractors, or consultants, (e.g., specific roles, expected performance levels), timelines, and financial compensation. At this pre-RFP/RFA stage, partners and subcontractors should submit capability statements, examples of similar past work, and résumés of key staff members who will participate in the proposed grant project. Consultants should submit résumés and brief biographical sketches that highlight past experience with similar projects. Federal and state grants often require that applications include local partners in support of proposed projects. Partners, subcontractors, and consultants should be active team players in planning the proposed project activities from the outset.

Grant Writers

When developing grant applications, upper administration must decide if there are internal staff members who have the knowledge and time to develop a proposal or if they need to hire outside grant writers to do the multitask activities associated with developing a grant application. There are several pros and cons for using internal staff members versus hiring outside grant writers. Hired grant writers are usually expensive but will often bring fresh ideas to the proposal development process. Using internal staff members is less expensive, but they may not have the expertise concerning the proposal development process. Upper administration must carefully weigh the pros and cons before making a decision whether to use internal staff members or hire external grant writers to develop a proposal. Before hiring a grant writer, administration should carefully check the individual's résumé for appropriate background and experience. Administration should also ask questions such as: How many proposals have you written? How much of the proposal did you actually write? What was your success rate? What government agencies have you submitted grant applications to? Can you provide us with a list of grant applications that have been submitted in the last two years? Can we see copies of at least two winning proposals and award letters? Can you provide the names and telephone numbers for at least two past clients? **See Exhibit 3-16**.

Exhibit 3-16

Using Internal Staff Members Versus External Grant Writers

Pros/ Cons	Internal Staff Members	External Grant Writers
Pros	Using internal staff members is an inexpensive way to develop grant applications; however, they often do not have the background to prepare winning grant applications. Internal staff members will be responsible for completing the daily activities identified in the proposed project, if the grant is awarded.	External grant writers bring a fresh perspective to the proposed project and usually have a thorough understanding of the grant development process and what it takes to win. External grant writers develop proposals without interrupting the daily duties of staff members.
Cons	Internal staff members may have a limited understanding about the grant development process and are often naive about what it takes to win. Grant development activities take time away from staff members to perform their daily duties.	External grant writers are usually expensive. Some grant writers charge a flat fee, while others charge a percentage of the total award. External grant writers will not be responsible for completing the daily activities identified in the proposed project, if the grant is awarded.

Upper administration must weigh the pros and cons before hiring external grant writers.

Write the Preliminary Proposal Narrative

Preliminary proposal narrative is developed prior to the release of the solicitation using a "model" solicitation and information obtained from intelligence-gathering activities. Most grant proposals include the following narrative sections:

Abstract—A one-page summary of the proposed project. Both subject-matter experts and the uninformed must be able to understand the content presented in the abstract.

Problem/Need—A persuasive essay that identifies a problematic situation supported by recent and relevant citations.

Goals/Objectives—Identify clear and concise project outcomes that are measurable, manageable, ambitious, but attainable.

Methods/Activities—A logical plan of work that indicates the project activities and events, key personnel, management plan, and project timeline.

Evaluation Plans—Assessment plans to determine if the project is proceeding as intended and meeting the project goals and objectives within a proposed timeline.

Preliminary proposal drafts should follow model solicitation guidelines, address proposal evaluation criteria, and provide information that is easy for the reviewer to locate and follow. Simple language that communicates clearly to the intended audience is the best. Write to express, not impress. Use tables, figures, charts, diagrams, and illustrations to supplement narrative.

Grant writers must develop proposals that inform government agencies about their organization and the services it will provide in response to the solicitation. Evidence of past experiences demonstrating similar work done well and on time should be included in the proposal, if requested. In addition, the proposal's tone should emphasize a commitment to the project by all personnel involved. Proposals must persuade government agency reviewers that your organization can meet the needs (requirements) and wants of the government agency. Remember, proposal competition is fundamentally an essay contest that must show that your project is better than those of other funding seekers. As such, proposals must describe the benefits of awarding funding to you rather than the competition. See Chapter 5 for detailed information about writing and editing the narrative.

Prepare the Preliminary Proposal Budget

Budgets should provide an estimate of costs associated with proposed activities to be completed during the performance period. Previously published solicitations from the government agency, proposals from past award recipients, and actual project costs are used to develop preliminary budgets.

Preliminary proposal budgets must consider direct costs, indirect (facilities and administrative) costs, and cost-sharing contributions, if required. *Direct costs* include personnel salaries and fringe benefits, travel and per diem, equipment and expendable supplies, contractual services, and other direct costs. *Indirect* costs are referred to as overhead or *facilities and administrative costs* and include expenditures not identified readily or specifically with a particular grant project or activity. Indirect costs include facility operation and maintenance expenses (e.g., utility costs, custodial service costs, and insurance premiums) and administrative expenses (e.g., accounting, payroll, and purchasing). *Cost sharing* is a requirement by some state and federal agencies that obligates the grant-seeking institution to make financial (matching funds) and/or resource (in-kind contributions) toward the completion of the proposed grant project. See Chapter 6 for a comprehensive discussion about preparing grant budgets.

If you are having a difficult time getting started with a grant application, consider the following advice:

> Assume that the government agency just sent your organization the funding necessary to complete the proposed grant project. Now, think about how you are going to spend the money.

Chapter Summary

Proposal planning and writing must be done before the RFP/RFA is released if a winning grant application is going to be prepared. To develop a winning grant application, funding seekers must understand both the government agency's needs (basic requirements included in the RFP/RFA) and wants (what the government agency would ideally like to see mentioned in the grant application).

Prior to release of the RFP/RFA, funding seekers should:

- identify a "good" project idea that addresses a problem/need,

- develop a proposal prospectus,

- search for funding opportunities,

- review potential solicitations,

- gather intelligence about solicitations,

- make a preliminary bid/no-bid decision,
  (Continue with this list, if the decision is to bid.)

- develop a "model" solicitation,

- identify a proposal director and key team members,

- determine needed partners, subcontractors, and consultants,

- write the preliminary proposal narrative, and

- prepare the preliminary proposal budget.

Funding seekers must start by identifying a clear, innovative, worthwhile, manageable, and cost-effective project idea that addresses a problem/need. Ask for feedback about the project idea as well as information about possible funding opportunities from knowledgeable colleagues.

Based on the project idea, the funding seeker should develop a proposal prospectus (1–2 page concept paper about the proposed project). The prospectus is used to communicate project plans to in-house administrators, staff members, and agency representatives.

Armed with a solid project idea, the funding seeker attempts to locate funding sources. Use the Internet and register for e-mail notifications about grant opportunities, and get on free mailing lists to obtain early alerts about grant opportunities so you have time to prepare a winning application. Funding sources include the *Catalog of Federal Domestic Assistance*, *Federal Register*, Grants.gov, Community of Science, grant funding source newsletters, agency websites, office of sponsored programs, and other sources.

Funding seekers should carefully review potential solicitations that seem to support your project idea. Pay special attention to the funding program's purpose, applicant eligibility, deadline date, specific regulations, selection criteria, and budget range of awards.

Gathering information prior to the release of the RFP/RFA is essential to successful grant seeking. Pre-solicitation activities involve obtaining relevant information from three sources: (1) the POC, (2) past award recipients, and (3) government agency proposal reviewers. Questions should be prepared prior to contacting these individuals. Funding seekers should also obtain and read grant applications from past award recipients.

After gathering intelligence about the solicitation, funding seekers should make a preliminary decision to develop a grant application or to terminate all activity. Funding seekers must decide if a match exists between what you want to do and what the government wants to support. Be extremely choosy about the grants you go after. State funds are often the easiest to obtain; federal funds are more difficult.

If a poor match exists between your proposed project goals and timeline and the government's purpose and period of performance, you should continue to search for other solicitations and/or revise the project idea and search for other potential funding opportunities.

If a good match exists between your project goals and the government agency's purpose or mission, you should develop a "model" solicitation, identify proposal staff members, determine if partners, subcontractors, or consultants are needed, and develop the preliminary grant narrative and budget.

Ultimately, the decision to go forward with developing or not developing a proposal is based on knowledge about the government agency's wants and needs and the funding seeker's ability to prepare a winning proposal. Making a decision to prepare a grant application or to terminate all activity should be based on answers to the following questions:

- Is your organization eligible to apply for this funding?

- Does the proposed project fit within your organization's strategic plan?

- Does your organization have the necessary intellectual workforce available to prepare a proposal within the time limits?

- What are your chances of winning?

- Can your organization do the work within the agency's budget range?

If the decision is to go forward and develop a grant application, the funding seeker should:

- Use the information gained from the intelligence-gathering effort to develop a "model" solicitation that will serve as a guide for developing the proposal.

- Identify a proposal director who will serve as the leader for the proposal development effort and proposal writers and financial staff members who will develop the narrative and budget sections of the grant application. Upper administration must determine if there are key internal staff members who have the knowledge, commitment, and time to develop a competitive proposal or if they need to hire outside grant writers to do the activities associated with developing a grant application. In addition, support staff members such as in-house reviewers, editors, graphic designers, and other support staff members need to be identified.

- Identify needed project partners, subcontractors, and/or consultants. Upper administration or management must understand their organization's capabilities and deficiencies when responding to government agency solicitations. If your organization has specific deficiencies, you should immediately identify partners, subcontractors, and/or consultants who can fill those voids. Partners, subcontractors, and consultants should be included only when it enhances your project. Formal written teaming agreements should be established with partners, subcontractors, and consultants before the grant application is submitted to the government agency.

- Write the preliminary proposal narrative based on information from intelligence-gathering activities. The preliminary proposal narrative should follow model solicitation guidelines, address proposal evaluation criteria, and provide information that is easy for the agency reviewers to locate. Simple language that communicates clearly to the intended audience is the best. Always provide the exact narrative sections requested in the solicitation.

- Prepare the preliminary proposal budget. Preliminary budgets should provide an estimate of costs associated with proposed project activities to be completed during the performance period. Preliminary budgets must consider direct costs, indirect costs, and cost-sharing contributions, if applicable.

Review Questions

(Answers to Review Questions are on p. 273.)

Directions: For statements 1–15, circle "T" for True or "F" for False.

T   F   1. Most institutions are neither prepared nor organized to write grant proposals due to lack of planning.

T   F   2. Grant writing is an essay contest.

T   F   3. A proposal prospectus is a brief concept paper about your proposed grant project.

T   F   4. The *Catalog of Federal Domestic Assistance* (*CFDA*) provides a comprehensive listing of government agency grant programs.

T   F   5. The *Federal Register* (*FR*) is the official government publication used by funding seekers to locate grant opportunities.

T   F   6. Grants.gov is a free online service that helps funding seekers find, apply, and manage federal grants.

T   F   7. When reviewing solicitations, funding seekers should pay special attention to eligibility requirements and program purpose.

T   F   8. Intelligence-gathering activities conducted prior to the release of a solicitation are vital to preparing a winning grant application.

T   F   9. Funding seekers formulate questions before contacting prospective government agency representatives.

T   F   10. When contacting a government agency representative, the first and most important question the funding seeker must ask is: Does the project idea fall under the government agency's mission?

T   F   11. The Freedom of Information Act allows the general public to have access to proprietary information and records.

T   F   12. Before making a preliminary decision to submit a grant application, funding seekers should take into account whether their organization has the necessary intellectual workforce to prepare a proposal.

T   F   13. A "model" solicitation is prepared by the government agency.

T   F   14. Teaming agreements are established with partners, subcontractors, and/or consultants after the grant application is submitted.

T   F   15. Preliminary budgets are developed before a solicitation is released using information from previous solicitations, grant applications from past award recipients, and actual project costs.

Exercise 3-1

Identify a Project Idea that Requires External Funding

Directions: Write spontaneously for seven minutes about a possible project idea you would like to complete in the near future that requires external funding. Don't worry about grammar or style. Just stick to your topic and write as fast as you can for the entire exercise. At the bottom of the page, identify keywords that can be used with search engines to locate possible funding opportunities.

List keywords to be used with search engines to locate funding opportunities.

Exercise 3-2

Develop a Proposal Prospectus

Directions: Answer the questions below to develop a proposal prospectus based on your project idea. Answer each question as completely as possible. Share your prospectus with colleagues and ask for feedback.

Project Title—What is a brief descriptive title of the proposed project?

Problem/Need—What is the problem? How will the project idea correct, reduce, or improve the problem? What evidence (data, reports, or trends) is available to support the need for this project?

Goals/Objectives—What is the overall purpose of this project? Are the goals and objectives specific and measurable? Can the goals/objectives be evaluated?

Methods/Activities—What is the plan of work for the proposed project? What are the qualifications, responsibilities, and time commitments for key personnel? What is the management structure of the project? When will activities be completed?

Evaluation Plans—What formative and summative evaluation strategies will be used to assess the project? Who will be responsible for conducting the project evaluation?

Estimated Cost—How much will the project cost? Are indirect costs applicable? Is cost sharing required? Do project costs fit within the agency's funding range?

Exercise 3-3

Locate and Review Solicitations

Funding seekers must be able locate what government agencies have funded in the past as well as what they intend to fund in the future. Experienced funding seekers are efficient and relentless solicitation hunters that are acquainted with traditional resource publications as well as search engines to prevent potential solicitations from being overlooked. Funding seekers must locate solicitations that match their project needs with the government's wants.

Directions: Locate the Catalog of Federal Domestic Assistance at www.cfda.gov. Review the CFDA programs that might provide funding for your project idea. Review one program announcement and provide the information below.

1. Name of federal agency:

2. Goals/objectives of program:

3. Eligibility requirements:

4. Total amount of funding available/number of awards given:

5. Brief summary of solicitation:

Exercise 3-3 continues on the next page.

Exercise 3-3 (Continued)

Locate and Review Solicitations

Directions: Visit the Federal Register website at http://www.gpoaccess.gov/fr/index.html *and locate potential grant solicitations related to your project idea. Choose one solicitation and provide the information below.*

1. *CFDA* #/solicitation title:

2. Sponsoring agency name and publication date:

3. Eligibility requirements:

4. Funding allocations:

5. Selection criteria:

6. Brief summary of solicitation:

Exercise 3-3 continues on the next page.

Exercise 3-3 (Continued)

Locate and Review Solicitations

Directions: Visit the Grants.gov website at http://www.grants.gov *and locate potential grant solicitations that are related to your project idea. Choose one solicitation and identify the information below.*

1. *CFDA* #/solicitation title:

2. Sponsoring agency name and publication date:

3. Eligibility requirements:

4. Funding allocations:

5. Selection criteria:

6. Brief summary of solicitation:

Exercise 3-4

Review a National Science Foundation (NSF) RFP

(Answers to Exercise 3-4 are on pp. 279–282.)

Use Adapted Program Solicitation NSF 07-543 (pp. 60–70) to complete this exercise.

Directions: Read the Solicitation "Course, Curriculum, and Laboratory Improvement" adapted from the National Science Foundation (pp. 60–70) and answer the following questions. Along with each answer, provide the page number in the RFP where you found the information.

NSF 1.   What is the purpose of the NSF?

NSF 2.   What is the purpose of the Course, Curriculum, and Laboratory Improvement program?

NSF 3.   Who is eligible to apply for funding?

NSF 4.   Who should be contacted regarding general inquiries about this program?

NSF 5.   How much funding is available for Phase 1, 2, and 3 projects? How long is the period of performance for Phase 1, 2, and 3 projects?

NSF 6.   What is the total anticipated funding amount for new and ongoing awards? How many estimated Phase 1, 2, and 3 awards will be made?

NSF 7.   In addition to the *Grant Proposal Guide* and *A Guide for the Preparation and Submission of NSF Applications,* what other information should be read before submitting a proposal?

Exercise 3-4 continues on the next page.

Exercise 3-4 (Continued)

Review a National Science Foundation (NSF) RFP

(Answers to Exercise 3-4 are on pp. 279–282.)

Use Adapted Program Solicitation NSF 07-543 (pp. 60–70) to complete this exercise.

NSF 8. What project components should be included in the proposal?

NSF 9. What important features should be included in the project proposal?

NSF 10. Who can submit grant applications?

NSF 11. What two NSF *criteria* are used to evaluate grant applications?

NSF 12. Who will review grant applications?

NSF 13. If awarded funding, what information will be included in the award letter?

NSF 14. If awarded, what project reporting is required?

NSF 15. How many proposals are submitted to NSF each year? How many are funded?

Exercise 3-4 continues on the next page.

Exercise 3-4: Review a National Science Foundation (NSF) RFP

Course, Curriculum, and Laboratory Improvement (Adapted from NSF 07-543)

SYNOPSIS OF PROGRAM

The Course, Curriculum, and Laboratory Improvement (CCLI) program seeks to improve the quality of science, technology, engineering, and mathematics (STEM) education for all undergraduate students. The program supports efforts to create new learning materials and teaching strategies, develop faculty expertise, implement educational innovations, assess learning and evaluate innovations, and conduct research on STEM teaching and learning. The program supports three types of projects representing three different phases of development, ranging from exploratory investigations to comprehensive projects.

I. INTRODUCTION

The CCLI program is intended to provide excellent STEM education for all undergraduate students. Toward this vision, the program supports projects based on high-quality science, technology, engineering or mathematics and recent advances in research on undergraduate STEM learning and teaching. The program seeks to stimulate, evaluate, and disseminate innovative and effective developments in undergraduate STEM education through the introduction of new content reflecting cutting-edge developments in STEM fields, the production of knowledge about learning, and the improvement of educational practice.

The CCLI program acknowledges the need for the development of exemplary courses and teaching practices and for assessment and research efforts in undergraduate STEM education that build on and contribute to the pool of knowledge concerning effective approaches in STEM undergraduate education. The program recognizes the value of STEM faculty committed to improving undergraduate STEM education and sharing their findings with each other. The report "Invention and Impact: Building Excellence in Undergraduate Science, Technology, Engineering and Mathematics Education" describes some of the successful efforts supported by the CCLI program and its predecessors.

II. PROGRAM DESCRIPTION

The CCLI program is based on a model depicting the relationship between knowledge, production, and improvement of practice in undergraduate STEM education. The model is adapted from the report, "Mathematical Proficiency for All Students." In this model, research findings about learning and teaching challenge existing approaches, thus leading to new educational materials and teaching strategies. The most promising of these developments are first tested in limited environments and then implemented and adapted in diverse curricula and educational institutions. These innovations are carefully evaluated by assessing their impact on teaching and learning. In turn, these implementations and assessments generate new insights and research questions.

Exercise 3-4 continues on the next page.

A. Project Components

All proposals must contribute to the development of exemplary undergraduate STEM education. Proposals may focus on one or more of the following project components.

Creating Learning Materials and Teaching Strategies. Guided by research on teaching and learning, by evaluations of previous efforts, and by advances within the disciplines, projects should develop new learning materials and tools, or create new and innovative teaching methods and strategies. Projects may also revise or enhance existing educational materials and teaching strategies, based on prior results. All projects should lead to exemplary models that address the varied needs of the nation's diverse undergraduate student population. They may include activities that help faculty develop expertise in adapting these innovations and incorporating them effectively into their courses.

Developing Faculty Expertise. Using new learning materials and teaching strategies often requires faculty to acquire new knowledge and skills and to revise their curricula and teaching practices. Projects should design and implement methods that enable faculty to gain such expertise. These can range from short-term workshops to sustained activities that foster new communities or networks of practicing educators. Projects must provide professional development for faculty so that new materials and teaching strategies can be implemented.

Implementing Educational Innovations. To ensure their broad-based adoption, successful educational innovations (such as learning materials, teaching strategies, faculty development materials, and evaluation tools) and the research relating to them should be widely disseminated. These innovations may come from CCLI projects or from other sources in the STEM community. Funds may be requested for local adaptation and implementation projects, including instrumentation to support such projects. Results from implementation projects should illuminate the challenges to and opportunities for adapting innovations in diverse educational settings, and may provide a foundation for the development of new tools and processes for dissemination. They may also provide a foundation for assessments of learning and teaching.

Assessing Student Achievement. Implementing educational innovations will create new needs to assess student learning. Projects for designing tools to measure the effectiveness of new materials and instructional methods are appropriate. Some projects may develop and share valid and reliable tests of STEM knowledge; other projects may collect, synthesize, and interpret information about student reasoning, practical skills, interests, or other valued outcomes. Projects that apply new and existing tools to conduct broad-based evaluations of educational programs or practices are appropriate if they span multiple institutions and are of general interest. Projects should carefully document population characteristics and context for abstracting what can be generalized. Results obtained using these tools and processes should provide a foundation that leads to new questions for conducting research on teaching and learning. Assessment projects likely to have only a local impact are discouraged.

Exercise 3-4 continues on the next page.

Conducting Research on Undergraduate STEM Education. Results from assessments of learning and teaching provide a foundation for developing new and revised models of how undergraduate STEM students learn. Research to explore how effective teaching strategies and curricula enhance learning is appropriate. Some research results may compel faculty to rethink STEM education for the future. Other projects will have a practical focus. All projects should lead to testable new ideas for creating learning materials and teaching strategies that have the potential for a direct impact on STEM educational practices. In all projects, testing to determine the effectiveness of the innovation should be appropriate to the stage of the project's development and implementation. In addition, evaluation results from within one component should influence the design of other components. For example, results from faculty development efforts may lead to refinement of learning materials and teaching strategies, and results from projects implementing educational innovations may identify the need for new approaches for developing faculty expertise.

B. Project Types

The CCLI program is accepting proposals under this solicitation for three types of projects representing different phases of development. These phases reflect the number of components included in the project; the number of academic institutions, students, and faculty members involved in the project; and the maturity of the proposed educational innovation.

Phase 1 Projects – total budget up to $150,000 ($200,000 when four-year colleges and universities collaborate with two-year colleges) for one-to three-years. Phase 1 projects typically will address one program component and involve a limited number of students and faculty members at one academic institution. Projects with a broader scope or larger scale can be proposed provided they can be done within the budget limitations. Proposed evaluation efforts should be informative, based on the project's specific expected outcomes, and consistent with the scope of a Phase 1 project. An extensive evaluation of student learning or use of an independent external evaluator may be included as appropriate but is not a requirement. To encourage collaboration between four-year colleges and universities and two-year colleges, projects involving such collaboration may request an additional $50,000. The distribution of effort and funds between the four-year institution and the community college should reflect a genuine collaboration. Results from Phase 1 projects are expected to be significant enough to contribute to the undergraduate STEM education knowledge base.

Phase 2 Projects – total budget up to $500,000 for two-to four-years. Phase 2 projects build on smaller-scale successful innovations or implementations, such as those produced by Phase 1 projects, and refine and test these on diverse users in several settings. Phase 2 projects carry the development to a state where the results are conclusive so that successful products and processes can be distributed widely or commercialized when appropriate. At a minimum, the innovation, if successful, should be institutionalized at the participating universities.

Exercise 3-4 continues on the next page.

Phase 3 Projects – total budget up to $2,000,000 for three-to five-years. Phase 3 projects should include an explicit discussion of the results and evidence produced by the work on which the proposed project is based. Such projects include a diversity of academic institutions and student populations. Evaluation activities are deep and broad, demonstrating the impact of the project's innovations on many students and faculty at a wide range of academic institutions. Dissemination and outreach activities that have national impact are an especially important element of Phase 3 projects, as are the opportunities for faculty to learn how to best adapt project innovations to the needs of their students and academic institutions.

Connections Between Phases

Although it is expected that some Phase 1 projects will lead to Phase 2 projects and some Phase 2 projects to Phase 3 projects, there is no requirement that a proposal be based on CCLI-funded work; however the antecedent(s) for all projects should be cited and discussed. While it is unlikely that the program would be able to support a single multi-year project to address all components in depth at a large scale, a succession of grants might support such an effort. In all cases the funds requested should be consistent with the scope and scale of the project.

C. Important Project Features

Although projects may vary considerably in the number of components they address, in the number of academic institutions involved, in the number of faculty and students that participate, and in their stage of development, all promising projects should include the following features:

Quality, Relevance, and Impact: Projects should address a recognized need or opportunity in the discipline, clearly indicate how they will meet this need, and be innovative in their production and use of new materials, processes, and ideas, or in their implementation of tested ones. They should have the potential to produce exemplary materials, processes, and models, or important assessment and research findings.

They should be based on an accurate and current understanding of the disciplinary field and utilize appropriate technology in student laboratories, classrooms, and other learning environments. These projects, even those that involve a local implementation, should address issues that have the potential for broad application in undergraduate STEM education. The results of these projects should advance knowledge and understanding within the discipline and within STEM education in general.

Student Focus: Projects should have a clear relation to student learning, with definite links between project activities and improvements in STEM learning. Moreover, they should involve approaches that are consistent with the nature of today's students, reflect the students' perspective, and, when possible, solicit student input in the design of the project.

Exercise 3-4 continues on the next page.

Use of and Contribution to Knowledge about STEM Education: Projects should reflect high-quality science, technology, engineering, and mathematics. They should have a clear and compelling rationale and use methods derived from existing knowledge concerning undergraduate STEM education and acknowledge existing projects of a similar nature. They should also have an effective approach for adding to this knowledge by disseminating their results.

STEM Education Community-Building: Projects should include interactions between the investigators and others in the undergraduate STEM education community. As appropriate to the scope and scale of the project, these interactions may range from informal contacts with a few colleagues to the establishment of a formal body of scholars. These interactions should enable the project to benefit from the knowledge and experience of others in developing and evaluating the educational innovation. This collaborating network should involve investigators working on similar or related approaches in the funding seeker's discipline or in other STEM disciplines and may also include experts in evaluation, educational psychology, or other related fields.

Expected Measurable Outcomes: Projects should have goals and objectives that have been translated into a set of expected measurable outcomes that can be monitored using quantitative and/or qualitative approaches. These outcomes should be used to track progress, guide the project, and evaluate its ultimate success. Expected measurable outcomes should pay particular attention to student learning, contributions to the knowledge base, and community-building.

Project Evaluation: All projects should have an evaluation plan that includes both a strategy for monitoring the project as it evolves to provide feedback to guide these efforts (formative evaluation) and a strategy for evaluating the effectiveness of the project in achieving its goals and for identifying positive and negative findings when the project is completed (summative evaluation). These efforts should be based on the project's specific expected measurable outcomes defined in the proposal and should rely on an appropriate mix of qualitative and quantitative approaches in measuring the outcomes.

D. Program Evaluation

The Division of Undergraduate Education (DUE) conducts an on-going program evaluation to determine how effectively the CCLI program is achieving its goal to stimulate, disseminate, and institutionalize innovative developments in STEM education through the production of knowledge and the improvement of practice. In particular, the program seeks to understand how effectively its projects are using current learning models in developing their innovations, contributing to the knowledge base on STEM education, and building a community of scholars in undergraduate STEM education. In addition to project-specific evaluations, all projects are expected to cooperate with this third-party program evaluation and respond to all inquiries, including requests to participate in surveys, interviews, and other approaches for collecting evaluation data.

Exercise 3-4 continues on the next page.

III. AWARD INFORMATION

NSF anticipates having $34 million for new and ongoing CCLI awards, pending the availability of funds. The awards will be made as standard or continuing grants. The number and size of awards will depend on the quality of the proposals received and the availability of funds. NSF expects to make the following number of awards:

- *Phase 1: Exploratory Projects*—70–90 awards expected.
- *Phase 2: Expansion Projects*—20–30 awards expected.
- *Phase 3: Comprehensive Projects*—2–5 awards expected.

For collaborative projects, these limits apply to the total project budget.

IV. ELIGIBILITY INFORMATION

Organization Limit: None Specified

Principal Investigator (PI) Limit: None Specified

Limit on Number of Proposals per Organization: None Specified

Limit on Number of Proposals per PI: An individual may be the PI on only one proposal submitted for any deadline. In applying this eligibility criterion, each proposal in a collaborative submission will be considered a separate proposal with a distinct PI. There is no restriction on the number of proposals for which an individual may serve as a co-PI.

Additional Eligibility Information: Proposals are invited from all organizations and in any field eligible under the standard Grant Proposal Guide (GPG). Specifically excluded are projects that address solely professional training in clinical fields such as medicine, nursing, and clinical psychology. There is no limit on the number of proposals an organization may submit.

V. PROPOSAL PREPARATION AND SUBMISSION INSTRUCTIONS

A. Proposal Preparation Instructions

Full Proposal Preparation Instructions: Proposers must submit proposals in response to this program solicitation via Grants.gov. Proposals submitted in response to this program solicitation via Grants.gov should be prepared and submitted in accordance with the NSF Grants.gov "Application Guide: A Guide for the Preparation and Submission of NSF Applications via Grants.gov." The complete text of the NSF Grants.gov application guide is available at: (http://www.nsf.gov/bfa/dias/policy/docs/grantsgovguide.pdf). To obtain copies of the application guide and application forms package, click on the "Apply" tab on the Grants.gov site, then click on the "Apply Step 1: Download a Grant Application Package and Application Instructions" link and enter the funding opportunity number (the program solicitation number without the NSF prefix) and press the "Download Package" button. Paper copies of the Grants.gov application guide may also be obtained from the NSF Publications Clearinghouse, telephone (703) 292-7827, or by e-mail from pubs@nsf.gov.

Exercise 3-4 continues on the next page.

Additional Full Proposal Instructions: The following information supplements the GPG and the NSF Grants.gov application guide. Funding seekers should make sure that their proposals respond to the list of questions provided both in the NSF general review criteria and in the additional program-specific review criteria. Additional information is at: http://www.nsf.gov/publications/pubsumm.jsp?odskey=nsf04016.

PIs are strongly encouraged to match their proposed budgets carefully to the scope and scale of the project. Excessive or poorly justified budgets indicate that the project is not well designed. Projects that plan to use the World Wide Web as a component of their overall dissemination strategy should connect the project's website to the National Science Digital Library (NSDL). The proposal should describe how the web pages would be tagged with descriptive metadata (see http://dublincore.org) so that the material becomes part of the NSDL. The website http://nsdl.org/ provides information and instructions for connecting the project's website.

All projects must comply with the section of the GPG on "Proposals Involving Human Subjects" (http://www.nsf.gov/publications/pub_summ.jsp?ods_key=gpg). The funding seeker should mark the "Human Subjects" box on the cover sheet and then indicate that the proposed project is exempt, approved, or pending. The process is pending if the Institutional Review Board (IRB) has not yet approved a submitted application or if the funding seeker has not yet submitted an application.

While all material relevant to determining the quality of the proposed work must be included within the 15-page project description or as part of the budget justification, funding seekers may, as a part of the supplementary documentation, include letters showing collaborator commitments and organizational endorsement. In addition, for those projects whose deliverables include a final product, samples of these products (e.g., excerpts from book chapters, assessment tools, screen shots of software, sample teaching modules, and other project deliverables) may be placed within the supplementary documentation section. These sample materials should be concise and relevant.

B. Grants.gov Requirements

For Proposals Submitted Via Grants.gov: Before using Grants.gov for the first time, each organization must register to create an institutional profile. Once registered, the applicant's organization can then apply for any federal grant on the Grants.gov website. The Grants.gov's "Grant Community User Guide" is a comprehensive reference document that provides technical information about Grants.gov. Funding seekers can download the user guide as a Microsoft Word document or as a PDF document. The Grants.gov user guide is available at: http://www.grants.gov/CustomerSupport. In addition, the NSF Grants.gov application guide provides additional technical guidance regarding preparation of proposals via Grants.gov. For Grants.gov user support, contact the Grants.gov Contact Center at 1-800-518-4726 or by e-mail: support@grants.gov. The Grants.gov Contact Center answers general technical questions related to the use of Grants.gov. Specific questions related to this program solicitation should be referred to the NSF program staff contact(s) listed in Section VIII of this solicitation.

Exercise 3-4 continues on the next page.

Submitting the Proposal: Once all documents have been completed, the Authorized Organization Representative (AOR) must submit the application to Grants.gov and verify the desired funding opportunity and agency to which the application is submitted. The AOR must then sign and submit the application to Grants.gov.

VI. NSF PROPOSAL PROCESSING AND REVIEW PROCEDURES

Proposals received by NSF are assigned to the appropriate NSF program and, if they meet NSF proposal preparation requirements, for review. A scientist, engineer, or educator serving as an NSF program officer and usually three to ten other persons outside NSF who are experts in fields represented by the proposal will carefully review all proposals. These reviewers are selected by program officers charged with the oversight of the review process. Proposers are invited to suggest names of persons they believe are especially well qualified to review the proposal and/or persons they would prefer not review the proposal. These suggestions may serve as one source in the reviewer selection process at the program officer's discretion. Care is taken to ensure that reviewers have no conflicts with the proposer.

A. NSF Review Criteria

All NSF proposals are evaluated through use of the two National Science Board (NSB)-approved merit review criteria: intellectual merit and the broader impacts of the proposed effort. In some instances, however, NSF will employ additional criteria as required to highlight the specific objectives of certain programs and activities.

The two NSB-approved merit review criteria are listed below. The criteria include considerations that help define them. These considerations are suggestions, and not all will apply to any given proposal. While proposers must address both merit review criteria, reviewers will be asked to address only those considerations that are relevant to the proposal being considered and for which the reviewer is qualified to make judgments.

What is the intellectual merit of the proposed activity? How important is the proposed activity to advancing knowledge and understanding within its own field or across different fields? How well qualified is the proposer to conduct the project? (If appropriate, the reviewer will comment on the quality of prior work.) To what extent does the proposed activity suggest and explore creative and original concepts? How well conceived and organized is the proposed activity? Is there sufficient access to resources?

What are the broader impacts of the proposed activity? How well does the activity advance discovery and understanding while promoting teaching, training, and learning? How well does the proposed activity broaden the participation of underrepresented groups? To what extent will it enhance the infrastructure for research and education, such as facilities, instrumentation, networks, and partnerships? Will the results be disseminated broadly to enhance scientific and technological understanding? What may be the benefits of the proposed activity to society? Examples of broader impacts can be found at www.nsf.gov/pubs/2004/nsf042/bicexamples.pdf.

NSF staff will give careful consideration to the following in making funding decisions:

Exercise 3-4 continues on the next page.

Integration of Research and Education. One of the principal strategies in support of NSF's goals is to foster integration of research and education through the programs, projects, and activities it supports at academic and research institutions. These institutions provide abundant opportunities where individuals may concurrently assume responsibilities as researchers, educators, and students and where all can engage in joint efforts that infuse education with the excitement of discovery and enrich research through the diversity of learning perspectives.

Integrating Diversity into NSF Programs, Projects, and Activities. Broadening opportunities and enabling the participation of all citizens—women and men, underrepresented minorities, and persons with disabilities—is essential to the health and vitality of science and engineering. NSF is committed to this principle of diversity and deems it central to the programs, projects, and activities it considers and supports.

Additional Review Criteria. In reviewing CCLI proposals, the standard criteria will be expanded to include the following additional review criteria as appropriate to the phase and main component of the proposed work:

Intellectual Merit. Will the project produce exemplary material, processes, or models that enhance student learning? Will it yield important assessment or research findings related to student learning, as appropriate to the goals of the project? Does the project build on the existing STEM education knowledge base? Are appropriate expected measurable outcomes explicitly stated, and are they integrated into an evaluation plan? Is the evaluation effort likely to produce useful information?

Broader Impacts. Will the project contribute to the STEM education knowledge base? Will the project help build the STEM education community? Will the project have a broad impact on STEM education in an area of recognized need or opportunity?

B. Review and Selection Process

A panel of experts will review proposals submitted in response to this program solicitation. Reviewers will be asked to formulate a recommendation to either support or decline each proposal. The program officer assigned to manage the proposal's review will consider the advice of reviewers and will formulate a recommendation. After scientific, technical, and programmatic review and consideration of appropriate factors, the NSF program officer recommends to the cognizant division director whether the proposal should be declined or recommended for award. NSF is striving to be able to tell applicants whether their proposals have been declined or recommended for funding within six months. The time interval begins on the date of receipt. The interval ends when the division director accepts the program officer's recommendation.

A summary rating and accompanying narrative will be completed and submitted by each reviewer. In all cases, reviews are treated as confidential documents. The program officer sends verbatim copies of reviews, excluding the names of the reviewers, to the principal investigator/project director. In addition, the funding seeker will receive an explanation of the decision to award or decline funding.

Exercise 3-4 continues on the next page.

In all cases, after programmatic approval has been obtained, the proposals recommended for funding will be forwarded to the Division of Grants and Agreements for review of business, financial, and policy implications and the processing and issuance of a grant or other agreement. Funding seekers are cautioned that only a grants and agreements officer may make commitments, obligations, or awards on behalf of NSF or authorize the expenditure of funds. No commitment on the part of NSF should be inferred from technical or budgetary discussions with an NSF program officer. A PI or organization that makes financial or personnel commitments in the absence of a grant or cooperative agreement signed by the NSF grants and agreements officer does so at their own risk.

VII. AWARD ADMINISTRATION INFORMATION

A. Notification of the Award
A grants officer in the Division of Grants and Agreements makes notification of the award to the submitting organization. The cognizant NSF officer administering the program will advise organizations whose proposals are declined as promptly as possible. Verbatim copies of reviews, not including the identity of the reviewer, will be provided automatically to the PI.

B. Award Conditions
An NSF award consists of: (1) the award letter, which includes any special provisions applicable to the award and any numbered amendments thereto; (2) the budget, which indicates the amounts, by categories of expense, on which NSF has based its support (or otherwise communicates any specific approvals or disapprovals of proposed expenditures); (3) the proposal referenced in the award letter; (4) the applicable award conditions, such as Grant General Conditions* or Federal Demonstration Partnership Terms and Conditions*; and (5) any announcement or other NSF issuance that may be incorporated by reference in the award letter. Cooperative agreements are also administered in accordance with NSF Cooperative Agreement Financial and Administrative Terms and Conditions and the applicable Programmatic Terms and Conditions. NSF awards are electronically signed by an NSF grants officer and transmitted electronically to the organization via e-mail. *Documents are at http://www.nsf.gov/awards/managing/general_conditions.jsp?org=NSF.

C. Reporting Requirements
For all multi-year grants (including both standard and continuing grants), the PI must submit an annual project report to the cognizant program officer at least 90 days before the end of the current budget period. (Some programs or awards require more frequent project reports.) Within 90 days after expiration of a grant, the PI also is required to submit a final project report. Failure to provide the required project reports will delay NSF review and processing of any future funding increments as well as any pending proposals for that PI. PIs should examine the formats of the required reports in advance to assure availability of required data.

Exercise 3-4 continues on the next page.

VIII. AGENCY CONTACTS

General inquiries regarding this program should be made to:

- Cameron Wiley, lead program director, telephone: (703) 292-XXXX, e-mail: cwiley@nsf.gov

- Matt Clark, lead program director, telephone: (703) 292-XXXX, e-mail: mclark@nsf.gov

- Amy Polk, lead program director, telephone: (703) 292-XXXX, e-mail: apolk@nsf.gov

IX. OTHER INFORMATION

The NSF website provides the most comprehensive source of information on NSF directorates (including contact information), programs and funding opportunities. Use of this website by potential funding seekers is strongly encouraged. In addition, "MyNSF" is an information-delivery system designed to keep potential funding seekers and other interested parties apprised of new NSF funding opportunities and publications, important changes in proposal and award policies and procedures, and upcoming NSF Regional Grants Conferences. Subscribers are informed through e-mail or the user's web browser each time new publications are issued that match their identified interests. "MyNSF" is available on NSF's website at http://www.nsf.gov/mynsf/.

Grants.gov provides an additional electronic capability to search for federal government-wide grant opportunities. NSF funding opportunities may be accessed via this new mechanism. Further information on Grants.gov is at http://www.grants.gov.

ABOUT THE NATIONAL SCIENCE FOUNDATION

NSF is an independent federal agency created by the National Science Foundation Act of 1950, as amended (42 USC 1861-75). The act states the purpose of the NSF is "to promote the progress of science; [and] to advance the national health, prosperity, and welfare by supporting research and education in all fields of science and engineering."

NSF funds research and education in most fields of science and engineering. It does this through grants and cooperative agreements to more than 2,000 colleges, universities, K–12 school systems, businesses, informal science organizations, and other research organizations throughout the United States. The foundation accounts for about one-fourth of federal support to academic institutions for basic research.

NSF receives approximately 40,000 proposals each year for research, education, and training projects, of which approximately 11,000 are funded. In addition, the foundation receives several thousand applications for graduate and postdoctoral fellowships. The agency operates no laboratories itself but does support National Research Centers, user facilities, certain oceanographic vessels, and Antarctic research stations. The foundation also supports cooperative research between universities and industry, U.S. participation in international scientific and engineering efforts, and educational activities at every academic level.

Chapter 4

Conduct Prewriting Activities After the RFP/RFA Is Released

With increasing competition for grant funds, prewriting activities are an essential prerequisite if funding seekers plan to be successful. Novice funding seekers often do not take the time to plan before responding to government solicitations, which typically results in mediocre proposals with little chance of winning.

Prewriting activities after the RFP/RFA is released involve (1) reviewing the solicitation and obtaining necessary clarification, and (2) making a formal bid/no-bid decision. If the formal decision is to bid, the proposal director should (1) determine the availability of proposal writers and reviewers; (2) distribute the RFP/RFA to all proposal team members; (3) prepare proposal planning tools, e.g., compliance checklist, proposal outline, and proposal schedule; and (4) hold a strategy meeting with proposal development team members. **See Exhibit 4-1**.

Prewriting activities must be completed prior to writing the proposal narrative and preparing the proposal budget. The adage "plan your work and work your plan" accurately describes this critical phase of the proposal development process.

Typically, prewriting activities involve three days of preparation and planning before developing a grant application. Day one involves analyzing the RFP/RFA and making a formal bid/no-bid decision. For the first time, the funding seeker has the official RFP/RFA in hand and must make a formal decision to submit a grant application or to terminate all activity. If the decision is to move forward (and prepare a grant application), then day two is focused on developing proposal planning tools necessary to guide writers and reviewers in preparing a grant application. During this period, the proposal director, in conjunction with institutional administrators, establishes proposal directives that provide guidance regarding how the proposed project would fit within the institution's mission. Day three involves holding a strategy meeting with writers and reviewers. During this meeting, the proposal director describes the overall purpose of the RFP/RFA with specific implications for the institution and uses the proposal prospectus to describe the goals, methods, and evaluation plans of the proposed project. The proposal director also discusses writing strategies and themes, assigns writing tasks, discusses major cost elements of the proposed project, and presents a schedule for writing, reviewing, editing, and submitting the grant application. **See Exhibit 4-2**.

Exhibit 4-1

Conduct Prewriting Activities After the RFP/RFA Is Released

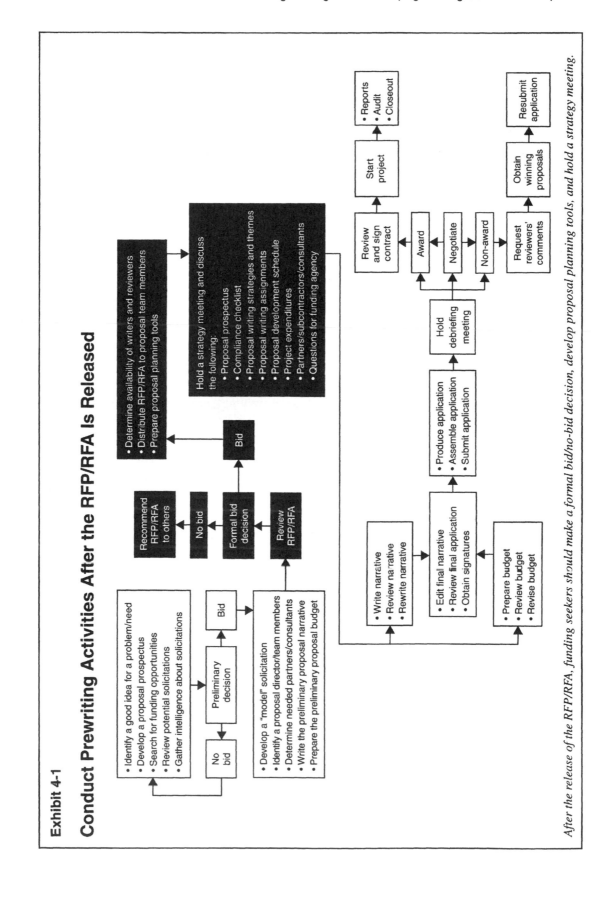

After the release of the RFP/RFA, funding seekers should make a formal bid/no-bid decision, develop proposal planning tools, and hold a strategy meeting.

Exhibit 4-2

First Three Days After the RFP/RFA Is Released

Day 1

- Analyze the RFP/RFA contents (e.g., eligibility, evaluation criteria, due date)
- Identify ambiguities and request clarification; discuss specific concerns with the POC
- Adjust/reevaluate the estimated probability of winning
- Make a formal bid/no-bid decision

Day 2*

- Determine the availability of proposal writers and reviewers
- Prepare a compliance checklist
- Prepare a proposal outline with specific writing assignments
- Prepare a proposal schedule with due dates for writing and budgeting assignments
- Prepare a proposal style sheet for all writers and reviewers to follow
- Distribute the RFP/RFA and proposal planning tools to key staff members

Day 3*

- Hold a proposal strategy meeting with all writers and reviewers
- Assign writing tasks based on the proposal outline and RFP/RFA criteria
- Establish specific due dates for reviewing, editing, and submitting the grant application
- Discuss budget assumptions and cost elements of the proposed project

*Completed only if there is a decision to submit a grant application.

Typically, prewriting activities involve three days of decision making, preparation, and planning before proposal writing and budget development will start.

Review the Solicitation and Obtain Necessary Clarification

A careful review of the RFP/RFA must be completed before a formal bid/no-bid decision is made. The first issue to consider before spending time developing a grant application is whether your organization is eligible to apply for funding. Some government agencies limit eligibility to selected organizations (e.g., state education agencies), organizations that serve only a particular population or group (e.g., K–12 students), or organizations that meet other specific criteria.

Proposal directors should analyze the entire solicitation and determine whether key information is different from what was anticipated. A careful review of the government solicitation will often lead to vague information that must be clarified before a formal bid/no-bid decision is made. Proposal directors should obtain clarification from the POC about any incomplete or unclear information found in the solicitation.

Specific questions should be developed before contacting a government agency representative. Always identify the solicitation by the RFP/RFA number and title before discussing questions with the government agency POC. Ask questions by referencing specific pages from the solicitation, when applicable. Take thorough notes and communicate information gained from conversations with the POC to proposal writers and reviewers. Use follow-up telephone calls or e-mails to resolve further questions, and always contact the same POC. In addition, the proposal director and key team members should attend agency pre-application conferences to more fully understand the RFP/RFA requirements.

Make a Formal Bid/No-Bid Decision

Based on the RFP/RFA and information from the POC, a formal bid/no-bid decision is made in conjunction with administration/management. The bid/no-bid decision is usually based on answers to the following questions:

- Is this project consistent with the organization's mission and goals?
- Is the organization qualified to complete the project in a timely manner?
- Are cost-sharing funds available (if required) to support this project?
- Is there commitment by the organization beyond the funding period?

A bid decision should be based on the (1) estimated value of the proposed work, (2) estimated effort in terms of person hours and cost to develop the proposal, (3) probable competition, (4) strengths and weaknesses of the institution in response to this funding opportunity, (5) arguments for and against bidding, and (6) estimated probability of winning. This information, coupled with the organization's readiness and support from upper administration, forms the basis for a "smart" bid decision. Institutions not in a good position to write a winning grant application are better off waiting for later competitions or looking for teaming partners who are in a better position to win. **See Exhibit 4-3.**

Determine the Availability of Proposal Writers and Reviewers

If an organization decides to develop a grant proposal in response to an RFP/RFA, the first activity is to reaffirm the availability of writers and reviewers. Upper administration should provide time and assistance to in-house writers and reviewers who will be developing the grant application. An ideal proposal team includes a proposal director, writers, reviewers, and support staff members. Proposal teams may also involve partners, subcontractors, and consultants. (See Exhibit 3-15 in Chapter 3.) Proposal directors must provide leadership during the proposal development process. Writers and reviewers must be interested in the proposed topic, have a proven record of delivering quality written documents, and be able to meet deadlines. Crafting a winning grant application requires committed leadership, creative and dedicated staff members, clear assignments, persuasive writing, realistic budgeting, a practical proposal development schedule, and upper administrative support.

Exhibit 4-3

Formal Bid Decision Form

Estimated $ Value of Grant

Estimated Effort (Person Hours/$ to Develop the Proposal)

Probable Competition

Major Strengths of the Grant-Seeking Institution/Organization

Major Weaknesses of the Grant-Seeking Institution/Organization

Arguments Pro

Arguments Con

Estimated Probability of Winning

Funding seekers use a formal bid decision form to make bid/no-bid proposal development decisions.

Develop Proposal Planning Tools

If the formal bid decision is to prepare a proposal, then day two is used to develop proposal-planning tools to assist writers in preparing the grant application. Specifically, the proposal director and key team members should develop a compliance checklist, proposal outline, proposal schedule, and style sheet.

Compliance Checklist

Based on a thorough analysis of the solicitation, the proposal director should develop a compliance checklist or work breakdown structure as a basis for generating proposal content and organization. A *compliance checklist* identifies every "shall" and "must" requirement in the solicitation. Identifying grant RFP/RFA requirements involves a careful reading of each solicitation sentence. A compliance checklist should (1) describe solicitation requirements as action statements (e.g., describe the qualifications of key personnel), (2) identify the page location within the solicitation, and (3) identify where the response will be described in the grant application. **See Exercise 4-4.**

Exhibit 4-4

Sample Compliance Checklist

RFP/RFA Requirement	Location in RFP/RFA	√	Location in Proposal	√
Demonstrate a detailed understanding of pertinent problems associated with the proposed topic.	Page 2 3rd paragraph	√	Page 1 1st paragraph	√
Identify project objectives that are observable and measurable.	Page 3 2nd paragraph	√	Page 6 3rd paragraph	√
Present a comprehensive plan to accomplish project objectives. Include a detailed management and staffing plan. Also include hours or percentage of time for each individual involved in the project.	Page 4 2nd paragraph	√	Page 8 2nd paragraph	√
Include a thorough evaluation plan that includes both formative and summative assessment strategies.	Page 5 1st paragraph	√	Page 17 3rd paragraph	√
List recent private and government clients (contract titles and numbers, as well as the name, address, telephone number, and e-mail address of previous work).	Page 7 3rd paragraph	√	Appendix	√
Include résumés of all key staff members and consultants involved in the proposed project. Résumés must include technical qualifications, such as duties, education, and experience.	Page 8 2nd paragraph	√	Appendix	√

Funding seekers use a compliance checklist to identify solicitation requirements that writers must address in the grant application. A work breakdown structure (WBS) can also used to identify specific solicitation requirements that serve as a guide to develop and organize the grant application.

Proposal Outline

A proposal outline must correspond with RFP/RFA requirements and identify proposal authors. An outline should include the RFP/RFA number, title, annotated RFP/RFA sections, and list of appendix items. A good proposal outline serves as a road map for developing a grant application. It should (1) use clear, concise, and descriptive headings; (2) be numbered sequentially; and (3) follow a logical order. Three levels of headings are generally used to develop a good proposal outline:

- level 1 headings are major content areas,

- level 2 headings are subdivisions of level 1 headings, and

- level 3 headings are subdivisions of level 2 headings.

If a proposal outline is provided in the RFP/RFA, follow it exactly. Do not leave anything up to the government agency reviewer's imagination. However, do not include extraneous information. Also note what the RFP/RFA prohibits from being included in the grant application. **See Exhibit 4-5.**

Proposal Schedule

A carefully planned schedule is an essential element in developing winning grant applications. Poor scheduling is a common mistake by funding seekers. Proposal schedules must allow sufficient time for writing, reviewing, and rewriting as well as for budgeting, reviewing, and rebudgeting project expenditures. A proposal schedule should especially be used if the proposed project involves (1) complex tasks, (2) numerous writers and reviewers, or (3) more than one partner.

Specifically, a proposal schedule should allow adequate time for:

- developing and reviewing at least two drafts of the narrative and budget,

- obtaining materials from partners, subcontractors, and/or consultants,

- developing appendix materials,

- editing the proposal narrative,

- producing and assembling proposal materials, and

- submitting the complete grant application to the government agency via electronic or non-electronic means before the deadline.

A proposal schedule should include a list of writers, reviewers, and support staff members involved in the proposal development process. A good technique for developing a proposal schedule is to determine the proposal due date and work backward to estimate the time needed to complete the writing and reviewing of each draft. Schedule proposal writing in small, but regular, amounts of time. The effort needed to write a proposal might seem insurmountable at first but is normally doable by using the "one step at a time" approach. **See Exhibit 4-6.**

Exhibit 4-5

Sample Proposal Outline

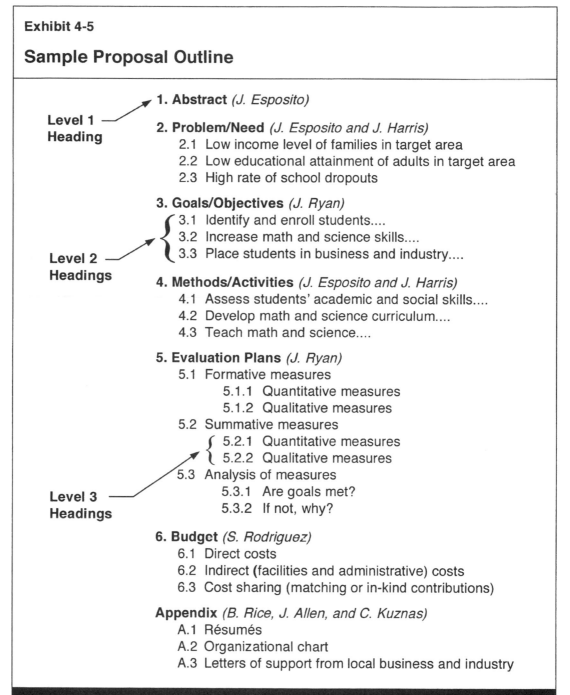

Level 1 Heading

1. Abstract *(J. Esposito)*

2. Problem/Need *(J. Esposito and J. Harris)*
   2.1 Low income level of families in target area
   2.2 Low educational attainment of adults in target area
   2.3 High rate of school dropouts

3. Goals/Objectives *(J. Ryan)*
   3.1 Identify and enroll students....
   3.2 Increase math and science skills....
   3.3 Place students in business and industry....

Level 2 Headings

4. Methods/Activities *(J. Esposito and J. Harris)*
   4.1 Assess students' academic and social skills....
   4.2 Develop math and science curriculum....
   4.3 Teach math and science....

5. Evaluation Plans *(J. Ryan)*
   5.1 Formative measures
         5.1.1 Quantitative measures
         5.1.2 Qualitative measures
   5.2 Summative measures
         5.2.1 Quantitative measures
         5.2.2 Qualitative measures
   5.3 Analysis of measures
         5.3.1 Are goals met?
         5.3.2 If not, why?

Level 3 Headings

6. Budget *(S. Rodriguez)*
   6.1 Direct costs
   6.2 Indirect (facilities and administrative) costs
   6.3 Cost sharing (matching or in-kind contributions)

Appendix *(B. Rice, J. Allen, and C. Kuznas)*
   A.1 Résumés
   A.2 Organizational chart
   A.3 Letters of support from local business and industry

Note: Italics indicate author or authors responsible for writing specific proposal sections.

A proposal outline includes headings and subheadings that writers follow when preparing narrative sections of the grant application.

Exhibit 4-6

Sample Proposal Schedule

Distribution: September 16, 20XX

Agency: U.S. Department of Education

CFDA #:   84.024A

Issue date: September 15, 20XX

Due date: October 15, 20XX

Tentative Schedule

Activity	Date	Time	Place or Person
Strategy meeting*	9/18	10:00 a.m.	Conference Room 210
1st draft to reviewers	9/24	5:00 p.m.	Kuznas
Reviewers' meeting*	9/26	11:00 a.m.	Conference Room 210
2nd draft to reviewers	10/5	5:00 p.m.	Kuznas
Reviewers' meeting*	10/8	1:00 p.m.	Conference Room 210
Edit final draft	10/11	Flow basis	Kuznas
Production and assembly	10/13	1:00 p.m.	Kuznas and Rice
Submit via Grants.gov	10/14	5:00 p.m.	Esposito and Kuznas
Grant application is due	10/15	4:00 p.m.	—

Writers
Harris, Esposito[1], Ryan, Rodriguez   *All writers and reviewers must attend.

Reviewers
Baker[2], Kraft, Esposito[2], Peters, Ryan[2], White

[1]Proposal director
[2]Final proposal review member

Support Staff Members
Rice, Allen, Kuznas

Proposal schedules identify activities to be accomplished within a specific time frame.

Proposal Style Sheet

Proposal writers usually have writing styles that vary, and thus the final proposal will often have numerous stylistic inconsistencies. If no format is recommended in the RFP/RFA, a style sheet developed in the early phases of the proposal will save considerable time and effort in the final stages of grant application preparation. A *style sheet* presents guidelines for document formatting, naming conventions, headings, use of illustrations, and other stylistic information. Style sheets are especially useful when developing large, complex proposals or when developing proposals that require large proposal teams to ensure that writers, reviewers, partners, subcontractors, and consultants use a consistent writing style. **See Exhibit 4-7.**

Exhibit 4-7

Sample Proposal Style Sheet

Directions: Writers, reviewers, and editors should follow the style guidelines below when preparing narrative sections of the grant application.

Title: Early Childhood Longitudinal Study–Kindergarten Cohort (ECLS-K)

Use this style sheet in conjunction with the proposal outline. Writers must use Microsoft Word for all narrative elements to eliminate formatting differences when sections are combined.

Naming Conventions

The official name of the proposal is indicated above; it is abbreviated "ECLS-K." The federal sponsor is the Department of Education, National Center for Education Statistics. Use the abbreviation "NCES/ED" for the sponsor.

Specific Jargon

In referring to school grades, please use "grade 1… grade 5," and "first grader" or "first grade students" (no hyphen).

Note that "kindergarten" is not capitalized; use "kindergarten student" rather than "kindergartner"; "preschool student" rather than "preschooler."

Note that Head Start is two words, both capitalized. State and local education agencies may be referred to as "SEAs" and "LEAs."

Headings

Section headings should be centered (e.g., "3. Methodology"). All other headings should be "flush left." Three levels of flush-left headings may be used in addition to the section heading. Additional headings should be treated as "run-in headings."

3. Methodology
[Centered Section Heading—14 pt. Helvetica Bold]

3.1 Project Initiation and Planning
[Flush left, first-level heading—12 pt. Helvetica Bold]

3.1.1 Meeting with NCES/ED
[Flush left, second-level heading—11 pt. Helvetica Bold]

3.1.1.1 Agenda
[Flush left, third-level heading—11 pt. Helvetica Bold Italic]

Style sheets present guidelines that writers and editors must follow when writing the narrative sections of a grant application.

Hold a Strategy Meeting

Three days after receipt of the RFP/RFA, a strategy meeting should be held with all writers and reviewers. The strategy meeting serves as both a serious working session and pep rally. Prior to the strategy meeting, the proposal director should distribute the RFP/RFA, compliance checklist, proposal schedule, proposal outline, proposal style sheet and other relevant documents to key team members so they have sufficient time to review them and come to the meeting with questions and comments.

During this meeting, the proposal director should provide an overview of the strategies/themes to be used in the proposal narrative and lead a discussion about key cost elements associated with the proposed project. The proposal director should also use this meeting to discuss specific proposal writing assignments and due dates for proposal drafts identified in the schedule. All staff members involved in the proposal development process must understand that grant application due dates are firm and cannot be missed.

The proposal director should also provide information about partners, subcontractors, consultants, and/or external grant writers (if used), and their roles and responsibilities. In addition, the proposal director should communicate all proposal development guidelines and schedule dates to external parties involved in the proposal development process.

Questions about the RFP/RFA are discussed and collected by the proposal director and submitted to the government agency representative (the POC) for answers. Answers from the government agency POC are distributed to internal and external parties involved in the proposal development process.

Immediately following the strategy meeting, grant writing and budget development activities must start on time to meet the planned writing and reviewing schedule. Support staff members should immediately start to collect appendix materials such as résumés, letters of support and commitment, and other documents from both internal and external parties.

Chapter Summary

Prewriting activities are fundamental to preparing a winning grant application. Funding seekers must make smart decisions about preparing or not preparing a grant application based on intelligence-gathering activities about the government agency and the solicitation.

Prewriting activities involve three days of preparation and planning before developing a grant application. Day one involves analyzing the RFP/RFA and making a formal bid/no-bid decision. Immediately after release of the RFP/RFA, the proposal director must analyze the entire solicitation and determine whether key information is different from what was anticipated. The proposal director should contact the POC to clarify any incomplete or unclear information in the RFP/RFA. Savvy proposal directors also attend any pre-application, pre-proposal, or technical workshops offered by the government agency.

Based on the RFP/RFA and feedback provided from the POC, a formal bid/no-bid decision should be made in conjunction with administration/management. Bid decisions are made based on answers to the following questions:

- Is the project consistent with the organization's mission and goals?

- Is the organization qualified to complete the project in a timely manner?

- Are cost-sharing funds available (if required) to support this project?

- Is there a commitment by the organization beyond the funding period?

A decision to prepare a grant application should be based on a good match between your project goals and timeline and the agency's mission and period of performance. Other deciding factors include the availability and commitment of key staff members and support from upper administration. If you do not have the time, commitment, or support to prepare a winning grant application, wait until you are in a better situation to compete for grant funds.

If the decision is to prepare a grant application, then day two is focused on reaffirming the availability of writers and reviewers and developing proposal planning tools to guide writers and reviewers in preparing the grant application. The proposal director, with assistance from key proposal team members, should develop a compliance checklist, proposal schedule, proposal outline, and proposal style sheet.

- A *compliance checklist* is a list of every RFP/RFA requirement. It is used as a basis for generating proposal content and organization.

- A *proposal outline* is a list of key RFP/RFA requirements and proposal authors. Funding seekers should always prepare an extensive outline of the project idea before writing the proposal narrative.

- A *proposal schedule* is a timeline for writing, budgeting, reviewing, and submitting the grant application.

- A *proposal style sheet* is a brief in-house document that provides format and style guidelines that writers, reviewers, and editors should follow in preparing a grant application. Style sheets usually include guidelines for text, headings, references, illustrations, and terminology specific to the solicitation.

Day three involves holding a planning session with writers and reviewers to discuss proposal strategies, themes, and major project cost expenditures. Specifically, the proposal director should provide an overview of the strategies and themes to be used in the proposal narrative and lead a discussion concerning budget assumptions associated with the proposal project.

The proposal director should also provide information about partners, subcontractors, consultants, and/or external grant writers (if used), and their roles and responsibilities. In addition, the proposal director should communicate all proposal development guidelines and schedule dates to external parties involved in the proposal development process.

Immediately after the strategy meeting, grant writing and budget development activities commence according to the proposal development schedule.

Review Questions

(Answers to Review Questions are on p. 273.)

(Answers to Review Questions are on p. 273.)

Directions: For statements 1–15, circle "T" for True or "F" for False.

T F   1. Prewriting activities after the RFP/RFA is released are completed prior to writing proposal narrative and preparing budgets.

T F   2. "Formal" bid decisions are made before solicitations are released.

T F   3. Prewriting activities after the RFP/RFA is released involve 10 days of preparation and planning.

T F   4. The adage "plan your work and work your plan" describes the prewriting phase of the proposal development process.

T F   5. Savvy funding seekers attend agency pre-application conferences.

T F   6. Before developing a proposal, funding seekers must determine if the organization has qualified staff members to develop the grant application in a timely manner.

T F   7. Funding seekers who have organizational and administrative support are in a better position to develop a grant application within the government's time frame.

T F   8. A compliance checklist is a list of solicitation requirements that are used as a guide in the development of a grant application.

T F   9. Proposal outlines correspond with RFP/RFA requirements and identify proposal authors.

T F   10. Carefully planned schedules are essential to developing winning grant applications.

T F   11. Good proposal schedules allow adequate time for developing and reviewing at least two drafts of grant application narrative.

T F   12. Style sheets provide formatting guidelines that writers, reviewers, and editors follow in preparing grant applications.

T F   13. Proposal planning tools (e.g., proposal outline) are distributed to key proposal team members prior to the strategy meeting.

T F   14. Strategy meetings are held with writers and reviewers to discuss proposal development activities and strategies.

T F   15. During the strategy meeting, the proposal director provides information about partners, subcontractors, consultants and/or external grant writers (if used), and their roles and responsibilities.

Exercise 4-1

Prepare a Compliance Checklist

(Answers to Exercise 4-1 are on pp. 283–285.)

Directions: Complete the compliance checklist form found on p. 86 after reading the solicitation OJP-92-R-008 "Drug Use Forecasting Program" found on pp. 87–90.

Situation: You are serving as a proposal director. One of your responsibilities is to review the following solicitation excerpts and create a comprehensive compliance checklist to guide writers in completing the proposal narrative.

To create a compliance checklist, you must read "Special Information for Developing Proposals." Look for "shall" and "must" statements to identify requirements.

Use the "Compliance Checklist" form to list every requirement that writers must address. In the column under the heading "RFP/RFA Requirements," describe each task briefly from the writer's perspective. Use an action statement, such as, "List management personnel by name, title, and projected percentage of time" (not simply "personnel list"). Be as specific as possible.

In the column under the heading "Location in RFP/RFA," indicate the section where you found each requirement (e.g., L-1-D). Finally, in the column under the heading "Location in Proposal," indicate where the requirement is addressed in the grant application.

Be sure to include all requirements identified in the solicitation. Remember that missing requirements may make the difference between a winning or losing proposal.

Exercise 4-1 continues on the next page.

Exercise 4-1 (Continued)
(Answers to Exercise 4-1 are on pp. 283–285)

Prepare a Compliance Checklist

Compliance Checklist Form

RFP/RFA Requirements	Location in RFP/RFA	√	Location in Proposal	√

Note: Reproduce this compliance checklist form if more space is needed.

Exercise 4-1 continues on the next page.

Exercise 4-1 (Continued)

Prepare a Compliance Checklist

Solicitation OJP-92-R-008: Drug Use Forecasting Program

The National Institute of Justice (NIJ) requests proposals in response to three tasks required by the Drug Use Forecasting (DUF) Program:

1. Rapid and high-quality editing, entry, preparation, and maintenance of data from DUF interviews and urine specimens available from 24 cities.

2. Publication of scheduled reports and special purpose analytical monographs, which are accurate and timely and meet high-editorial and graphic standards.

3. Consistent and attentive procedural training at all local DUF sites and technical assistance to local criminal justice agencies interested in DUF methodology.

Special Information for Developing Proposals

L-1: Technical Proposal Preparation

A. The contract will comprise one base year and three one-year options.

B. The proposal should be structured to accommodate all requirements and the evaluation criteria.

C. The offeror shall describe how work set forth in this proposal will be carried out.

D. The offeror shall submit a background statement stating its experience and qualifications to perform the resultant contract. The offeror shall include résumés of all principal staff and consultants involved in data entry, data analysis, data preparation, editing of text, technical editing, and graphic design under this RFP as well as the primary contact for inquiries relating to contract compliance issues. The offeror shall include technical qualifications, such as current duties, education, and experience.

E. The offeror shall list private and government clients with whom they recently (within the last three years) have had contracts. The references will be contacted as part of the evaluation of offerors. The offeror shall provide the following information: name and number of contract, name of client, address, telephone number, and contact person.

F. The offeror shall describe in detail the quality control procedures that will be followed in accomplishing the work set forth in this RFP, including data entry, data preparation, data editing, site training, technical editing, and graphics.

G. The offeror shall include a detailed management and staffing plan, including the hours or percentage of time for each individual and/or position identified.

H. The offeror shall list all equipment that will be used in accomplishing the work set forth in the RFP.

Exercise 4-1 continues on the next page.

I. Suggestions for Preparation

   1. After a thorough analysis of the statement of work, the offeror shall present a plan to accomplish the objectives. This section should demonstrate an understanding of the pertinent problems involved and methods of overcoming them. The technical proposal should be presented in a clear and concise manner to assist in the evaluation effort.

   2. The offeror should address each of the specific tasks contained in the statement of work, specifying methodology/approach for accomplishing and indicating number of person hours estimated for each task. (Note: Person hours for each task should also be indicated in the cost proposal.) Offerors should provide an approach to each task, including the necessary procedures, formats, and designs to indicate how they will meet the requirements of and manage the tasks listed in the statement of work.

L-2: Special Requirements

A. Task 1: Data Editing, Entry, Preparation, and Maintenance

   1. Offerors should know that the DUF interview instrument will change over time.

   2. Offerors are required to show their expertise in using SPSS or SPSSPC and show their ability to modify data entry programs and log programs, which will be provided by the NIJ as needed.

   3. Offerors shall describe procedures to ensure quality and shall demonstrate experience in maintaining data integrity during data entry of interviews, multi-source data merging, and data reporting. Offerors are encouraged to identify other problems that may occur in completing tasks specified in this RFP and to recommend procedures to prevent or resolve them.

      a. The DUF program involves data collection in booking facilities from diverse sites with changing local staff. Data are continually being generated and submitted to the contractor. Given the realities of urban booking center operations, instructions provided to DUF site personnel regarding data collection and editing may not always be followed exactly. The offeror must show an understanding and mastery of the complex practical issues involved in organizing, tracking, processing, and reporting results from a national multi-site data collection program.

      b. Offerors must demonstrate successful implementation of quality control measures and availability of personnel to respond to quality control issues. Offerors shall propose procedures for attaining the following goals and cite recent experience in successfully accomplishing similar goals on projects involving collection of data from multiple independent sites:

         (1) Ensure that the total number of interviews per gender/age group received from a site is processed.

Exercise 4-1 continues on the next page.

(2) Ensure that all interview data are reported.

(3) Ensure that the total number of specimen results received from the laboratory is processed.

(4) Ensure that the total number of specimen results received from the laboratory is reported.

(5) Ensure that data are reported separately for each site and each quarter.

(6) Ensure that data are reported separately for each gender/age group.

(7) Ensure that all data are entered accurately.

(8) Ensure contract compliance with schedules outlined in this RFP.

(9) Ensure confidentiality of site results.

(10) Ensure confidentiality of DUF data, e.g., DUF data cannot be released without written approval.

(11) Ensure accuracy in matching interview data and urine data when merging files.

(12) Ensure that data sets are free from errors for all files, e.g., data files, system files and merged files.

B. Task 2: Publication of Special Reports

1. Quality control issues

Offerors are required to respond to the quality control issues described in this RFP concerning editing, graphics, and layouts of DUF publications. Offerors may suggest other layouts, that may improve the publication. Offerors may also suggest problems, which may occur in the publication tasks specified in this RFP, and propose solutions or procedures to prevent them.

2. Graphics and presentation of data

a. Offerors should propose new graphics in their proposals for NIJ review.

b. Offerors shall propose procedures to ensure a high-quality presentation of data. Also, offerors shall demonstrate experience in accurately representing quantitative data and shall provide points of contact for substantiation.

3. Publication

a. DUF data are published annually and quarterly in the National Institute of Health's *Research In Brief* series (*RIB*). Special analyses of DUF research findings are also published in monographs. For purposes of this RFP, offerors should assume two monograph publications per year, averaging 16 pages each. (Copies of the *RIB*s and monographs may be viewed in the Office of Justice Programs reading room or may be ordered from the contracting officer.) The offerors must demonstrate an understanding of the issues involved in publishing results from a national program under tight time schedules.

Exercise 4-1 continues on the next page.

    b. Offerors must demonstrate experience in graphic design, editing, and report development. Offerors must further demonstrate that sufficient quality control measures are in place and that personnel are available to respond to diverse quality control issues. Offerors shall propose procedures for attaining the following goals and cite recent experience in successfully accomplishing similar goals on projects involving quantitative information for publication:

      (1) Ensure that data received from NIJ are accurately transposed into graphic layouts.

      (2) Ensure that all materials are presented according to NIJ specifications.

      (3) Ensure that data presented in tables, graphs, or charts are consistent with corresponding text.

      (4) Ensure that a final review of the entire publication is conducted with emphasis on accuracy within the publication.

      (5) Ensure compliance with respect to timelines set out in this RFP.

      (6) Ensure confidentiality of data until publication is released.

C. Task 3: Procedural Training

    1. For purposes of this proposal, offerors should assume four trips per year to provide technical assistance. Trips dedicated to technical assistance are in addition to the 12 DUF site visits.

    2. Offerors are encouraged to submit samples of weekly reports and monthly reports with their technical proposals. Also, offerors should provide a modified sample of the quarterly report along with their technical proposals. A sample financial report should be submitted with the technical proposal.

    3. Offerors are required to demonstrate their capability to accomplish subitems A (meet with the Contracting Office Technical Representative in Washington D.C. on a regular basis and sometimes on short notice) and B (identify and enter into an agreement with a pool of consultants to provide a number of diverse tasks) of the Special Requirements.

L-3: Management Portion of Technical Proposal

A. The management proposal should set forth all relevant information concerning the offeror's ability to run and effectively manage a project of this type, including a detailed discussion of its experience and familiarity in this subject area. Description of the offeror's managerial staff, along with résumés of each of the staff members, shall also be submitted. It should also demonstrate the degree of importance that offerors attach to projects of this nature.

B. Organizational Structure proposed should be included as part of the Management Proposal.

C. Résumés of key personnel to be employed on this contract must be included.

Exercise 4-2

Prepare a Proposal Outline and Schedule

(Answers to Exercise 4-2 are on pp. 286–287.)

Directions: Read the memorandum and RFP from the State Community College Board (pp. 92–96) and prepare a proposal outline and schedule. Assume that you have 30 days to prepare the proposal. Also assume that funding is for one year (July 1 through June 30). Grants may be continued up to four additional years.

Proposal Outline

Develop a proposal outline that:

- corresponds with solicitation requirements,
- includes major proposal sections and proposed authors, and
- lists appendix materials.

Proposal Schedule*

Develop a proposal schedule that:

- allows sufficient time for proposal writing and budget preparation,
- identifies writers, reviewers, and support staff members, and
- allows sufficient time for reviewing, editing, producing, assembling, and submitting the proposal to the government agency.

*Note: A good way to develop a schedule is to determine the due date and work backward, estimating the time needed to complete the writing and reviewing of each proposal draft.

Exercise 4-2 continues on the next page.

State Community College Board
401 East Highway Road
Capital City, IN 58765-1234

STATE COMMUNITY
COLLEGE BOARD

Memorandum

Date: March 15, 20XX

To: Community College Presidents

From: Dr. Jean E. Thomas, Chief Financial Officer

Subject: Innovative Programs to Increase Information Technology Graduates
RFP #SCCB 315

The State Community College Board (SCCB) received an appropriation for a new special initiative grant program. Since the State will be facing a critical shortage of qualified workers in the field of Information Technology (IT), $300,000 in grant funds will be dedicated to support innovative programs designed to increase the number of IT professionals graduating or receiving certification from community colleges. To address this need, SCCB is conducting a competitive Request for Proposal (RFP) to fund 8–10 projects with budgets of $25,000–$50,000. No facilities and administrative (indirect) costs are allowed.

Attached is the RFP for the special initiative. Proposals are due April 15, 20XX. Grant awards will be made in June. The period of performance is from July 1 through June 30.

Grants may be continued up to four additional years. Additional funding is based upon availability of funds and the progress of the local partnership in meeting its proposed program objectives.

If you have questions, please do not hesitate to contact me at jthomas@sccb.org.

Exercise 4-2 continues on the next page.

Innovative Programs to Increase
Information Technology Graduates
RFP #SCCB 315

Background/Purpose

In the next fiscal year, the State Community College Board (SCCB) will support innovative programs designed to increase the number of Information Technology (IT) professionals graduating or receiving certification from state community colleges. Funds will be awarded to support the development and implementation of programs to (1) increase high school students' awareness of career opportunities in IT, and (2) increase the number of high school graduates who enroll in IT programs at the postsecondary level.

Proposed high school/college linkages should be designed to support the development and implementation of new programs or enhance and expand existing programs in the IT field that (1) begin with the junior year of high school and move through a certificate or AAS degree, and (2) provide students with connections to workplace experiences. Proposals must include at least one high school partner and at least one business partner. The following executive summary article may contain several helpful suggestions concerning IT:

> Meares, C.A. & Sargent, Jr., J.F. (20XX). *The Digital Work Force: Building Infotech Skills at the Speed of Innovation.* Washington, DC: U.S. Department of Commerce Office of Technology Policy.

Each college applicant is required to contribute a cash match of at least 25 percent of the total amount requested from SCCB. For example, if an application is for a $40,000 grant, the college must contribute a cash match of $10,000 or more. No indirect (facilities and administrative) funds are allowed. Consortia of two or more colleges are encouraged to apply.

Selection Criteria

Grant applications should include a detailed description of project activities and costs. Include the following information in the application package (note the weighted value of each component in brackets):

- Application Cover Sheet and Project Abstract [see p. 95] (10 points)
- Problem/Need (15 points)
- Project Goals and Objectives (10 points)
- Project Activities and Timeline (20 points)
- Project Leadership and Partners (20 points)
- Budget (20 points)
- Appendix (5 points)

Exercise 4-2 continues on the next page.

In addition to the selection criteria, funding seekers should also consider the following questions before submitting the grant application:

- Does the abstract present a comprehensive overview of the project, and is it fewer than 200 words?

- Is the problem/need statement supported by recent and relevant citations?

- Do goals and objectives identify measurable project outcomes?

- Is there a logical and detailed description of project activities designed to accomplish the proposed project objectives?

- Are personnel qualifications, responsibilities, and time commitments identified?

- Is there a management plan that shows the organizational structure of the project?

- Is there a reasonable timeline for completing the major project activities within the agency's period of performance?

- Do evaluation plans describe formative and summative procedures to measure the project's objectives?

- Is the budget reasonable, and does it include 25 percent matching funds?

- Do the appendix items include important materials that support the proposed project?

Application Submittal

The narrative section of the proposal is limited to five pages. A complete grant application must include a proposed budget that is reasonable and cost effective. Budget detail (e.g., three computers @$1,200 = $3,600) and narrative should also be provided to explain complex or unusual project expenditures.

Each community college district is eligible to submit one grant application. Colleges are encouraged, but not required, to work together to achieve broader project impacts.

Please submit the grant application to:
    State Community College Board
    Attn: Dr. Jean E. Thomas, CFO
    401 East Highway Road
    Capital City, IN 58765-1234

The application must be received no later than 4:00 p.m. CST on April 15, 20XX. Questions should be directed to Dr. Jean E. Thomas at jthomas@sccb.org.

Exercise 4-2 continues on the next page.

Application Cover Sheet and Project Abstract
RFP #SCCB 315

Name of college:

Contact person:

Office address:

Telephone:

Fax:

E-mail:

Descriptive title of grant application

Grant abstract (no more than 200 words)

Exercise 4-2 continues on the next page.

Budget RFP #SCCB 315			
Name of college:			
CFO name:			
CFO signature:			
Line Item Description	**Government Agency**	**Matching Funds**	**Total Amount**
Personnel Salaries			
Fringe Benefits			
Travel and Per Diem			
Equipment and Expendable Supplies			
Contractual Services			
Other Direct Costs			
Total Project Costs*			

*Note: No indirect (facilities and administrative) costs are allowed.

Chapter 5

Write, Review, Rewrite, and Edit the Proposal Narrative

Writing, reviewing, rewriting, and editing several drafts of narrative before the final proposal is submitted to a government agency is key to developing a winning grant application. Grant proposals are only as good as the effort invested. Government agencies receive far more good grant applications than they can fund. A winning proposal is based on good ideas that are expressed in a clear and understandable manner. A well thought out and succinct grant proposal will always have the best chance to win funding. Winning proposals are based on innovative project ideas that provide clear objectives, describe feasible tasks, present quality personnel, and identify clear evaluation procedures. Perfect writing cannot turn a bad project idea into a winning proposal; however bad writing can turn a good project idea into a poor proposal.

Prepare to Write the Proposal Narrative

Grant writers must possess subject-matter knowledge, writing skills, analytical and creative expertise, and marketing savvy. If one or more of these attributes is missing, it will be evident in the final grant submission. In addition, grant writers must have a place to write, tools for writing, and time to write. The place to write must be a comfortable atmosphere that is away from distractions. Interruptions from the telephone, co-workers, children, etc., will hinder grant proposal writing. Grant writers must get away from daily activities and focus on writing tasks. Tools for writing include the RFP/RFA, winning grant proposals from similar competitions, proposal prospectus, proposal outline, and proposal schedule. Finally, grant writers must block out specific time for writing and have reasonable writing goals. The key is to avoid procrastination and maintain a consistent writing schedule until the grant application is finished. **See Exhibit 5-1**.

Experienced grant writers (1) follow RFP/RFA guidelines, (2) read examples of past winning grant proposals, and (3) follow a good proposal outline that organizes thoughts and captures the RFP/RFA evaluation criteria. Proposal narrative headings should match RFP/RFA criteria so reviewers don't have to "hunt" for critical information. When developing the first draft of proposal narrative, grant writers should write ideas quickly without worrying about style. Grammar and syntax can be improved later. **See Exhibit 5-2**.

Exhibit 5-1

Write, Review, Rewrite, and Edit the Proposal Narrative

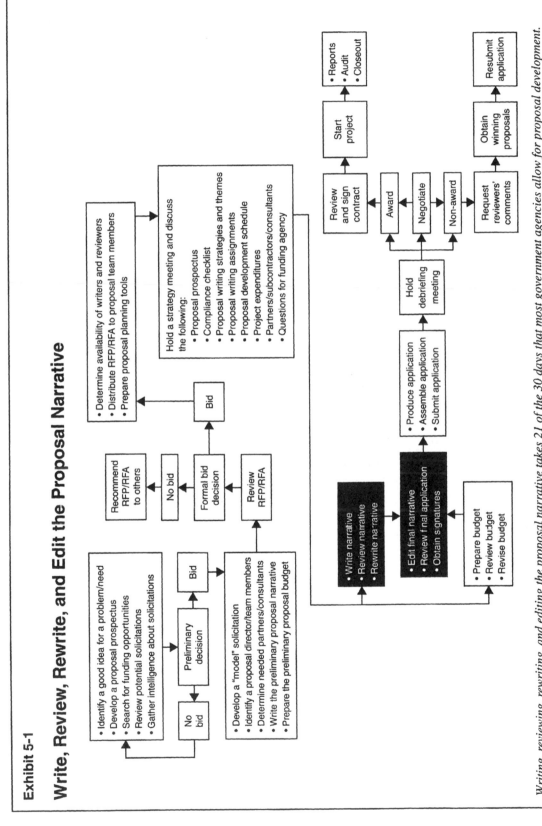

Writing, reviewing, rewriting, and editing the proposal narrative takes 21 of the 30 days that most government agencies allow for proposal development.

Exhibit 5-2

Guidelines for Writing Grant Proposals

Follow RFP/RFA Guidelines and Read Other Grant Proposals.
- Read the complete RFP/RFA—follow specific guidelines.
- Read and reread all grant application forms—follow directions.
- Be responsive to evaluation criteria to be used by government agency reviewers.
- Read examples of prior winning grant applications.

Use Proposal Planning Tools.
- Use a compliance checklist that corresponds with RFP/RFA requirements.
- Follow a proposal outline with clear headings and author writing assignments.
- Adhere to a proposal schedule with specific due dates.
- Use a proposal style sheet to ensure that writers follow a consistent style.

Write Proposal Narrative.
- Write narrative that follows the proposal outline.
- Know your audience—write your grant application for the agency reviewer.
- In case of writer's block, insert "??" in the narrative and keep on writing.
- Write to inform, not to impress—use concise and accurate language.
- Present major ideas—make it easy for reviewers to understand the big picture.
- Make your application attractive—use graphics, tables, and figures.
- Avoid in-house jargon, unusual acronyms, and abbreviations.
- Avoid words that plant doubt (e.g., "We will try to develop....").
- Avoid long sentences and paragraphs—use white space effectively.
- Use bulleted lists to highlight important project steps, procedures, or strategies.
- Use emphasized narrative (bolded, italicized, or underlined) sparingly.
- Use recent and relevant citations and references.

Ask for Constructive Feedback from Colleagues Prior to Submission to the Agency.
- Ask content experts to review your proposal.
- Ask readers outside your area of expertise to review your proposal.
- Ask style experts to review your proposal.

Experienced grant writers follow RFP/RFA guidelines, use proposal-planning tools, write several drafts of proposal narrative, and seek feedback from content and style experts.

When completing narrative drafts, grant writers should strive to develop a project idea that presents proposal themes and benefits in an easy-to-read format. Grant writers should adhere to the five "C's" of good writing: content, communication, clarity, commitment, and consistency. Specifically, grant writers must:
- have a thorough understanding of the proposed project *content,*
- *communicate* information to the reading audience,
- seek *clarity* in proposal narrative,
- *commit* to completing the grant-writing tasks within a specified time, and
- be *consistent* with format and presentation of information.

Proposal writers must (1) aim for clarity of thought and expression, (2) specify clear objectives, and (3) provide a detailed description of project activities. Funding seekers always have the burden of proof and must demonstrate how the solicitation criteria will be met. Grant writers must provide exactly what is required in the RFP/RFA. Experienced funding seekers keep their writing clear, factual, supportable, and professional. Well-written grant proposals include concise writing with short words, short sentences, and short paragraphs to avoid unnecessary verbiage and reduce reader fatigue. In addition, graphics and textboxes should be used to illustrate and highlight key proposal concepts. Writing must be as specific as possible and substantiate all claims with measurable data (e.g., "the proposal director has 23 years of experience overseeing 55 projects," rather than, "the proposal director has overseen numerous projects"). Grant writers should provide simple and straightforward narrative, be politically correct, and avoid jargon, sexist language, and acronyms. Finally, grant writers should always write in the third person. **See Exhibit 5-3.**

Exhibit 5-3

Tips to Improve Grant Writing

Gather intelligence. Read past agency solicitations, review winning proposal examples, and examine other relevant agency publications. Talk with the government agency POC, colleagues who have won grants, and staff members from the office of sponsored programs about your proposed project.

Start with a proposal prospectus. Start with a proposal concept paper that captures the major ideas of your proposed project. Share your concept paper with upper administration and staff members from the office of sponsored programs for support and advice. Finally, use the concept paper as a guide to locate appropriate funding opportunities.

Use an outline. Include major points to be addressed in the grant application. Use proposal outline headings that correspond with RFP/RFA requirements.

Use clear, concise, accurate, and vivid language. Plan your message carefully and state it succinctly. Good writing means using words your audience will comprehend. Use the active voice: Say, "We serve 350 people," instead of, "A total of some 350 people were served." The active voice is more forceful and easier to follow. The most effective writing paints a picture of the situation. Use statistics, figures, tables, and charts to support the narrative and illustrate major proposal points.

Make it easy for the agency reviewers to understand your proposal. Reviewers may or may not be content experts—make it easy for them to understand your project. Develop a straightforward application that makes it easy for reviewers to locate information directly related to solicitation criteria. Finally, serve as a grant reviewer before submitting a grant application to understand the reviewers' roles and responsibilities.

Experienced proposal writers plan their message for a specific audience.

All grant proposals require persuasive writing to produce convincing narrative that will positively influence government agency reviewers. Proposal narrative sections must always consider the reading audience and thoroughly describe the "why," "what," "how," "who," "where," and "when" of the proposed project.

- Why   — Identifies the need, significance, or rationale for the project.
- What   — Describes the purpose, goals, or objectives of the project.
- How   — Describes the project activities and procedures.
- Who   — Describes the participants who will be served.
- Where — Identifies the place where the project will be completed.
- When   — Provides a detailed timeline for completing project activities.

Common Narrative Components Found in Grant Applications

Some narrative components can be adapted from previously written material, while other components must be written fresh for each proposal. In either case, all narrative must adapt the message to meet the needs and wants of the government agency. Although each proposal is unique, most funding agencies require the following narrative components:

- Cover Sheet
- Table of Contents*
- Abstract
- Introduction*
- Problem/Need
- Goals/Objectives
- Methods/Activities
- Evaluation Plans
- References and Bibliography*
- Appendix*

> Proposal narrative requirements will vary from agency to agency. Always use the specific narrative components identified in the RFP/RFA as headings in your grant application.
>
> *Indicates an optional proposal narrative component.

Cover Sheet

Most government agencies require a standard cover sheet as the first page of the grant application. Funding seekers should carefully follow instructions for completing information about the applicant and employer, proposed project, estimated project funding, and authorized organization representative. Typical required information includes the title of the project, name and address of the applicant's organization, project dates, total budget requested, and the name, degree, and contact information for the Principal Investigator (PI) or Project Director (PD). Always check standard forms for completeness and accuracy. The cover sheet and other standard forms are available at most government agency websites. **See Exhibit 5-4.**

Exhibit 5-4

Sample Grant Application Cover Sheet

COVER SHEET FOR PROPOSAL TO THE NATIONAL SCIENCE FOUNDATION

PROGRAM ANNOUNCEMENT/SOLICITATION NO./CLOSING DATE/If not in response to a program announcement/solicitation enter NSF 00-2	FOR NSF USE ONLY
NSF XX-XXX	NSF PROPOSAL NUMBER

FOR CONSIDERATION BY NSF ORGANIZATIONAL UNIT(S) (Indicate the most specific unit known, i.e., program, division, etc.)

Computing and Technology

DATE RECEIVED	NUMBER OF COPIES	DIVISION ASSIGNED	FUND CODE	DUNS # (Data Universal Numbering System)	FILE LOCATION
				060215493	

EMPLOYER IDENTIFICATION NUMBER (EIN) OR TAXPAYER IDENTIFICATION NUMBER (TIN)	SHOW PREVIOUS AWARD NO. IF THIS IS ☐ A RENEWAL ☐ AN ACCOMPLISHMENT-BASED RENEWAL	IS THIS PROPOSAL BEING SUBMITTED TO ANOTHER FEDERAL AGENCY? YES ☐ NO ☒ IF YES, LIST ACRONYM(S)
123456789		

NAME OF ORGANIZATION TO WHICH AWARD SHOULD BE MADE	ADDRESS OF AWARDEE ORGANIZATION, INCLUDING 9 DIGIT ZIP CODE
Hoosier State University	**Hoosier State University**
AWARDEE ORGANIZATION CODE (IF KNOWN)	**123 Main Street**
0016268000	**Hoosier, IN 45321-3303**
NAME OF PERFORMING ORGANIZATION, IF DIFFERENT FROM ABOVE	ADDRESS OF PERFORMING ORGANIZATION, IF DIFFERENT, INCLUDING 9 DIGIT ZIP CODE
PERFORMING ORGANIZATION CODE (IF KNOWN)	

IS AWARDEE ORGANIZATION (Check All That Apply)
(See GPG II.D.1 For Definitions)   ☐ FOR-PROFIT ORGANIZATION   ☐ SMALL BUSINESS   ☐ MINORITY BUSINESS   ☐ WOMAN-OWNED BUSINESS

TITLE OF PROPOSED PROJECT **Innovative Programs to Increase Information Technology Graduates**

REQUESTED AMOUNT	PROPOSED DURATION (1-60 MONTHS)	REQUESTED STARTING DATE	SHOW RELATED PREPROPOSAL NO., IF APPLICABLE
$2,007,665	**36 months**	**10/1/20XX**	

CHECK APPROPRIATE BOX(ES) IF THIS PROPOSAL INCLUDES ANY OF THE ITEMS LISTED BELOW

☐ BEGINNING INVESTIGATOR (GPG I.A.3)
☐ DISCLOSURE OF LOBBYING ACTIVITIES (GPG II.D.1)
☐ PROPRIETARY & PRIVILEGED INFORMATION (GPG I.B, II.D.7)
☐ NATIONAL ENVIRONMENTAL POLICY ACT (GPG II.D.10)
☐ HISTORIC PLACES (GPG II.D.10)
☐ SMALL GRANT FOR EXPLOR. RESEARCH (SGER) (GPG II.D.12)

☐ VERTEBRATE ANIMALS (GPG II.D.12) IACUC App. Date _____
☐ HUMAN SUBJECTS (GPG II.D.12)
Exemption Subsection _____ or IRB App. Date _____
☐ INTERNATIONAL COOPERATIVE ACTIVITIES: COUNTRY/COUNTRIES _____
☐ FACILITATION FOR SCIENTISTS/ENGINEERS WITH DISABILITIES (GPG V.G.)
☐ RESEARCH OPPORTUNITY AWARD (GPG V.H)

PI/PD DEPARTMENT	PI/PD POSTAL ADDRESS
Engineering Technology	**123 Main Street**
PI/PD FAX NUMBER	**Hoosier, IN 45321-3303**
219-834-XXXX	**United States**

NAMES (TYPED)	High Degree	Yr of Degree	Telephone Number	Electronic Mail Address
PI/PD NAME **Patrick Smith**	**Ph.D.**	**1985**	**219-834-XXXX**	**psmith@hoosierstate.edu**
CO-PI/PD **David Johnson**	**M.A.**	**2002**	**219-834-XXXX**	**djohnson@hoosierstate.edu**
CO-PI/PD				
CO-PI/PD				

NSF Form 1207

Most government agencies require a cover sheet as the first page of the grant application. Funding seekers should carefully follow instructions for completing information about the applicant and employer, proposed project, and estimated project funding. The cover sheet and other standard forms are available at most government agency websites.

Table of Contents

Many solicitations require a table of contents (TOC) as part of the grant application, especially if the narrative is lengthy and/or complex. The TOC should include major proposal narrative headings and subheadings along with specific page numbers. The TOC is used to help agency reviewers locate material quickly and efficiently. Because grant application requirements vary from agency to agency, funding seekers must follow agency guidelines for preparing the TOC. Once the proposal is done, page numbers for all narrative sections identified in the TOC should be checked before the application is submitted. It is also a good practice to include a separate TOC as a preface to numerous appendix materials.

Abstract

An *abstract* is a cogent one-page summary of the proposed project written in third person. Even though the abstract is usually not scored, it represents the first impression of your organization and as such must educate agency reviewers about your proposed project. Abstracts must be informative to the content specific reviewer, but yet written in plain English so the lay reader can interpret the project idea. Funding seekers must allow sufficient time to write a clear and comprehensive abstract—while the abstract is usually the proposal opening and last section written, it should not be written at the last minute. The abstract must (1) follow RFP/RFA guidelines, (2) be checked by a style editor to ensure that every sentence has meaning, and (3) convince agency reviewers that the project is significant and worthy of funding.

Introduction

The *introduction* is an optional proposal component that is used to familiarize agency reviewers with your organization, institutional mission and philosophy, programs, target population, and past and present operations. The introduction is a short description of who you are and what you do. It should provide specific quantitative information (e.g., census and/or chamber of commerce data) that is responsive to the RFP/RFA criteria. The introduction might also include pertinent background information about the number of people in the community and/or organization and number of individuals to be served as a result of the proposed project.

If the government agency does not require a separate introduction section, it is recommended that funding seekers include this information at the beginning of the problem/need statement. In either case, the introduction should clearly describe the local or regional area and how the institution's professional and organizational qualifications relate to the proposed grant project.

Grant application introductions should use up-to-date information that provides descriptive detail about the community to be served. Illustrations are used in the introduction section to make information stand out and to break up the monotony of the narrative. Regional areas to be served are often presented in mapform, supplemented by demographic information. Introductions also identify the institution's mission and goals, establish institutional eligibility, provide evidence of previous accomplishments, set the context for the proposed project, and lead logically to the problem/need statement. **See Exhibit 5-5**.

Exhibit 5-5

Sample Narrative and Map Used in a Proposal Introduction

The Yukon-Kuskokwim (Y-K) Delta is located in Southwestern Alaska and encompasses 75,000 square miles (about the size of South Dakota) of wetlands, tundra, and mountains. Summers have almost 20 hours of daylight with maritime temperatures of more than 60 degrees F. Winters are harsh and dark with windchill temperatures well below 50 degrees F. The geography and climate of the Y-K Delta region pose severe transportation limitations. There are no existing road systems linking the

villages within the area. The Kuskokwim River system and a network of lakes provide links between villages by boat in summer and by snow machines, trucks, or all-terrain vehicles along rivers and their tributaries after freezing.

Experienced funding seekers use regional or community maps to identify the area to be served.

Proposal introductions should paint vivid pictures about the community to be served in the minds of agency reviewers. Textboxes are often used in proposal introductions to present brief snapshots of the community, organization, and/or target population. Textboxes should include up-to-date information supported by recent and relevant statistics to grab government agency reviewers' attention. **See Exhibit 5-6**.

Exhibit 5-6

Sample Textbox Used to Describe a Target Population

Anytown State College (ASC) was established in 1960, and the Nursing Department began instruction in 1966. ASC's student population is culturally diverse, with 45 percent African American or Hispanic. The nursing program is also culturally distinct, with 46 percent minority students. The

Anytown State College Fall 20XX	
ASC Students	**ASC Nursing Students**
• 4,792 total students	• 112 nursing students
• Mean age 29; median age 24	• Mean age 30; median age 30
• 60% female; 40% male	• 93% female; 7% male
• 55% Caucasian	• 54% Caucasian
• 34% African American	• 38% African American
• 11% Hispanic	• 8% Hispanic

college's economic strata is equally diverse. ASC's district spans from the impoverished community of City Heights (one of the poorest communities in the United States) to fairly affluent communities of Wright Fields and Richville. Twelve percent of students receive PELL grants.

Textboxes are used in grant applications to highlight key points about the proposed project.

Problem/Need

The *problem/need* section is a persuasively written essay that convinces agency reviewers a problem exists that needs to be solved, corrected, improved, or reduced. The problem/need section must be compelling and establish why the proposed project is important and timely. Finally, the problem/need should cite studies that provide quantitative results. Problem/need statements should avoid the use of "lack of" or the "need for" in their description. The "lack of" or "need for" goods or services is not a justification or rationale. **See Exhibit 5-7.**

Exhibit 5-7

Poor and Better Problem/Need Statements

Poor Problem/Need Statements

1. Lack of adequate equipment to support students in mathematics courses.

2. There is a need for a park in our community.

Better Problem/Need Statements

1. Thirty percent of Madison County students fail key mathematics courses (MCM, 20XX).

2. Based on survey data, 87% of homeowners would use/benefit from a community park.

Winning grant applications must address an important problem/need. Funding seekers should avoid statements that only declare the problem/need as the "lack of" or the "need for" something."

Specifically, the problem/need section should:

- Document a problem/need that relates to the government agency's interest. Be succinct, but use sufficient evidence to provide a convincing argument.

- Identify a problem/need of reasonable size that is manageable.

- Describe a problem/need within a context. Use comparison data to show how your problem/need compares to others.

- Provide an original and innovative project idea, approach, or vision to solve, reduce, or improve the problem. Avoid painting a hopeless situation.

The problem/need should be supported by information that is recent (within the last three years) and relevant (e.g., census, local, and community data). Facts, statistical data, and research results are often used to demonstrate need for funding a project that will correct or reduce a problem in a reasonable period of time. Use well-documented contemporary comparative information from local, state, and federal documents to support problem/need statements (e.g., demonstrate how local community needs are different from state or national statistics). Proposals that do not establish a pressing problem/need supported by documented data are seldom selected for funding. **See Exhibit 5-8**.

Exhibit 5-8

Problem/Need Supported by Recent and Relevant Information

Northern Plains includes seven counties with an average of 42.3% of families classified as low income, which is more than 13% higher than the state average (29.1%).

Table 1 Low-Income Families in Northern Plains Below Poverty Level			
Target Area	**Families**	**Number of Low-Income Families**	**Percent of Low-Income Families**
Banks County	13,928	5,181	37.2%
Franklin County	10,514	4,825	45.9%
Henry County	16,953	6,577	38.8%
Lake County	5,814	2,674	46.0%
Martin County	18,218	7,287	40.0%
Pitts County	12,931	5,883	45.5%
Russ County	4,025	1,720	42.7%
Northern Plains	**82,383**	**34,147**	**42.3%**
State	**1,847,796**	**537,708**	**29.1%**
Source: U.S. Census Bureau, 20XX			

Recent and relevant information is used to support the problem/need.

Graphics (pie charts, bar charts, etc.) are used to illustrate statistical comparison information and drive home key points to agency reviewers. The major purpose of the problem/need statement is to convince agency reviewers that a problem exists and grant funds are necessary to improve the situation. Finally, the problem/need section should serve as a foundation for the proposal's goals/objectives, methods/activities, and evaluation plans. **See Exhibit 5-9**.

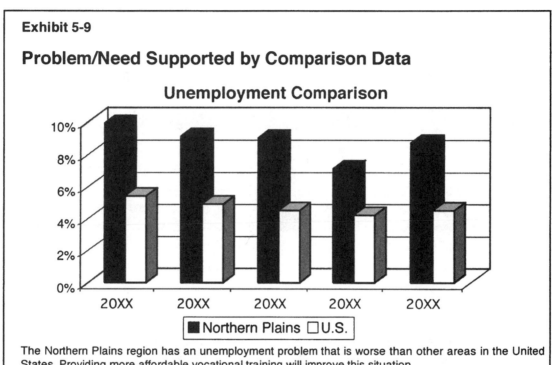

Exhibit 5-9

Problem/Need Supported by Comparison Data

Unemployment Comparison

■ Northern Plains ☐ U.S.

The Northern Plains region has an unemployment problem that is worse than other areas in the United States. Providing more affordable vocational training will improve this situation.

Comparison information is often used to illustrate a local problem/need against national information.

Goals/Objectives

Goals/objectives are the intellectual heart of a grant application and should provide a clear idea of the project's direction. Goals/objectives should directly relate to the government agency's wants and needs. Goals (ultimate) are broad conceptual outcomes and objectives (intermediate) are smaller stepping-stones to each goal. Each goal should have several objectives and flow logically from the problem/need. Goals/objectives form a basis for designing and sequencing project activities within a time frame. Goals/objectives indicate what will be done, under what conditions, and how the target population will be affected as a result of the proposed activities. Goals/objectives also help the funding seeker consider what resources, people, time, and equipment are necessary to complete the project. In addition, measurable goals/objectives provide a premise for evaluating project accomplishments, which are used as a basis for describing the level of project success in progress reports provided to the government agency. **See Exhibit 5-10**.

Exhibit 5-10

Sample Goal/Objectives Stemming from Problem/Need

Problem/Need

According to the Information Technology Association of America, more than 840,000 Information Technology (IT) jobs have gone unfilled this past year. There is a virtual explosion of IT job opportunities; however, many local high school students are not prepared for these jobs (Roberts, 20XX).

Goal

Increase high school students' enrollment in IT college programs throughout the district.

Objectives

- Recruit 150 high school students to enroll in IT programs.
- Provide 100 high school students with a core curriculum in computer networking.
- Provide 50 high school students with workplace experiences.

Methods/Activities

- Develop IT marketing program to inform and recruit high school students.
- Develop IT courses for high school students that articulate with college-level courses.
- Send instructors to training workshops in preparation for IT courses.
- Schedule workplace visitations and job shadowing activities for high school students at local businesses.

Evaluation Plans

- Assess the IT marketing program to inform and recruit students. For example:
  - 500 brochures, 10 press releases, and 4 newspaper ads were developed.
  - Three IT informational meetings were held for students and parents at local schools.
- Assess the IT courses developed for high school students. For example:
  - Objectives and daily activities were developed for each course.
  - Textbooks and lab manuals for courses were purchased.
  - Seven instructors attended IT training workshops.
- Determine the number of high school students enrolled in IT courses and the number of students who were provided IT workplace experiences at local businesses.

Time Frame

- January 1, 20XX to December 31, 20XX.

Goals/objectives stem from the problem/need and form the basis for sequencing project activities and identifying project outcomes within a time frame. Project goals/objectives must be measurable, tangible, specific, concrete, and realistic. Funding seekers should avoid stating outcomes that cannot be met within the government agency's period of performance.

Good project objectives are clear and concise statements that are:

- listed in chronological order of achievement,

- measurable in quantitative terms,

- ambitious, but attainable (ask yourself if you have the time and resources to accomplish the objectives), and

- practical and cost effective. **See Exhibit 5-11.**

Never include objectives in your proposal that are not required in the RFP/RFA. If you receive the grant, you will be held accountable for these extra objectives, which will create additional unpaid work and make the project more difficult to complete within the agency's period of performance.

Exhibit 5-11

Sample Project Objective

Objective	Relates to Problem/Need	Measurable	Ambitious, but Attainable
Assist target area participants so that 60% of all high school graduates will undertake a program of post-secondary education.	Only 45% percent of high school graduates in the target area currently undertake a program of postsecondary education, and only 34% of these graduate (TIM, 20XX). This objective seeks to encourage students to complete a postsecondary education.	Specific number of target-area adults undertaking a program of postsecondary education is quantifiable and can be measured by graduates self-reporting as well as college registrar reports.	The objective is ambitious because it seeks to increase the number of high school graduates undertaking a program of postsecondary education by 15%. The objective is attainable because the program will use a variety of proven workshops, informational media, and guest speakers, as well as experienced college counselors to encourage students to undertake a program of postsecondary education.

Objectives relate to the problem/need and are measurable, ambitious, but attainable.

Methods/Activities

The proposal *methods/activities* section is a plan of work that describes the tasks and procedures necessary to achieve the project goals and objectives and ultimately address the project problem/need. Methods/activities are project means to meet the objectives/goals (project ends). Proposal methods provide a logical and detailed description of project activities and events to be completed within the performance period. Specifically, this section should describe the "how," "who," "where," and "when" of the project. **See Exhibit 5-12.**

Exhibit 5-12

Sample Project Methods/Activities Chart

Anytown State College's Project Implementation Activities			
Objective: To identify and serve at least 1,000 participants each year of the project			
Activities/Methods	**Staff Member(s)**	**Time Schedule**	**Resources**
Recruit prospective participants by implementing a comprehensive marketing campaign.	Project Director, Coordinator	Monthly	**Community** • Community agencies • Local businesses • Local civic organizations • Local church groups • Recreation centers • Secondary schools • Postsecondary schools • Veteran groups • Employment services **College** • Public relations office • Communications group • Foundations office • Mailing/duplication center • College newspaper **Local Public Relations** • Radio and television • Websites
Distribute public service messages via websites, television, and radio stations in the target area.	Project Director	Monthly	
Distribute brochures to businesses and community groups throughout the target area with contact information about outreach activities.	Project Director, Coordinator	Ongoing	
Contact postsecondary institutions in the target area to promote services and request referrals.	Project Director	Monthly	
Contact secondary schools in the target area to promote services and request referrals.	Project Director, Coordinator	Monthly	
Contact community agencies in the target area to promote services and request referrals.	Project Director, Coordinator	Ongoing	

Project activities must be adequately developed, well integrated, directly tied to objectives, and identify staff members responsible for completing specific tasks. Proposed activities must match the background and experience of the project director (PD) and other key team members.

Plan of Work

A *plan of work* identifies specific tasks that must be accomplished to meet the project goals/objectives within the government agency's period of performance. Time-and-task charts are excellent planning tools used by funding seekers to summarize, illustrate, and communicate the scope and sequence of tasks and subtasks to be completed in one- or multi-year grant projects. Start the project timeline when your organization is likely to receive grant funding. Realistic timelines help agency reviewers visualize full implementation of project tasks and activities. Project tasks must be reasonable and completed with available resources and within the government agency's deadline. Time-and-task charts can be created with Microsoft Excel™ or Microsoft Project.™ **See Exhibit 5-13.**

Exhibit 5-13

Sample Project Time-and-Task Chart

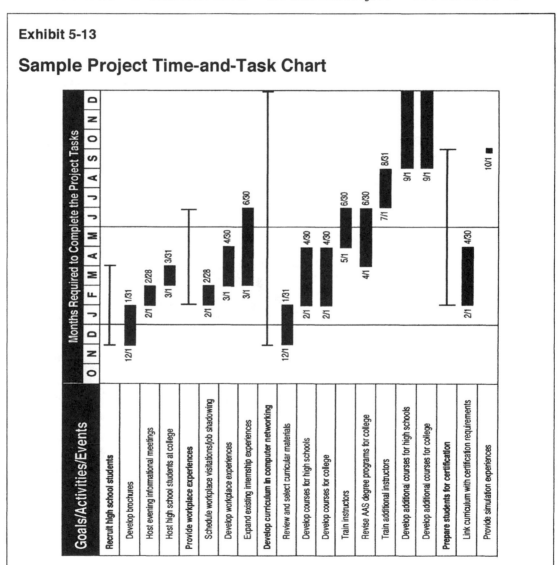

Time-and-task charts provide a sequence of project tasks to be completed within a specific time period. Avoid using pastel colors with time-and-task charts because some colors will not reproduce.

The plan of work should also identify when staff meetings will be held (e.g., monthly or bimonthly). Regular project meetings should:

- review major project developments and challenges,

- take corrective action or recommend project changes and/or amendments when either the timeline or objectives are not being met, and

- indicate project progress information on a quarterly basis to both internal management and the government agency.

Management Plans

A management plan should identify the names and titles of key personnel to be used in the project as well as indicate the lines of authority within the organization. The Principal Investigator (PI) or Project Director (PD) should have day-to-day responsibility and authority for implementing and managing the project. Project personnel must be appropriately trained and well suited to complete the proposed project. **See Exhibit 5-14**.

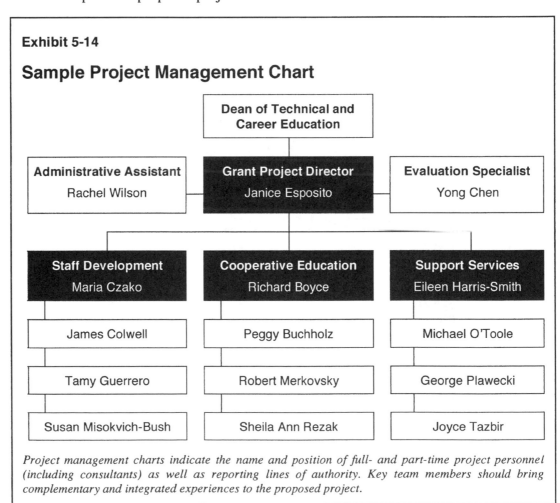

Exhibit 5-14

Sample Project Management Chart

Dean of Technical and Career Education

Administrative Assistant Rachel Wilson	Grant Project Director Janice Esposito	Evaluation Specialist Yong Chen

Staff Development Maria Czako	Cooperative Education Richard Boyce	Support Services Eileen Harris-Smith
James Colwell	Peggy Buchholz	Michael O'Toole
Tamy Guerrero	Robert Merkovsky	George Plawecki
Susan Misokvich-Bush	Sheila Ann Rezak	Joyce Tazbir

Project management charts indicate the name and position of full- and part-time project personnel (including consultants) as well as reporting lines of authority. Key team members should bring complementary and integrated experiences to the proposed project.

Management plans should also show where the proposed project fits within the grant-seeking organization. The grant PI/PD and other key personnel should show close ties to upper management in the institution's organizational chart. **See Exhibit 5-15**.

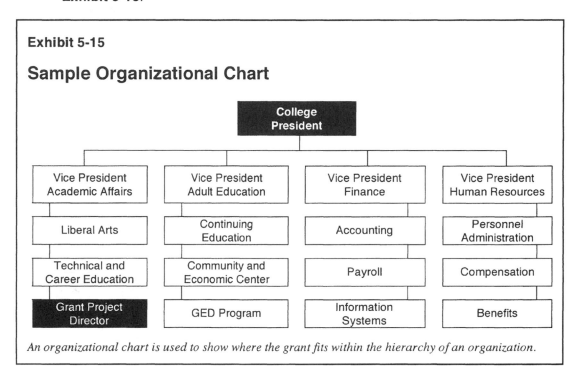

Exhibit 5-15

Sample Organizational Chart

An organizational chart is used to show where the grant fits within the hierarchy of an organization.

Key Personnel Qualifications

Specific information about the duties and responsibilities of the PI/PD as well as co-PIs/PDs and other senior personnel who will make substantive contributions to the proposed project should be discussed in the management plan. Biographical sketches with documented credentials should be submitted for all key personnel (including consultants) that will be discussed in the budget. Biographical sketches should present a well-crafted synthesis of each project member's professional preparation and qualifications.

Detailed résumés or curricula vitae of key personnel that emphasize recent and relevant experience (e.g., professional appointments, significant publications, and other major accomplishments) pertinent to the proposed project are often required in the grant application appendix. Funding seekers should avoid padding personnel résumés with manuscripts in progress, degrees in progress, etc. Government agency reviewers use biographical sketches, résumés, and other personnel credentials to evaluate the qualifications of project staff members who are identified to complete specific project tasks. **See Exhibit 5-16**.

Exhibit 5-16

Sample Qualifications of Key Project Personnel

Position	Education		Relevant Experience
PI/PD	Ph.D. M.S. B.S.	Administration Counseling Counseling	14 years as an administrator 7 years as a counselor 8 years as a grant director
Education Specialist	M.S. B.S.	Education Education	4 years as an administrator 10 years as a teacher 5 years as a counselor
Counseling Director	M.A. B.A.	Counseling Liberal Arts	6 years as a counseling director 5 years as a site coordinator 6 years as a counselor
Site Coordinator #1	M.A. B.A.	Divinity Liberal Arts	10 years as a site coordinator 12 years as a social worker 5 years as a high school teacher
Site Coordinator #2	M.A. B.A.	Counseling Psychology	5 years as a site coordinator 16 years as a counselor 3 years as a high school teacher

Personnel qualifications are often presented in summary tables when grant applications have page limitations. Résumés for the PI/PD and other key staff members are placed in the appendix.

Key Personnel Time Commitments

The key personnel section of a management plan should indicate staff members' time commitment to the project. This section must demonstrate that the proposed project team has dedicated sufficient personnel and time to ensure successful completion of the project. **See Exhibit 5-17.**

Exhibit 5-17

Sample Time Commitments of Key Project Personnel

Name	Project Position	Time Commitment
George Abramowitz	Principal Investigator	100%
Bruce Wilson	Education Specialist	100%
Zhou Chenn	Counseling Director	100%
Linda Black	Site Coordinator for Area 1	50%
Joyce Weather	Site Coordinator for Area 2	50%
Gregory Steinz	Financial Manager	25%

The name, position, and time commitment of all key personnel in the proposed project should be identified in the methods/activities section of the proposal. Some solicitations require that key personnel must have a minimum time commitment to the proposed project.

Job Description/Announcement

A *job description/announcement* is a presentation of duties, responsibilities, and required qualifications of key personnel to be hired for the proposed grant project. A job description/announcement summary is often included in the proposal narrative, and a complete job announcement is placed in the appendix. All job descriptions/announcements must reference and be compliant with the Americans with Disabilities Act (ADA) and Equal Opportunity Employer (EOE) statements. Remember that agency reviewers want to support carefully planned activities led by experienced PIs/PDs who will expend grant funds in an appropriate manner to ensure a successful grant project. **See Exhibit 5-18.**

Exhibit 5-18

Sample Job Description/Announcement Summary

Title: Systems Analyst

Classification: Administrative Staff

Supervisor: Director of Administrative Computing

Position Summary
The Systems Analyst is responsible for assisting the Director of Administrative Computing in the design and implementation of the digital achievement portfolio.

Duties and Responsibilities
- Develop interface between digital achievement portfolio and local area network.
- Work with college committees and the Director of Administrative Computing to identify and select software for the achievement portfolio development project.
- Develop a digital achievement portfolio model for implementation.
- Develop, test, and implement a fully operational digital achievement portfolio with digitized data and audio elements.
- Identify, purchase, develop, and test a prototype system for digitized video storage and retrieval that can become part of the achievement portfolio.
- Maintain the security and reliability of data in the achievement portfolio.
- Perform system administration tasks, provide technical assistance to users, monitor system security, and conduct other duties as assigned.

Qualifications
Minimum qualifications: Bachelor's degree in computer systems analysis or related field, three years experience in a client/server network environment, and knowledge in multimedia application development.

Preferred qualifications: Master's degree in computer systems analysis, five years experience in a client/server network environment, and knowledge in multimedia application development.

Job descriptions/announcements include specific duties and responsibilities required of staff members to be hired for the proposed grant project.

Evaluation Plans

Reporting outcomes of federally funded projects has become increasingly important with the establishment of the Government Performance and Results Act (GPRA). According to GPRA, "all federal agencies are required to manage their activities with attention to the consequences of those activities." Each government agency interprets GPRA in different ways to reflect accountability; however, government agencies must report annually on the accomplishments of all federally funded projects. Consequently, PIs/PDs must consider GPRA before they submit reports that include quantitative and qualitative data about the status of their funded projects to the federal government agency.

Project evaluation involves the collection of information to determine whether funded grants are proceeding as planned and whether grants are meeting project goals and objectives within a proposed time frame. *Evaluation plans* describe systematic data-gathering procedures used to measure the projects' worth, merit, or success at different stages or benchmarks during the period of performance. Evaluation plans must (1) identify qualified individuals or organizations that will be responsible for the evaluation process, (2) design evaluation procedures and data-gathering instruments to assess project objectives, (3) collect and analyze data, (4) specify information to be included in the government agency reports, and (5) describe how results will be disseminated to internal and external individuals. Strong evaluation plans use quantifiable methods to measure project success. The evaluation process will frequently provide new insights that were not anticipated, which may prove to be very informative and useful in determining project results. **See Exhibit 5-19.**

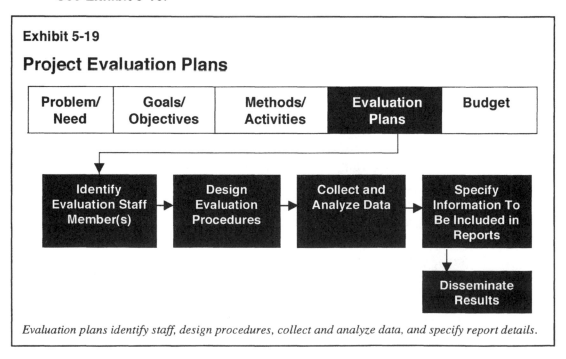

Exhibit 5-19

Project Evaluation Plans

| Problem/ Need | Goals/ Objectives | Methods/ Activities | Evaluation Plans | Budget |

Identify Evaluation Staff Member(s) → Design Evaluation Procedures → Collect and Analyze Data → Specify Information To Be Included in Reports → Disseminate Results

Evaluation plans identify staff, design procedures, collect and analyze data, and specify report details.

In-house or external evaluators may be used to complete project evaluation tasks. If an external evaluator is a requirement in the RFP/RFA, be sure to check the individual's prior experience and establish a clear written agreement that identifies specific responsibilities and project deadlines. Also make sure the costs for the external evaluator's services are in line with the overall budget. Evaluators should not gain personally or professionally from project results. In high-stakes or political situations, it is strongly recommended that an external evaluator, who is seen as objective and unbiased, be hired to review the evaluation design and assess the validity of project findings. Evaluation plans must incorporate procedures that make independent and objective decisions about the quality and effectiveness of grant projects and should not be thought of as an "add on" to the grant project. Rather, evaluation should be an integral part of the grant from the project's beginning to end, with evaluative data examined on an ongoing basis to accurately determine the project's success in relation to the intended outcomes.

The two types of evaluation used to assess grant projects are formative and summative. *Formative evaluation* is concerned with monitoring the initial and ongoing progress of grant projects. Formative evaluation assesses project activities at several points in the life cycle of the project and provides regular reports about (1) meeting project objectives, (2) completing project activities, (3) measuring participants' progress, and (4) assessing project staff members' performance. *Summative evaluation* is concerned with judging the overall quality or worth of a grant at the end of a defined project period. Summative evaluation activities should provide quantitative and qualitative information that is directly tied to project goals and objectives. Summative evaluation reports are prepared using formative reports and follow-up data from project participants. Quantifiable data obtained from evaluation plans are used to describe project accomplishments in reports sent to funding agencies. Any unanticipated findings should also be discussed in the reports. **See Exhibit 5-20**.

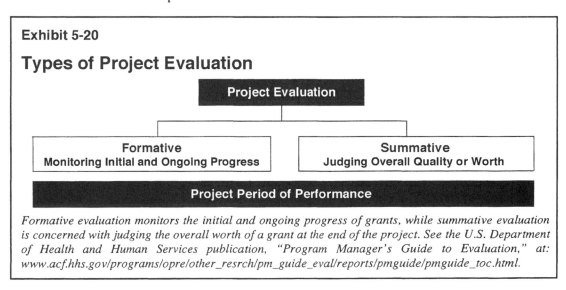

Exhibit 5-20

Types of Project Evaluation

Project Evaluation

| Formative | Summative |
| Monitoring Initial and Ongoing Progress | Judging Overall Quality or Worth |

Project Period of Performance

Formative evaluation monitors the initial and ongoing progress of grants, while summative evaluation is concerned with judging the overall worth of a grant at the end of the project. See the U.S. Department of Health and Human Services publication, "Program Manager's Guide to Evaluation," at: www.acf.hhs.gov/programs/opre/other_resrch/pm_guide_eval/reports/pmguide/pmguide_toc.html.

Proposed Grant Project Summary Tables

Proposed grant project overviews are often summarized in tables to provide a "snapshot" of major narrative components (problem/need, goals/objectives, methods/activities, and evaluation plans) included in most grant applications. Summary tables are often used when proposals are limited to a specific number of pages. **See Exhibits 5-21 and 5-22.**

Exhibit 5-21

Grant Project Summary Table Guidelines

Problem/Need	Goals/Objectives	Methods/Activities	Evaluation Plans
Convince agency reviewers that a problem exists and describe how the project idea will correct, reduce, or improve the problem.	Indicate what you intend to change through your project.	Describe the specific activities ("means") that will be conducted to meet each project goal/objective ("ends").	Describe procedures and instruments that will be used to assess the project. Identify who will evaluate the project.
Provide a rationale or justification for the project.	Identify project aims, i.e., "The purpose of this project is to ...." (Your purpose must match the government agency's mission.)	Provide a clear, logical progression of tasks to be completed within the grant period.	Explain how data will be collected and analyzed.
Use facts, statistical data, or research results from tests, records, reports, questionnaires, or literature reviews.	Write outcomes that are specific, measurable, and sequential.	Use a time-and-task chart to summarize, illustrate, and sequence the "how," "who," "where," and "when."	Indicate how data will be used to demonstrate what has been achieved.
Identify the population or sample to be affected by the proposed project.	Write outcomes that are ambitious but attainable.	Describe key personnel qualifications, experiences, and time commitments.	Describe what reports will be generated. Explain how project data will be disseminated.
Leave room for hope that the problem can be improved; must not be hopeless.	Identify multiple objectives for each goal.	Explain project management plans and where the project fits within the organization.	Indicate how the project will continue after grant funds end.
Number all problem/ need statements.	Number objectives to correspond with problem/need statements.	Number methods/ activities to correspond with problem/need and goals/objectives.	Number evaluation plans to correspond with problem/need, goals/objectives, and methods/ activities.

Project summary table guidelines provide funding seekers with strategies for developing commonly used narrative components found in most grant applications. These guidelines may or may not be inclusive of the RFP—always be responsive to specific requirements found in the government agency's solicitation.

Exhibit 5-22

Sample Summary Table for Two-Year Grant Project

Year	Problem/Need	Goals/Objectives	Methods/Activities	Evaluation Plans
1	1 Faculty members have limited community-based knowledge and experience as compared to other state colleges (AACN, 20XX).	1 Provide community-based training for 15 faculty members.	1a Send 15 faculty members to community-based training. 1b Send 15 faculty members to national nursing conferences. 1c Schedule 15 faculty member clinical site visitations.	1a 15 faculty members provide reports about community-based training. 1b 15 faculty members provide reports about conference proceedings. 1c 15 faculty members provide reports about clinical site visitations.
	2 Outdated community-based nursing curriculum (ANCC, 20XX).	2 Update the nursing curriculum and instructional materials to include a community-based component.	2 Revise nursing curriculum and instructional materials to include a community-based component.	2 All nursing syllabi and instructional materials include a community-based component.
	3 Outdated health/wellness services (ANCC, 20XX).	3 Provide up to date health/wellness services to college community.	3 Conduct needs analysis of services and update as necessary.	3 Offer up to date health/wellness services to college community.
2	4 Limited hands-on community-based experiences for nursing students (ANCC, 20XX).	4 Provide hands-on community-based experiences for 30 nursing students per semester.	4 Schedule hands-on community-based experiences for 30 nursing students per semester.	4 30 nursing students will pass a hands-on community-based experiences state test.
	5 No on-campus health/wellness program exists (ANCC, 20XX).	5 Develop a health/wellness program for college and community participants by fall, 20XX.	5a Renovate space and equip wellness center. 5b Develop health/wellness record keeping and documentation system. 5c Implement health/wellness center to serve 250 clients per month.	5a Wellness center is functional by fall, 20XX. 5b Record keeping and documentation system is fully operational by fall, 20XX. 5c Monthly report of clients served and client satisfaction results.

Note: Corresponding numbers are used to show how components are linked.

Grant project summary tables provide an overview of the problem/need, goals/objectives, methods/activities, and evaluation plans.

References or Bibliography

References represent a compilation of documents (books, articles, government records, etc.) specifically cited in the narrative of a grant application. A *bibliography* includes all documents reviewed (both those cited and not cited) in the narrative of a grant application. Reference and bibliography entries should be relevant, current, and arranged alphabetically by the first author's surname. The purpose of a reference or bibliography list is to demonstrate to agency reviewers that you are familiar with the literature associated with the grant topic under investigation. The formatting of a reference or bibliography list will vary; authors should follow an accepted style manual.

Appendix

The *appendix* contains supplemental information too detailed to include in the proposal narrative. Generally, this appendage information is considered valuable but too bulky to include in the main body of the grant application. A table of contents should precede appendix materials. Examples of appendix items include:

- organizational mission statements;

- résumés of key project members or job descriptions of staff to be hired;

- letters of support and commitment from all collaborators, including individuals and organizations that will not receive monetary compensation from the grant;

- evaluation instruments (tests, questionnaires, etc.); and

- annual reports and other supplemental documentation.

Letters of Support

Letters of support are an endorsement of the merit of the proposed project from individuals or groups of individuals within or outside the institution applying for a grant (e.g., politicians, community leaders, and local business and industry representatives) who do not have an active role in the proposed project. Supporters believe the project is a good idea and it will have a positive impact on the intended audience. Obtaining letters of support can be a difficult and time-consuming task because you must first educate the writer about the project to be supported. Before asking someone to write a letter of support, funding seekers should provide them with a one or two page prospectus that indicates who the grant will serve and why funding is necessary to complete the project. The prospectus should include a concise description of the project's problem/need, purpose (goals/objectives), methods/activities, and evaluation plans. It is recommended that funding seekers provide supporters with several mock-up letters that can be used as examples. All letters of support should be customized and written on the supporting institution's letterhead with a signature from a high-level manager/administrator and dated. Funding seekers should provide the following information to individuals who will write letters of support:

- name and address of the organization applying for the grant,

- name, title, and position of the PI/PD who will oversee the proposed project (person to whom the letter should be sent),

- title of grant for which you are applying (e.g., Title III, Part A: Strengthening Institutions Program),

- name of your project, if applicable,

- name of the agency that will provide funding for grant activities (e.g., U.S. Department of Education), and

- deadline when the letter of support is needed. **See Exhibit 5-23.**

Exhibit 5-23

Sample Institutional Letter of Support

March 15, 20XX   **Letter Addressed to the Proposed PI/PD**

Dr. Susan Bishop, Dean
College of Education
Hoosier State University
Hoosier, IN 45321-3303

Dear Dr. Bishop: **Title of Grant**

Global Technologists is pleased to provide this letter of support for the Title III, Part A: Strengthening Institutions Program at Hoosier State University. The grant will provide substantial professional development to Hoosier State University faculty members and advisors in an effort to improve their understanding, skills, and responsiveness to the diverse learning needs of students who would not otherwise experience this new and challenging program. Most importantly, this grant will provide Hoosier State University with the opportunity to give many minority students first-hand experiences with local business and industry and thus make them better prepared for tomorrow's world of work.

We are excited about the possibility of having a Title III project at our local university and the advantages it will bring to students, faculty members, and representatives from local business and industry.

Sincerely,   **Signature from High-Level Manager**

Jose Ortiz

Jose Ortiz, President

Letters of support are from individuals who do not have an active role in the proposed project. Each letter should be unique—avoid using identical letters. Address letters to the PI/PD. Funding seekers should obtain letters of support during the early stages of the proposal's development effort.

Letters of Commitment

Letters of commitment come from individuals or organizations that will be actively involved in the proposed project. These letters document specific financial and non-financial commitments (personnel time, office equipment, materials, supplies, building space, etc.) to the project. The purpose of the letter of commitment is to show the collaborator's specific roles or responsibilities in the project. The letter should also indicate any cash contributions and/or dollar value for any in-kind contributions. For example, if a partner is providing the use of a computer laboratory for a specific number of days, the rental value of that space should be calculated and reported in the commitment letter. **See Exhibit 5-24**.

Exhibit 5-24

Sample Partner Commitment Letter

GENERIC UNIVERSITY

March 12, 20XX

Name, Title, and Position of Proposed PI/PD

Dr. Susan Bishop, Dean
College of Education
Hoosier State University
Hoosier, IN 45321-3303

Dear Dr. Bishop:

Generic University is pleased to join in partnership with Hoosier State University and local area businesses in developing opportunities for students to obtain cooperative experiences as part of the U.S. Department of Education's Title III, Part A: Strengthening Institutions Program. To promote these student opportunities, Generic University is committed to supporting Hoosier State University in the following ways:

- developing and disseminating recruiting materials for 2,000 students,

- providing transportation for 50 students per year to cooperative business sites,

- training 25 faculty members per year about cooperative experiences, and

- providing an annual recognition banquet with certificates for 100 students who complete one or more semester of cooperative experience.

Sincerely,   *Administrator's Signature*

John Lebowski

John Lebowski,
Vice President of Academic Affairs

Commitment letters detail partners' contributions to the proposed project and should not just be a generic letter of support. Always include original letters of commitment in the grant application appendix.

Human Research Protection

Grant proposals that involve the use of human subjects, animals, and hazardous materials must adhere to federal, state, institutional, and local laws and regulations governing the proposed project activities before funding can be committed by a government agency. Grant applications that involve the use of human subjects at an institution of higher education must comply with regulations for protecting human subjects and seek approval from an Institutional Review Board. An *Institutional Review Board (IRB)* consists of selected staff members of an institution who review and approve research to ensure that the rights and welfare of human subjects are protected. The IRB does not judge the science or worth of the research effort, but rather is an ethical review of the proposed research. *Research* is a systematic investigation that may include development, testing, and/or evaluation designed to contribute to generalizable knowledge. A *human subject* is a living individual about whom an investigator conducting research obtains data through:

- intervention or interaction with the individual (use of questionnaires, manipulation of an individual's environment, drawing blood, etc.), or

- identifiable private information (i.e., information that can be linked to specific individuals).

The PI/PD of the grant application is responsible for submitting the necessary information to the IRB for initial and subsequent annual reviews. For more information about regulations and guidelines concerning human subjects, see the website of the Office of Human Research Protection at http://hhs.gov/ohrp.

The PI/PD must obtain informed consent from individuals involved in research efforts conducted at institutions of higher education. *Informed consent* is where participants have been adequately informed about the research and participate willingly. Special protection is required for children, prisoners, mentally handicapped individuals, and other vulnerable populations. Voluntary participation means that participants have received adequate information in order to give genuine informed consent. **See Exhibit 5-25**.

Certification and Assurance Forms

Various requirements are imposed by government agencies as conditions for receiving grant awards. Solicitations include certification and assurance forms that funding seekers must sign concerning federal laws, regulations, and/or executive orders. Examples of conditions include certifications that the recipient maintains a drug-free workplace or assurances related to the Civil Rights Act of 1964. Some government agencies require only a few conditions, while other agencies require numerous certifications and/or assurances as part of the grant application process. **See Exhibits 5-26 and 5-27**.

Exhibit 5-25

Informed Consent Information Provided to Grant Participants

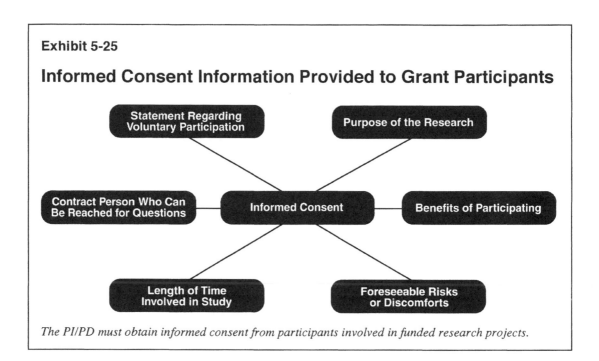

The PI/PD must obtain informed consent from participants involved in funded research projects.

Exhibit 5-26

Selected Government Certifications and Assurances

- Antidiscrimination—The Civil Rights Act of 1964 prohibits discrimination on the basis of race, color, or national origin in any program receiving federal assistance.

- Drug-Free Workplace—The Drug-Free Workplace Act of 1988 requires each grantee to certify that it will maintain a drug-free workplace. Funding seekers must establish drug-free awareness programs that meet certain requirements.

- Lobbying Restrictions—The Anti-Lobbying Amendment applies to recipients of grants over $100,000, prohibiting use of appropriated funds for lobbying the executive or legislative branches of the federal government. Funding seekers are required to disclose lobbying activities financed with non-federal funds.

- Others
    - Sex and age discrimination
    - Health, safety, and welfare of human subjects
    - Public employee standards
    - Etc.

Government agencies require funding seekers to complete and sign certification and/or assurance forms as part of the grant application process.

Exhibit 5-27

Sample Grant Application Certification Page

CERTIFICATION PAGE

Certification for Principal Investigators and Co-Principal Investigators

I certify to the best of my knowledge that:

(1) the statements herein (excluding scientific hypotheses and scientific opinions) are true and complete, and

(2) the text and graphics herein as well as any accompanying publications or other documents, unless otherwise indicated, are the original work of the signatories or individuals working under their supervision. I agree to accept responsibility for the scientific conduct of the project and to provide the required project reports if an award is made as a result of this proposal.

I understand that the willful provision of false information or concealing a material fact in this proposal or any other communication submitted to NSF is a criminal offense (U.S.Code, Title 18, Section 1001).

Name (Typed)	Signature	Social Security No.*	Date
PI/PD **Walter Waverly**	*Walter Waverly*	233-4509876	5/1/20XX
Co-PI/PD **Kenneth Filmore**	*Kenneth Filmore*	657-678-3452	5/1/20XX
Co-PI/PD			
Co-PI/PD			
Co-PI/PD			

Certification for Authorized Organizational Representative or Individual Applicant

By signing and submitting this proposal, the individual applicant or the authorized official of the applicant institution is: (1) certifying that statements made herein are true and complete to the best of his/her knowledge; and (2) agreeing to accept the obligation to comply with NSF award terms and conditions if an award is made as a result of this application. Further, the applicant is hereby providing certifications regarding Federal debt status, debarment and suspension, drug-free workplace, and lobbying activities (see below), as set forth in the *Grant Proposal Guide (GPG)*, NSF 00-2. Willful provision of false information in this applica- and its supporting documents or in reports required under an ensuing award is a criminal offense (U.S. Code, Title 18, Section 1001).

In addition, if the applicant institution employs more than fifty persons, the authorized official of the applicant institution is certifying that the institution has implemented a written and enforced conflict of interest policy that is consistent with the provisions of *Grant Policy Manual* Section 510; that to the best of his/her knowledge, all financial disclosures required by that conflict of interest policy have been made; and that all identified conflicts of interest will have been satisfactorily managed, reduced or eliminated prior to the institution's expenditure of any funds under the award, in accordance with the institution's conflict of interest policy. Conflicts that cannot be satisfactorily managed, reduced or eliminated must be disclosed to NSF.

Debt and Debarment Certifications   (If answer "yes" to either, please provide explanation.)

Is the organization delinquent on any Federal debt?　　　　　　　　　　　　　　Yes ☐　　No ☒

Is the organization or its principals presently debarred, suspended, proposed for debarment, declared ineligible, or voluntarily excluded from covered transactions by any Federal Department or agency?　　Yes ☐　　No ☒

Certification Regarding Lobbying

This certification is required for an award of a Federal contract, grant or cooperative agreement exceeding $100,000 and for an award of a Federal loan or a commitment providing for the United States to insure or guarantee a loan exceeding $150,000.

Certification for Contracts, Grants, Loans and Cooperative Agreements

The undersigned certifies, to the best of his or her knowledge and belief, that:

(1) No Federal appropriated funds have been paid or will be paid, by or on behalf of the undersigned, to any person for influencing or attempting to influence an officer or employee of any agency, a Member of Congress, an officer or employee of Congress, or an employee of a Member of Congress in connection with the awarding of any federal contract, the making of any Federal grant, the making of any Federal loan, the entering into of any cooperative agreement, and the extension, continuation, renewal, amendment, or modification of any Federal contract, grant, loan, or cooperative agreement.

(2) If any funds other than Federal appropriated funds have been paid or will be paid to any person for influencing or attempting to influence an officer or employee of any agency, a Member of Congress, and officer or employee of Congress, or an employee of a Member of Congress in connection with this Federal contract, grant, loan, or cooperative agreement, the undersigned shall complete and submit Standard Form LLL, "Disclosure of Lobbying Activities," in accordance with its instructions.

(3) The undersigned shall require that the language of this certification be included in the award documents for all subawards at all tiers including subcontracts, subgrants, and contracts under grants, loans, and cooperative agreements and that all subrecipients shall certify and disclose accordingly.

This certification is a material representation of fact upon which reliance was placed when this transaction was made or entered into. Submission of this certification is a prerequisite for making or entering into this transaction imposed by Section 1352, Title 31, U.S. Code. Any person who fails to file the required certification shall be subject to a civil penalty of not less than $10,000 and not more than $100,000 for each such failure.

AUTHORIZED ORGANIZATIONAL REPRESENTATIVE	SIGNATURE	DATE
NAME/TITLE (TYPED) **Beverly V. Marquis**	*Beverly V. Marquis*	5/1/20XX
TELEPHONE NUMBER **708-456-7890**	ELECTRONIC MAIL ADDRESS **bvmarquis@genericu.edu**	FAX NUMBER **708-456-7812**

*SUBMISSION OF SOCIAL SECURITY NUMBERS IS VOLUNTARY AND WILL NOT AFFECT THE ORGANIZATION'S ELIGIBILITY FOR AN AWARD. HOWEVER, THEY ARE AN INTEGRAL PART OF THE NSF INFORMATION SYSTEM AND ASSIST IN PROCESSING THE PROPOSAL. SSN SOLICITED UNDER NSF ACT OF 1950, AS AMENDED.

Various requirements are imposed by government agencies as conditions for receiving grant awards. Always check government forms for completeness and accuracy before signing.

Review and Rewrite the Proposal Narrative

Most winning grant applications go through an in-house review by content experts for continuity, clarity, and reasoning before submission to government agencies. In-house reviewers read each proposal draft to ensure that writers have addressed the evaluation criteria in the RFP/RFA and have presented a comprehensive, coherent, and persuasive essay. The primary job of an in-house reviewer is to make sure the grant proposal is compliant and that all information requested by the government agency is included in the narrative. Proposal review meetings should be held after reviewers have had sufficient time to read each proposal draft. The primary purpose of a proposal review meeting is to ensure that writers and reviewers have an open forum to discuss ways of improving the grant application. Reviewers should discuss general comments about the proposal followed by specific comments. Stylistic comments should not be the focus of this meeting, but rather handled by a style editor after the narrative has been completely written. Reviewers should provide writers with specific written suggestions for improvement. In-house reviewers should also discuss issues of consistency between the narrative and budget. Proposal team leaders who have ultimate authority over the grant application should review the final proposal. An administrator who has sign-off authority should be a review team member and evaluate the final proposal in relation to the institutional mission. Proposals must be complementary rather than tangential to the institution's goals.

Edit the Proposal Narrative

Editors must have adequate time to read and edit the final proposal narrative prior to submission. Generally there are two types of editing: (1) content editing and (2) style editing. *Content editing* focuses on the accuracy and completeness of the proposal ideas (by checking claims, facts, names, terms, titles, etc.). Content editors understand the proposal subject matter and closely compare the narrative sections with the compliance checklist and RFP/RFA guidelines. *Style editing* focuses on clarity and readability of ideas. Style editors understand consistency of writing and closely check manuscripts for grammar, punctuation, tone, presentation, formatting, and appropriate use of diagrams, charts, and figures. Style editors review manuscripts according to a style sheet that was distributed at the strategy meeting. The style editor's goal is to provide a reader-friendly and clearly written proposal. The following questions serve as guides for editors to answer in proofreading manuscripts.

- Can revising, reducing, rearranging, and/or rewriting improve the proposal?
- Are all major proposal sections presented in a logical order?
- Does the proposal use language that communicates to non-specialists?
- Would shorter words, sentences, or paragraphs express the same thoughts better?
- Is the proposal readable and attractive in terms of layout and graphic design?

Common tips to use in proofreading proposals include:

- limit sentences to 15 words or less on average,

- check for subject-verb agreement,

- use non-sexist language,

- use the computer to spell check narrative (but don't totally rely on this),

- check spelling of proper names and accuracy of numbers, and

- check all references for accuracy and completeness. **See Exhibit 5-28.**

Exhibit 5-28

Editing Guidelines

Desirable	**Undesirable**
· Active voice	· Passive voice
· Fewest words	· Wordy
· Variety	· Repetitious
· Understandable terms	· Jargon
· Lively phrasing	· Flat, dull language
· Clear syntax	· Misinterpretation
· Complete sentences	· Choppy sentences
· Key points visible	· Key points hidden
· Facts, examples	· Vague, too general

Editors rework narrative in an effort to present a clear message to agency reviewers. Complex proposals developed by several authors must be edited for style to ensure a unified voice.

The only way to win grant funding is to submit quality applications. There is no shortcut to good writing. The only way to become a good writer is to write a lot, and the best way to learn how to write a grant proposal is to write one.

Tables, Figures, and Illustrations

Savvy grant writers recognize that a picture is worth a thousand words and will often use charts, figures, exhibits, or diagrams to illustrate important content and break up the monotony of the narrative. Proposal graphics are used to supplement narrative. Graphics should be numbered (e.g., Figure 1) and include a descriptive caption immediately below the illustration. *Callouts* are used to identify specific parts, components, or processes in illustrations. Callouts may be one word or a brief descriptive sentence. References to graphics in the narrative (e.g., see Figure 1) are used to refer readers to specific illustrations. **See Exhibit 5-29.**

Tables present a comprehensive and attractive way of providing related summary information to agency reviewers. Inaccuracy in tables—especially budget tables—can be very detrimental to grant applications. Tables should be checked and rechecked for missing or incorrect information prior to submitting a grant application to the government agency. **See Exhibit 5-30.**

Exhibit 5-29

Sample Figure Used to Support Grant Narrative

Figure 1: Student Enrollment by Ethnicity and Gender

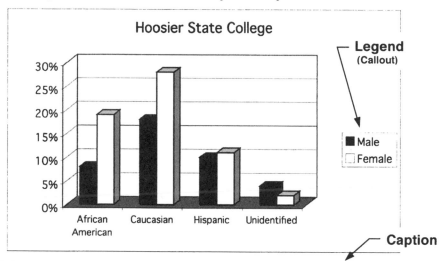

Hoosier State College enrollment was 6,934 students in fall 20XX. Student ethnicity was 27% African American, 46% Caucasian, 21% Hispanic, and 6% unidentified. Gender was 60% female and 40% male.

Grant proposals use charts, figures, and diagrams to illustrate the proposal narrative.

Exhibit 5-30

Sample Table Used to Support Grant Narrative

Anytown State College Fall 20XX Enrollment			
Academic Programs	**Full-Time Students**	**Part-Time Students**	**Total Enrollment**
Business and Management	297	285	582
Technology	212	54	266
Fine Arts and Humanities	224	123	347
Nursing	132	58	190
Professional Communication	168	102	270
Science and Mathematics	191	45	236
Social Science and Humanities	112	25	137
Total	**1,336**	**692**	**2,028**

Tables must be checked and rechecked for accuracy. Always follow the agency formatting requirements and include citations when appropriate.

Boilerplate Material

Institutions that apply for numerous grant applications will often use boilerplate material for the first proposal draft. *Boilerplate* material includes well-written documents that are reused to prepare grant proposals. Boilerplate material often provides an excellent starting point for writers; however, these generic files must not be thought of as final proposal sections. Rather, these documents should be customized to meet the government agency's needs and wants to be effective. An example of boilerplate material organized by proposal sections is shown below.

Introduction
- Institutional mission and purpose statements
- Institutional strategic plan with implications for the proposed project
- Institutional fact sheet that includes current demographic data

Problem/Need
- Reports from studies, community forums, and case studies that document current problems that will be addressed as a result of grant funding
- Supportive data from state and federal legislators, universities, community agencies, professional organizations, and chambers of commerce

Goals/Objectives
- Goals/Objectives from approved proposals completed by your organization
- Goals/Objectives from approved proposals completed by other organizations

Methodology/Activities
- Time-and-task charts, organizational charts, and project management charts
- Description of data-gathering instruments used in similar projects
- Management plans, qualifications, and time commitments of key personnel

Evaluation Plans
- Successful evaluation strategies
- Names and résumés of project evaluators

Budget
- List of components included in your institution's fringe benefits package
- Indirect (facilities and administrative) cost rate used with similar grant applications (including the indirect cost-rate agreement)

Proprietary Information

Proprietary information is private information that funding seekers only want grant agency reviewers to read. To protect proprietary information, funding seekers should include the following statement on the cover page: "A portion of the material contained in this proposal is considered proprietary and should not be released other than to those involved in the evaluation of the proposal. Pages XX through XX are subject to this proprietary restriction." Place the following footnote on the bottom of each page with proprietary information: "Use or disclosure of information on this page is subject to the restrictions on the title page of this proposal." Always check government agency policies regarding proprietary information before submitting the proposal.

Chapter Summary

Grant writing is an essay contest. Government agencies receive far more good grant applications than they can fund. A well thought out and succinct grant proposal will always have the best chance to win government funding. Successful grant writers must possess subject-matter knowledge, writing skills, analytical skills, creative expertise, and marketing savvy.

All grant proposals require persuasive writing to produce convincing narrative that will positively influence agency reviewers. Proposal narrative sections must always consider the reading audience and thoroughly describe the "why," "what," "how," "who," "where," and "when" of the proposed project.

Use rules of writing that make the proposal narrative shine:

- Use current government agency language; write to express, not to impress.

- Develop two to three proposal drafts.

- Use headings and subheadings to organize the proposal content.

- Use figures, tables, and charts to break up the monotony of the narrative.

Some narrative sections can be adapted from boilerplate materials while other sections must be written fresh for each proposal. In either case, all narrative must adapt the message to meet the needs and wants of the government agency. Although each proposal is unique, there are basic narrative sections standard to most grant proposals. Most government agencies require the following narrative sections:

- Cover Sheet—first page of the grant application that provides information about the applicant and employer, proposed project, estimated project funding, and PI/PD.

- Table of Contents—listing of major proposal narrative headings and subheadings with specific page numbers.

- Abstract—comprehensive project summary that highlights the features and benefits of the proposed project. The abstract should be a stand-alone document that explains why the proposed project is important.

- Introduction—brief upfront proposal section that introduces agency reviewers to your organization, institutional mission and philosophy, programs, target population, and past and present operations.

- Problem/Need—persuasively written narrative that should convince agency reviewers that a problem exists that must be improved or solved. Funding seekers should avoid painting a hopeless situation, but rather provide a vision for solving the problem. Demonstrate the existence of a problem with recent and relevant statistics.

- Goals/Objectives—indicate what will be done, under what conditions, and how the target population will be affected as a result of the proposed activities. Provide quantifiable outcomes that are realistic and attainable considering the project time frame and budget.

- Methods/Activities—detailed, convincing, and logical plan of work that describes the project activities and procedures necessary to achieve project goals and objectives. This section must also describe project management plans, key personnel qualifications (especially grant management experience), and personnel time commitments. This section should also identify the specific tasks to be completed by partners, subcontractors, and consultants.

- Evaluation Plans—systematic data-gathering procedures and strategies to measure the worth, merit, or success of a project at different stages during the period of performance. Evaluation plans must (1) identify qualified individuals or organizations that will be responsible for the evaluation process, (2) design evaluation procedures and data-gathering instruments to assess project objectives, (3) collect and analyze data, (4) specify information to be included in the government agency reports, and (5) describe how results will be disseminated.

- References or Bibliography—listing of documents cited or reviewed in order to prepare the grant application.

- Appendix—supplemental information too detailed to include in the proposal narrative (e.g., résumés, letters of support and commitment, evaluation instruments, and annual reports).

Grant proposals that involve the use of human subjects, animals, and hazardous materials must adhere to federal, state, and local laws and regulations governing the proposed project activities before funding can be committed by the government agency. Grant applications that involve the use of human subjects at an institution of higher education must comply with regulations for protecting human subjects and seek approval from an Institutional Review Board.

In-house reviewers should read the proposal narrative prior to submitting the grant application to a government agency to ensure that writers have addressed the evaluation criteria in the RFP/RFA and have presented a comprehensive, coherent, and persuasive essay. The primary job of an in-house reviewer is to ensure the grant application is compliant and that all information requested by the government agency is included in the narrative. Proposal narrative should also be edited for style to guarantee a reader-friendly and clearly written proposal. Finally, funding seekers should use charts, figures, exhibits, or diagrams to illustrate important content and break up the monotony of continuous narrative.

Review Questions

(Answers to Review Questions are on p. 274.)

(Answers to Review Questions are on p. 274.)

Directions: For statements 1–15, circle "T" for True or "F" for False.

T F   1. To develop a winning grant application, grant writers must be knowledgeable about the proposed subject matter.

T F   2. When developing the first draft of grant narrative, writers should develop ideas quickly without worrying about style.

T F   3. A winning grant proposal is based on good ideas that are expressed in a clear and understandable manner.

T F   4. Grant writers must provide exactly what is required in the RFP/RFA.

T F   5. Effective proposal writing uses the passive voice.

T F   6. Grant narrative describes the "why," "what," "how," "who," "where," and "when" of the proposed project.

T F   7. Recent and relevant information is used to support the grant application problem/need statement.

T F   8. Goals and objectives provide direction for the proposed project.

T F   9. Résumés for key personnel are placed in the proposal narrative.

T F   10. A job description/announcement should include a comprehensive presentation of duties and responsibilities required of key personnel to be hired for the proposed project.

T F   11. Evaluation plans describe specific procedures to measure grant project success.

T F   12. Formative evaluation is concerned with judging the overall quality or worth of grant programs at completion of the project.

T F   13. Government agencies require funding seekers to sign certifications and/or assurances as part of their grant application process.

T F   14. In-house reviewers ensure that grant applications are compliant and that all information requested by the government agency is included in the grant application prior to submission.

T F   15. Content editing focuses on clarity and readability of project ideas.

Exercise 5-1

Plan the Proposal Narrative

Directions: Follow the guidelines identified in Exhibit 5–21 to brainstorm the major narrative sections for a grant proposal.

Evaluation Plans	
Method/Activities	
Goals/Objectives	
Problem/Need	

Exercise 5-2

Prepare a Grant Application

(Answers to Exercise 5-2 are on pp. 288–296.)

Directions: Prepare a transmittal (cover) letter and grant application in response to the State Community College Board RFP SCCB 315 for a new special initiative grant program designed to increase the number of Information Technology (IT) graduates.

Use the proposal outline and schedule developed in Exercise 4-2 (p. 91), reread the memorandum (found on p. 92) and RFP (found on pp. 93–96), and develop a grant proposal that includes the following components:

1. Grant application cover sheet and project abstract (see p. 95)

2. Proposal narrative (maximum five pages)

3. Appendix

Exercise 5-3

Edit the Narrative

(Answers to Exercise 5-3 are on p. 297.)

Unnecessary Words and Phrases

Directions: Rewrite the following sentences to eliminate unnecessary words.

Sentence 1
The proposed project will afford participants the opportunity to master contemporary computer skills.

Sentence 2
Local colleges are producing highly skilled graduates in light of the fact that community businesses are requiring a stronger technical workforce.

Sentence 3
Outside consultants will conduct an evaluation of the entire project.

Sentence 4
The end-of-the-year annual performance report will be submitted at the end of each program year.

Sentence 5
Each and every report shall conform to the government agency's instructions.

Exercise 5-3 continues on the next page.

Exercise 5-3 (Continued)

Edit the Narrative

(Answers to Exercise 5-3 are on p. 297.)

Unnecessary Words and Phrases

Directions: Rewrite the following sentences to eliminate unnecessary words.

Sentence 6
The grantee is directed to submit the necessary project reports.

Sentence 7
It is the duty of the grantee to submit documented financial reports.

Sentence 8
The grantee shall submit project reports for the reason that the government agency's approval is mandatory.

Sentence 9
Partners will make annual contributions of $1,000 a year.

Sentence 10
A comprehensive job description listing all duties connected with the proposal manager's position is included in the appendix.

Chapter 6

Prepare, Review, and Revise the Proposal Budget

Sound budgets identify realistic project expenditures that are an essential part of a winning grant application. Budget amounts requested must be (1) necessary to meet project objectives, (2) follow the government agency's guidelines, and (3) be considered "allowable" according to the Office of Management and Budget (OMB). Usually, several budget drafts are prepared and revised before all project expenditures are identified. When developing one-year or multi-year budgets, funding seekers should (1) adhere to solicitation specifications, (2) use budget information from other grants, and (3) present actual costs for project expenditures. Budgets include direct and indirect (facilities and administrative) costs, unless the government agency indicates that indirect costs are not allowed. Cost sharing may also be a grant application requirement. **See Exhibit 6-1**.

Direct Costs

Direct costs are expenditures identified with a particular sponsored project or that can be directly assigned to such activities readily with a high degree of accuracy. Direct costs include (1) personnel salaries and fringe benefits, (2) travel and per diem, (3) equipment and expendable supplies, (4) contractual services, and (5) other direct costs. Some agencies may identify cost ranges or exclude one or more budget categories. Most government agencies provide standard forms for budget preparation, which experienced funding seekers supplement with budget detail and narrative to provide an accurate explanation of project expenditures. Funding seekers must follow OMB circulars for determining allowable project costs. OMB Circular A-21 provides cost principles for educational institutions; OMB Circular A-110 provides uniform administrative requirements for grants and agreements with institutions of higher education, hospitals, and other nonprofit organizations; and OMB Circular A-133 provides cost principles for state and local governments and nonprofit organizations. **See Exhibit 6-2**.

Personnel Salaries

Personnel salaries or wages (professional and support staff) are identified as either replacement costs or stipends. Funding seekers should use *full-time equivalents (FTEs)* or a *percent of effort* when calculating costs for full-time or part-time personnel. For example, the budget line item for a full-time PI/PD with an annual salary of $85,000 can be presented as FTE or percent of effort multiplied by the annual salary (e.g., 1.0 FTE or 100% x $85,000 = $85,000). Multi-year projects must consider annual personnel raises, cost-of-living allowances, and expected changes in fringe benefit rates.

Exhibit 6-1

Prepare, Review, and Revise the Proposal Budget

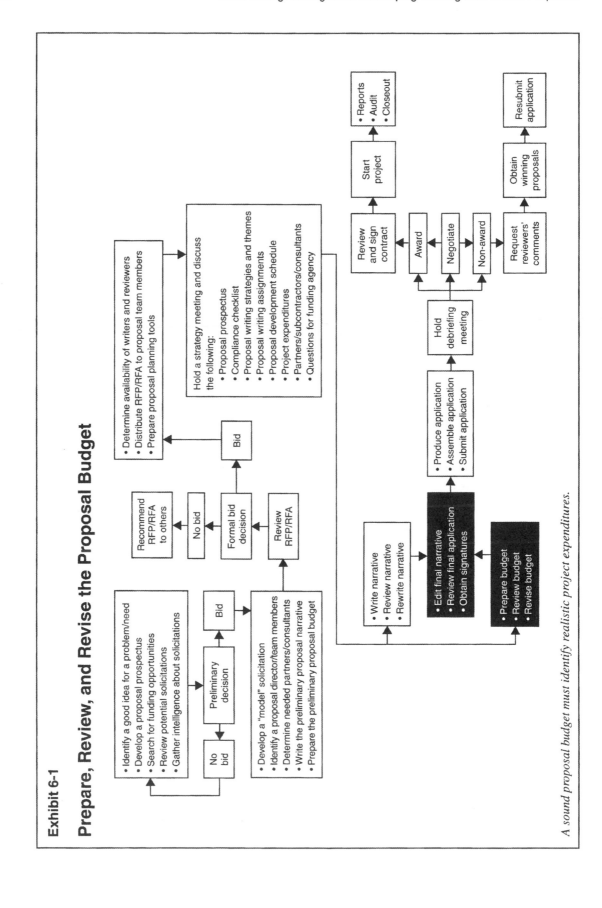

A sound proposal budget must identify realistic project expenditures.

Exhibit 6-2

Allowable Costs for Sponsored Projects

OMB A-21, C.2

	Grant budgets must only include allowable project expenditures. "Allowable" costs are reasonable, allocable, and handled in a consistent manner according to OMB circulars.
Reasonable	A cost may be considered reasonable if the nature of the goods or services acquired or applied, and the costs involved, reflect the action that a prudent person would have taken under the circumstances prevailing at the time the decision to incur the cost was made.
Allocable	A cost is allocable to a particular cost objective (i.e., a specific function, project, sponsored agreement, department, or the like) if the goods or services involved are chargeable or assignable to such cost objective in accordance with relative benefits received or other equitable relationship.
Consistent Treatment	Costs must be given consistent treatment through application of those generally accepted accounting principles appropriate to the circumstances.
Conform to Limitations	Costs must conform to limitations or exclusions set forth in these principles or in the sponsored agreement as to types or amounts of cost items.

Allowable costs are eligible for reimbursement from the federal government. Generally, it is not the type of cost that determines allowability, but rather the purpose and circumstances of the expenditure.

Fringe Benefits

Fringe benefits are part of personnel costs and represent various nonwage compensations provided to employees in addition to their normal salaries. These benefits must be consistent with the funding seeker's institutional policies. Fringe benefits are expressed as a percentage of personnel costs. **See Exhibit 6-3.**

Exhibit 6-3

Sample Fringe Benefits

Medical and dental insurance	20.57%
Life insurance	1.25%
Workers' compensation and unemployment	.73%
FICA (Social Security and Medicare)	1.07%
Retirement pension	8.67%
Total	**32.29%**

Personnel salaries and fringe benefits usually account for the majority of the project's direct costs. Fringe benefits will vary for different personnel categories (e.g., administrative, faculty, or clerical).

Travel and Per Diem

Travel costs are used to reimburse personnel working on grant projects for allowable domestic and international travel. Travel costs should indicate the traveler's name, purpose of the trip, as well as the destination and duration. Economy (round-trip) airfare or the latest government per-mile cost for personal ground transportation is used to calculate travel expenditures. In compliance with the Fly American Act, grant recipients must use American airlines to fly abroad.

Per diem costs are cost per day for lodging, meals, registration fees, and related incidental expenses associated with the proposed travel. Budget staff members must carefully consider per diem costs if project personnel need to travel to locations with higher than average cost-of-living expenses (e.g., New York City). Federally approved per diem rates for U.S. regions are established annually by the U.S. General Services Administration (see: http://www.gsc.gov).

Equipment and Expendable Supplies

Some government agencies define nonexpendable equipment as any item with an expected service life of two or more years and costs at least $5,000 per unit (other agencies allow a lower per unit cost). Proposed project equipment should indicate the manufacturer's name, model number, unit cost, quantity (e.g., 30 Dell computers [model # PP07L] @ $1,500 = $45,000), and shipping costs. Supplies are reasonable consumable items used in a project. Supplies include software, books, chemicals, and instructional materials. When listing supplies, it is advisable to indicate cost detail (e.g., 200 Wilson 1" notebooks @ $2.50 = $500).

Contractual Services

Contractual services include expenses for subcontractors and consultants, rentals, tuition, service contracts, equipment repairs, and other purchased services. Consultants are used for services too urgent, temporary, or technical to be provided by in-house staff members. When using consultants, indicate the proposed number of days to be worked and the daily consultant fee (e.g., five days @ $500 = $2,500) plus other related costs (e.g., travel and per diem). Some government agencies will limit the maximum daily cost amount that can be charged by consultants. Institutions may also enter into written agreements with other institutions as subcontractors under a sponsored award. Subcontractors must identify all direct and indirect costs before a proposal is submitted to the agency.

Other Direct Costs

Other direct costs (e.g., publications, postage, or communications) are expenses not specified under the categories above but are necessary for project success. All other direct costs must be reasonable and justified in the budget narrative.

Indirect (Facilities and Administrative) Costs

Indirect or *facilities and administrative (F&A) costs* are expenditures incurred for common objectives and therefore cannot be identified specifically with a sponsored project. General indirect costs are subtle expenditures associated with grant projects that include (1) facility operation and maintenance expenses (e.g., utility costs, custodial service costs, non-capital improvements, and insurance premiums), (2) library charges (books, library facilities, and library administration), (3) general administrative expenses (e.g., accounting, payroll, and purchasing), (4) departmental administrative expenses, (5) office of sponsored programs administrative expenses, and (6) student services. **See Exhibit 6-4.**

Exhibit 6-4

Indirect (Facilities and Administrative) Costs

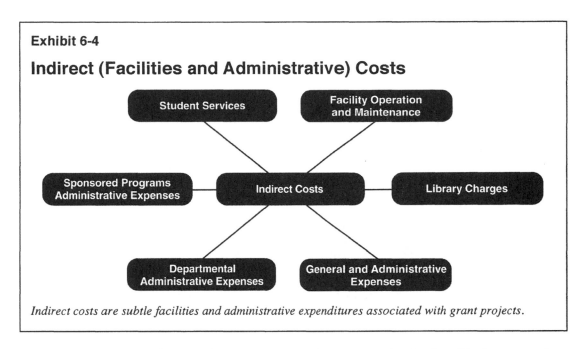

Indirect costs are subtle facilities and administrative expenditures associated with grant projects.

Organizations that develop grant proposals on a regular basis will often negotiate an indirect cost-rate agreement with a cognizant agency that is honored by other government agencies when applying for grants. A *cognizant agency* is a federal agency responsible for approving indirect or F&A rates for institutions on behalf of all federal agencies. *Indirect cost-rate agreements* establish a specific indirect cost percentage of the total direct costs (TDC) or modified total direct costs (MTDC). Indirect cost-rate agreements are negotiated with a federal agency every three years. Some agencies will not allow recovery of indirect costs, while other agencies may limit the indirect cost rate percentage that can be charged. There may also be restrictions on indirect cost rate computation and how indirect rates are applied in grant applications. Funding seekers must follow OMB guidelines and government agency restrictions for determining appropriate indirect costs.

Indirect or F&A costs are calculated as a percentage of the TDC or MTDC. *Total Direct Costs* are all direct costs charged to a project. For example, if the TDC for a proposed project is $100,000, and the allowable indirect cost rate is 35% ($100,000 [TDC] x 35% = $35,000), the total project costs (TPC) would be $135,000. *Modified total direct costs* are total direct costs excluding equipment and capital expenditures, patient care, tuition remission, rental costs, scholarships and fellowships, and subawards in excess of $25,000. For example, if the TDC for a proposed project is $100,000 of which $20,000 is for equipment, and the allowable indirect cost rate is 35% ($100,000 − $20,000 = $80,000 [MTDC] x 35% = $28,000), the TPC would be $128,000. OMB Circular A-21 requires that indirect costs be allocated on the basis of modified total direct costs. **See Exhibits 6-5 and 6-6.**

Exhibit 6-5

Sample Indirect Costs Based on Total Direct Costs

Personnel Salaries	100,000
Fringe Benefits	25,000
Travel and Per Diem	15,000
Equipment	10,000
Expendable Supplies	3,000
Contractual Services (subcontract)	30,000
Other Direct Costs	5,000
Total Direct Costs	188,000
Indirect @ 25% of TDC ($188,000 x 25% = $47,000)	47,000
Total Project Costs	$235,000

The total direct costs for the proposed project are $188,000, and the allowable indirect cost rate is 25% ($188,000 x 25% = $47,000), thus the total project costs are $235,000.

Exhibit 6-6

Sample Indirect Costs Based on Modified Total Direct Costs

Personnel Salaries	100,000
Fringe Benefits	25,000
Travel and Per Diem	15,000
Equipment	10,000
Expendable Supplies	3,000
Contractual Services (subcontract)	30,000
Other Direct Costs	5,000
Total Direct Costs	188,000
Indirect @ 25% of MTDC ($188,000–[10,000+ 5,000] = 173,000 x 25% = $43,250)	43,250
Total Project Costs	$231,250

Modified total direct costs are total direct costs excluding equipment and capital expenditures, patient care, tuition remission, rental costs, scholarships, fellowships, and subcontracts in excess of $25,000.

The total direct costs for the proposed project are $188,000, of which $10,000 is for equipment and $5,000 is for a subcontract that exceeds the allowable $25,000 times the allowable indirect cost rate of 25% ($188,000 – $15,000 = $173,000 x 25% = $43,250), thus the total project costs are $231,250.

Cost Sharing

Cost sharing is that portion of project costs that are not borne by the government agency, but rather obligate the grant-seeking institution to provide financial and/or resource contributions toward the project. Cost sharing is the difference between actual cost and the amount requested from the government agency. Cost sharing may be (1) mandatory as part of the eligibility requirement for proposal submission, (2) voluntary contributions made by the grant-seeking institution (voluntary cost sharing is not recommended since these costs are auditable and may have a negative impact on the institution's F&A rate), or (3) not required. Cost sharing made in a proposal becomes part of the award, whether or not the cost sharing was required. If awarded, grant recipients are obligated to meet all cost-sharing commitments.

In accordance with OMB Circular 110, cost sharing must be:

- verifiable and auditable within the organization's accounting system,

- necessary and reasonable to accomplish the project objectives,

- allowable in accordance with applicable cost principles (OMB Circular A-21), terms of the agreement, and institutional costing policies,

- funded from non-federal sources, unless authorized by federal statute, and

- incurred during the term of the agreement.

Cost-sharing contributions are grouped into two categories: (1) in-kind and (2) matching funds. *In-kind contributions* are non-financial donations to the proposed project from the grant-seeking institution, partners, and local business and industry. In-kind contributions include direct costs (e.g., percentage of personnel time, percentage of building space used for the project, purchase or use of equipment and expendable supplies, or use of miscellaneous services such as accounting, security, or cleaning) and indirect costs (e.g., utility costs, telephone expenses). For example, if a PI/PD is planning to work 50 percent of the time on a project but only 25 percent of his/her salary is requested, the remaining 25 percent of salary and benefits can be shown as in-kind costs. If office space is provided as an in-kind contribution, it is advisable that a floor plan with approximate square footage or room dimensions be included in the grant application. Equipment, furniture, supplies, and services that are being provided as in-kind contributions should include detailed information about the quantity of items as well as the name of the institution or partner making the contribution. When indicating in-kind contributions, grant seekers should provide a separate summary table to indicate specific contributions. **See Exhibit 6-7.**

Exhibit 6-7

Sample In-Kind Contributions

In-Kind Contributions	Lincoln		Partners	
	#	$ Value	#	$ Value
Computer Equipment and Software				
Dell desktop computers model 9200	20	20,000	5	5,000
HP laser printers model 5400	5	5,000	3	3,000
HP scanners model 3200	5	1,000	3	600
Dell laptop computers model 9300	12	18,000	0	0
Microsoft software licenses	20	4,000	5	1,000
Office Furniture and Equipment				
Computer desk and chair	25	12,500	0	0
Bookcases (12" x 48" x 72")	15	7,500	0	0
Office desks (48" x 72")	25	12,500	0	0
Four drawer file cabinets	5	2,000	20	8,000
Credenza (24" x 72")	10	5,000	5	2,500
Office Services				
Telephone service	25	3,000	0	0
Internet access	25	3,000	0	0
Photocopying and multimedia	25	5,000	0	0
Total Value		$98,500		$20,100

In-kind contributions should indicate the item, quantity, value, and contributor.

Matching funds are cash that come from the institution's general operating funds, private donations, foundation funds, or other sources. Matching contributions are not allowed to come from other federal or state grant awards. When completing proposal budgets that require matching funds, it is a good practice to establish a three-column budget. The first column indicates grant funds requested from the agency, the second column indicates the institution's matching contribution, and the third column indicates the totals for each line item. Funding seekers should obtain written cost-sharing commitments from their own institution and any partners or subcontractors prior to proposal submission. **See Exhibit 6-8**.

Exhibit 6-8

Sample Three-Column Budget

Direct Costs Line Item	Grant Funds	Matching Funds	Total Costs
Personnel Salaries	30,000	9,000	39,000
	30,000	**9,000**	**39,000**
Fringe Benefits @ 32%	9,600	0	9,600
	9,600	**0**	**9,600**
Travel and Per Diem			
Travel for Instructors	12,000	4,000	16,000
	12,000	**4,000**	**16,000**
Equipment and Expendable Supplies			
Equipment	16,000	7,700	23,700
Instructional Supplies	17,000	0	17,000
Outreach Supplies	3,000	3,000	6,000
	36,000	**10,700**	**46,700**
Contractual Services			
Consultant to Develop Curriculum	4,000	0	4,000
Cabling for Classrooms and Labs	0	3,000	3,000
	4,000	**3,000**	**7,000**
Other Direct Costs	0	0	0
	0	**0**	**0**
Total Project Costs*	**$91,600**	**$26,700**	**$118,300**

*Note: No indirect (facilities and administrative) costs are used in this sample budget.

Funding seekers use a three-column budget when agencies require matching contributions. Funding from one grant cannot be used to provide matching funds for another grant. Funding seekers should use a spreadsheet when calculating budget costs to minimize arithmetic errors.

Not all government agencies require cost sharing. In addition, some agencies only require a nominal percentage of the total project cost to satisfy the cost-sharing commitment. For example, the National Science Foundation currently only requires a cost-sharing commitment of 1 percent of the proposed project costs.

If cost sharing is specified in a proposal and the grant application is funded, the cost-sharing commitment becomes part of the grant award (even if only by reference). Grant recipients must produce the full cost-sharing commitment, or the total award amount may be lowered by the government agency.

Budget Detail and Narrative

Budget detail is a brief description of how project expenditures were determined (e.g., three computers @ $1,500 = $4,500). These parenthetical statements must explain each line item so information is clear to reviewers. *Budget narrative* provides a written explanation of complex or unusual expenditures. Narrative is not necessary when costs are straightforward. **See Exhibits 6-9, 6-10, and 6-11.**

Exhibit 6-9

Sample Budget Detail

Personnel Salaries and Fringe Benefits

PI/PD (100% of full-time salary)	57,400
Project Coordinator (100% of full-time salary)	54,000
Financial Manager (10% of six months of full-time salary)	3,400
Secretary (10 hours per week for 26 weeks @ $7.50 hourly)	1,950
Total personnel costs	116,750
Fringe benefits (28.29% x $116,750)	33,029
	$149,779

Travel and Per Diem

PI/PD (3 trips x $800 airfare)	2,400
Project Coordinator (2 trips x $800 airfare)	1,600
Financial Manager (1 trip x $800 airfare)	800
PI/PD (12 days x $48 per diem)	576
Project Coordinator (8 days x $48 per diem)	384
Financial Manager (4 days x $48 per diem)	192
	$5,952

Equipment and Expendable Supplies

Computers (20 Dell [model # PP343] computers x $1,250)	25,000
Removable hard drives (60 Dell hard drives [model # PP321] x $150)	9,000
Laser printers (3 Hewlett Packard printers [model # PP364] x $1,500)	4,500
Recruitment materials (2,000 two-color brochures x $.50)	1,000
Instructional materials (100 textbooks x $60)	6,000
	$45,500

Contractual Services

Consultants (2 consultants x 5 days x $250)	2,500
Van rental (5 days x $100)	500
	$3,000

Total Direct Costs	**$204,231**
Indirect (Facilities and Administrative) Costs @ 45%	**$91,904**
Total Project Costs	**$296,135**

Budget detail provides a brief parenthetical description of proposed project expenditures. NIH requires funding seekers to prepare budgets using modules of $25,000 and detail is not required.

Exhibit 6-10

Sample Budget Narrative

Personnel

The Activity Director is a new permanent full-time employee for the project. This individual will devote 100% time to the project for five years. Funding is requested to support this position 100% in years one and two, 75% in year three, 50% in year four, and 25% in year five. The college will support this position after the grant-funding period. The Activity Director's salary is based on current college salaries for faculty members with upper-level experience.

A Network Administrator will be hired as a new permanent full-time employee for the project. This individual will work with the Activity Director to assist with project implementation and will devote 100% time to the project. The college will support this position after the grant-funding period. The salary for the Network Administrator is based on current salaries for personnel in the administrative computing department.

Travel and Per Diem

To keep abreast of national developments in technology, the Activity Director will attend a professional development conference each year of the grant. The information gained from attending these conferences will be used by the Activity Director to train faculty and develop networking programs.

Equipment and Expendable Supplies

In year one, the infrastructure for the campus-wide network will be installed. Funds are requested each year of the project to cover the infrastructure equipment cost of $856,616. Specific equipment needed for the infrastructure includes:

- communications server and expansion port network,
- switching and network access equipment,
- management firewall protector, and
- fiber optic and copper cable.

To complete the network infrastructure, fiber optics and structural wiring will be run to every building on campus. The installation of this equipment will permit access to the intra-campus network, the Internet, and voice communication in all buildings on campus including all faculty and staff member offices, residence hall rooms, classrooms, computer labs, and other applicable locations. The college has already secured a tentative agreement with Lucent Technologies to provide the campus infrastructure equipment.

The server operating system will integrate a variety of network services needed to run the campus network. The operating system will allow centralized management of the network and will provide a means to automate common tasks and use logon scripts to effectively distribute software upgrades, standardize desktops, and enforce security. Licenses will be purchased for 120 users. This will cover the computers in student labs, faculty offices, and administrative offices. Licenses will be purchased as needed for students in residence halls.

Budget narrative provides a thorough explanation of complex or unusual project expenditures.

Exhibit 6-11

Sample Budget With Detail and Narrative

Northern Plains Educational Center	
Government Funds Requested	
Personnel and Fringe Benefits	**Costs**
PI/PD (100% of full-time salary)	57,000
Educational Specialists (100%) (4 Specialists x $30,000)	120,000
Counselor (100% of full-time salary)	38,000
Project Secretary (100% of full-time salary)	24,000
Subtotal	**$239,000**
Fringe Benefits @ 30%	$ 71,700
Total Personnel and Fringe Benefits	**$310,700**

The budget includes full-time personnel costs for the PI/PD, four educational specialists to serve seven regions in the target area, a counselor, and project secretary. Salaries are consistent with the state classified compensation plan. The standard college fringe benefits of 30% consist of FICA (7.65%), retirement (11.34%), health insurance (9.38%), group life insurance (.80%), and disability insurance (.83%). Proposed personnel will be able to provide individual attention to the learning needs and academic growth of participants in the target area.

Equipment and Expendable Supplies	**Costs**
Dell computer model # 9300 (30 x $1,500)	45,000
Microsoft Office software license (30 x $200)	6,000
Hewlett Packard laser printer (6 x $3,000)	18,000
Computer station (desk and chair) (30 x $750)	22,500
Assessment and testing materials (500 x $13.40)	6,700
Instructional materials (100 workbooks x $30)	3,000
Total Equipment and Expendable Supplies	**$101,200**

Equipment and supply expenses include 30 computers and six laser printers to equip the main instructional area to be used by project participants. Microsoft Office licenses will be obtained for all computer stations. Thirty computer stations will be purchased with adjustable keyboards and tabletops. Assessment and testing materials will be used to screen 500 participants so proper placement will take place (costs will include testing analysis fees). Instructional materials include workbooks for 100 participants.

Budgets should provide detail and narrative to clarify project costs. When there is inadequate justification for expenditures, government agencies may suggest a reduced budget. If cuts are greater than 10% of the total budget, the applicant should submit a revised budget and scope of work to reflect the reduced budget.

Review and Revise the Budget

At least two grant application budget drafts should be prepared and thoroughly checked by in-house reviewers. Reviewers should assess the budget in relationship to project activities and RFP/RFA requirements. Specifically, in-house reviewers should ask the following questions:

- Does the budget include all essential direct costs necessary to meet the project objectives?

- Does the budget consider personnel raises, cost-of-living allowances, and inflation when calculating a multi-year budget?

- Does the budget provide detail and narrative so agency reviewers will understand how unusual or complex expenditures were calculated?

- Does the budget include appropriate indirect costs, if allowed?

- Does the budget specify cost-sharing (matching and/or in-kind) contributions, if applicable?

- Does the budget present a plan for project sustainability (to demonstrate long-term financial viability of the project after depletion of grant funds)?

Proposal team leaders should review the final budget (direct and indirect costs as well as any cost-sharing commitments) in conjunction with the proposal narrative. A style editor should review the grant application budget narrative for clarity. The financial administrator/manager, who is a member of the final proposal review team, should provide final sign-off for grant expenditures.

Government agencies operate under different fiscal years and under different budget terms and conditions. For some projects, July 1 through June 30 is a fiscal year, as is the case for many state-funded projects. The federal government's fiscal year is October 1 through September 30. Some government agencies use different deadlines or annual calendars. Grant application budgets are similar to bank accounts where funding is drawn for the life of the grant project. The key is to complete all proposal commitments and spend all available funds within the constraints prescribed by the funding source.

Funding seekers complete one or more standard budget forms when submitting grant applications to most government agencies: (1) federal funds for non-construction programs (direct and indirect costs for the proposed project) and (2) non-federal funds (matching funds, if required by the agency). Funding seekers must carefully read and follow specific instructions when completing government agency budget forms and supplement them with budget detail and narrative to provide explanation. In addition, funding seekers should prepare a contingency budget with prioritized budget needs in case the government agency provides only partial support for the proposed grant project. **See Exhibit 6-12**.

Exhibit 6-12

Sample Grant Budget Forms and Instructions

U.S. DEPARTMENT OF EDUCATION
BUDGET INFORMATION
NON-CONSTRUCTION PROGRAMS

OMB Control Number: 1894-0008
Expiration Date: 02/28/2011

Name of Institution/Organization
Hoosier State University

Applicants requesting funding for only one year should complete the column under "Project Year 1." Applicants requesting funding for multi-year grants should complete all applicable columns. Please read all instructions before completing form.

SECTION A - BUDGET SUMMARY
U.S. DEPARTMENT OF EDUCATION FUNDS

Budget Categories	Project Year 1 (a)	Project Year 2 (b)	Project Year 3 (c)	Project Year 4 (d)	Project Year 5 (e)	Total (f)
1. Personnel	238,401	245,553	252,918	260,512	268,327	1,265,711
2. Fringe Benefits	56,311	58,004	59,737	61,532	63,377	298,961
3. Travel	27,632	28,461	29,315	30,194	32,819	148,421
4. Equipment	0	0	0	0	0	0
5. Supplies	13,825	14,143	14,482	14,815	13,448	70,713
6. Contractual	0	0	0	0	0	0
7. Construction	0	0	0	0	0	0
8. Other	0	0	0	0	0	0
9. Total Direct Costs (lines 1-8)	336,169	346,161	356,452	367,053	377,971	1,783,806
10. Indirect Costs*	26,894	27,794	28,721	29,676	30,660	143,745
11. Training Stipends	0	0	0	0	0	0
12. Total Costs (lines 9-11)	363,063	373,955	385,173	396,729	408,631	1,927,551

*Indirect Cost Information (To Be Completed by Your Business Office):

If you are requesting reimbursement for indirect costs on line 10, please answer the following questions:

(1) Do you have an Indirect Cost Rate Agreement approved by the Federal government? _X_Yes ____ No

(2) If yes, please provide the following information
     Period Covered by the Indirect Cost Rate Agreement: From: 10/1/20XX To: 9/30/20XX (mm/dd/yyyy)
     Approving Federal agency: _X_ED ____ Other (please specify): _____

(3) For Restricted Rate Programs (check one) -- Are you using a restricted indirect cost rate that:
     ____ Is included in your approved Indirect Cost Rate Agreement? or _X_ Complies with 34 CFR 76.564(c)(2)?

ED 524

Government agencies usually provide budget forms or templates for preparing a budget as part of the application package. Budget form (Section A) is used to summarize federal funds requested from the government agency to complete the proposed project. The proposal narrative should always drive the budget. Multi-year budgets must anticipate inflation and salary adjustments.

Exhibit 6-12 (Continued)

Sample Grant Budget Forms and Instructions

Name of Institution/Organization

Hoosier State University

Applicants requesting funding for only one year should complete the column under "Project Year 1." Applicants requesting funding for multi-year grants should complete all applicable columns. Please read all instructions before completing form.

SECTION B - BUDGET SUMMARY
NON-FEDERAL FUNDS

Budget Categories	Project Year 1 (a)	Project Year 2 (b)	Project Year 3 (c)	Project Year 4 (d)	Project Year 5 (e)	Total (f)
1. Personnel	0	0	0	0	0	0
2. Fringe Benefits	0	0	0	0	0	0
3. Travel	0	0	0	0	0	0
4. Equipment	0	0	0	0	0	0
5. Supplies	17,550	17,550	17,550	17,550	17,550	87,750
6. Contractual	0	0	0	0	0	0
7. Construction	0	0	0	0	0	0
8. Other	9,900	9,900	9,900	9,900	9,900	49,500
9. Total Direct Costs (Lines 1-8)	27,450	27,450	27,450	27,450	27,450	137,250
10. Indirect Costs	0	0	0	0	0	0
11. Training Stipends	0	0	0	0	0	0
12. Total Costs (Lines 9-11)	27,450	27,450	27,450	27,450	27,450	137,250

SECTION C – BUDGET NARRATIVE (see instructions)

ED 524

Budget form (Section B) is used to summarize non-federal funds (e.g., matching and other non-federal resources) contributed by the funding seeker to complete the proposed project.

Exhibit 6-12 (Continued)

Sample Grant Budget Forms and Instructions

Instructions for ED 524

General Instructions

This form is used to apply to individual U.S. Department of Education (ED) discretionary grant programs. Unless directed otherwise, provide the same budget information for each year of the multi-year funding request. Pay attention to applicable program specific instructions, if attached. You may access the Education Department General Administrative Regulations, 34 CFR 74 – 86 and 97-99, on ED's website at: http://www.ed.gov/policy/fund/reg/edgarReg/edgar.html

You must consult with your Business Office prior to submitting this form.

Section A - Budget Summary
U.S. Department of Education Funds

All applicants must complete Section A and provide a break-down by the applicable budget categories shown in lines 1-11.

Lines 1-11, columns (a)-(e): For each project year for which funding is requested, show the total amount requested for each applicable budget category.

Lines 1-11, column (f): Show the multi-year total for each budget category. If funding is requested for only one project year, leave this column blank.

Line 12, columns (a)-(e): Show the total budget request for each project year for which funding is requested.

Line 12, column (f): Show the total amount requested for all project years. If funding is requested for only one year, leave this space blank.

Indirect Cost Information: If you are requesting reimbursement for indirect costs on line 10, this information is to be completed by your Business Office. (1): Indicate whether or not your organization has an Indirect Cost Rate Agreement that was approved by the Federal government. (2): If you checked "yes" in (1), indicate in (2) the beginning and ending dates covered by the Indirect Cost Rate Agreement. In addition, indicate whether ED or another Federal agency (Other) issued the approved agreement. If you check "Other," specify the name of the Federal agency that issued the approved agreement. (3): If you are applying for a grant under a Restricted Rate Program (34 CFR 75.563 or 76.563), indicate whether you are using a restricted indirect cost rate that is included on your approved Indirect Cost Rate Agreement or whether you are using a restricted indirect cost rate that complies with 34 CFR 76.564(c)(2). Note: State or Local government agencies may not use the provision for a restricted indirect cost rate specified in 34 CFR 76.564(c)(2). Check only one response. Leave blank, if this item is not applicable.

Section B - Budget Summary
Non-Federal Funds

If you are required to provide or volunteer to provide cost-sharing or matching funds or other non-Federal resources to the project, these should be shown for each applicable budget category on lines 1-11 of Section B.

Lines 1-11, columns (a)-(e): For each project year, for which matching funds or other contributions are provided, show the total contribution for each applicable budget category.

Lines 1-11, column (f): Show the multi-year total for each budget category. If non-Federal contributions are provided for only one year, leave this column blank.

Line 12, columns (a)-(e): Show the total matching or other contribution for each project year.

Line 12, column (f): Show the total amount to be contributed for all years of the multi-year project. If non-Federal contributions are provided for only one year, leave this space blank.

Section C - Budget Narrative [Attach separate sheet(s)]
Pay attention to applicable program specific instructions, if attached.

1. Provide an itemized budget breakdown, and justification by project year, for each budget category listed in Sections A and B. For grant projects that will be divided into two or more separately budgeted major activities or sub-projects, show for each budget category of a project year the breakdown of the specific expenses attributable to each sub-project or activity.

2. For non-Federal funds or resources listed in Section B that are used to meet a cost-sharing or matching requirement or provided as a voluntary cost-sharing or matching commitment, you must include:

   a. The specific costs or contributions by budget category;
   b. The source of the costs or contributions; and
   c. In the case of third-party in-kind contributions, a description of how the value was determined for the donated or contributed goods or services.

   [Please review ED's general cost sharing and matching regulations, which include specific limitations, in 34 CFR 74.23, applicable to non-governmental entities, and 80.24, applicable to governments, and the applicable Office of Management and Budget (OMB) cost principles for your entity type regarding donations, capital assets, depreciation and use allowances. OMB cost principle circulars are available on OMB's website at: http://www.whitehouse.gov/omb/circulars/index.html]

3. If applicable to this program, provide the rate and base on which fringe benefits are calculated.

4. If you are requesting reimbursement for indirect costs on line 10, this information is to be completed by your Business Office. Specify the estimated amount of the base to which the indirect cost rate is applied and the total indirect expense. Depending on the grant program to which you are applying and/or your approved Indirect Cost Rate Agreement, some direct cost budget categories in your grant application budget may not be included in the base and multiplied by your indirect cost rate. For example, you must multiply the indirect cost rates of "Training grants" (34 CFR 75.562) and grants under programs with "Supplement not Supplant" requirements ("Restricted Rate" programs) by a "modified total direct cost" (MTDC) base (34 CFR 75.563 or 76.563). Please indicate which costs are included and which costs are excluded from the base to which the indirect cost rate is applied.

   When calculating indirect costs (line 10) for "Training grants" or grants under "Restricted Rate" programs, you must refer to the information and examples on ED's website at: http://www.ed.gov/fund/grant/apply/appforms/appforms.html

   You may also contact (202) 377-3838 for additional information regarding calculating indirect cost rates or general indirect cost rate information.

5. Provide other explanations or comments you deem necessary.

Paperwork Burden Statement

According to the Paperwork Reduction Act of 1995, no persons are required to respond to a collection of information unless such collection displays a valid OMB control number. The valid OMB control number for this information collection is 1890-0018. The time required to complete this information collection is estimated to vary from 13 to 22 hours per response, with an average of 17.5 hours per response, including the time to review instructions, search existing data sources, gather the data needed, and complete and review the information collection. If you have any comments concerning the accuracy of the time estimate(s) or suggestions for improving this form, please write to: U.S. Department of Education, Washington, D.C. 20202-4537. If you have comments or concerns regarding the status of your individual submission of this form, write directly to (insert program office), U.S. Department of Education, 400 Maryland Avenue, S.W., Washington, D.C. 20202.

The U.S. Department of Education provides specific instructions for completing budget forms. Budgets must be based on real costs. If specific instructions are not provided for developing a budget, it should be prepared using the major budget categories.

Common Budget Problems

Grant budgets are credibility statements. Incomplete budgets signal poor preparation. Inflated budgets indicate waste. Low budgets cast doubt on the applicant's planning ability. Funding seekers must strive to establish realistic budgets that are complete, unambiguous, and reflect good project planning. Funding seekers must carefully check and recheck budgets before submitting grant applications. Common problems with grant budgets are presented below.

Arithmetic Errors in Subtotals and Totals. Arithmetic errors reflect sloppy preparation. Budget totals and subtotals must be checked and rechecked for accuracy. Errors and omissions detract from the overall proposal credibility.

Lack of Budget Detail. Budget detail provides information about how totals and subtotals were determined. For example, 25 computers @ \$2,000 = \$50,000; 200 books @ \$50 = \$10,000; 10% of \$70,000 annual salary = \$7,000. Always provide sufficient detail so government agency reviewers can easily determine how budget items were calculated.

Unrealistic Costs for Budget Items. Budget items must reflect actual costs, not inflated costs. Government agency reviewers usually identify budget items that exceed a normal cost range. Never pad a budget. In addition, be prepared to prioritize grant project budget needs.

Budget Items Inconsistent with Proposal Narrative. Proposal narrative and budget items must be carefully reviewed for internal consistency and compliance with the RFP/RFA. Cost items identified in the grant application narrative must always be reflected in the budget. Conversely, budget items must be justified in the proposal narrative.

Little or No Budget Narrative. Budget narrative explains and clarifies cost expenditures. Budget narrative should accompany large projects with complex or unusual expenditures.

Vague and Unexplained Source(s) for Cost-Sharing Dollars. Specific detail must be provided for cost-sharing contributions. Matching funds should include the financial contribution for each budget category. In-kind contributions should indicate the item, quantity, value, and contributor.

Indirect Costs Are Missing From Budgets. If allowed, funding seekers should always include indirect costs in proposal budgets. Some agencies will only allow a limited percentage of the total budget to count as indirect costs. Other agencies will allow grant seekers to apply the maximum indirect cost percentage established via an indirect cost-rate agreement with a cognizant government agency.

Chapter Summary

Grant budgets must be realistic and credible. Budgets may include direct and indirect costs as well as require cost-sharing contributions.

Direct costs are specific expenditures necessary to complete the grant project. These included expenditures for (1) personnel salaries and fringe benefits, (2) travel and per diem, (3) equipment and expendable supplies, (4) contractual services, and (5) other direct costs.

Funding seekers must follow the OMB circulars for determining allowable costs. An allowable cost is eligible for reimbursement from the federal government. An allowable cost must be:

- *Reasonable.* A prudent businessperson would have purchased this item and paid this price.

- *Allocable.* It can be assigned to the activity on some reasonable basis.

- *Consistently treated.* Like costs must be treated the same in like circumstances, as either direct or indirect costs.

Unallowable costs may be grouped into activities and transactions. Unallowable activities include such tasks as lobbying and fundraising. Unallowable transactions include such dealings as the purchase of decorations, alcoholic beverages, and entertainment not directly tied to grant business.

Indirect costs are referred to as overhead or facilities and administrative costs and include expenditures not identified readily or specifically with a particular grant project or activity. General indirect costs include:

- facility operation and maintenance expenses (e.g., utility costs, custodial service costs, noncapital improvements, and insurance premiums),

- library charges (books, library facilities, and library administration),

- general administrative expenses (e.g., accounting, payroll, and purchasing),

- departmental administrative expenses,

- office of sponsored programs administration expenses, and

- student services.

Indirect costs are calculated as a percentage of the total direct costs or modified total direct costs. *Total direct costs* are all direct costs charged to a project. Modified total direct costs are total direct costs excluding equipment and capital expenditures, patient care, tuition remission, rental costs, scholarships, fellowships, and subawards in excess of $25,000. OMB Circular A-21 requires that indirect costs be allocated on the basis of MTDC.

Organizations that develop grant proposals on a regular basis will often negotiate an indirect cost-rate agreement with a cognizant government agency that is honored by other government agencies. Indirect cost-rate agreements establish an indirect cost percentage of the TDC or MTDC. Indirect cost-rate agreements are negotiated every three years.

Cost sharing is a requirement by some state and federal agencies that obligates the grant-seeking institution to provide financial and/or resource contributions toward the grant project. Cost sharing may be (1) mandatory as part of the eligibility requirement for proposal submission, (2) voluntary contributions made by the grant-seeking institution, or (3) not required. Cost-sharing contributions are grouped into two categories: (1) in-kind and (2) matching funds. In-kind contributions are non-financial donations to the proposed project from the grant-seeking institution, partners, and local business and industry. Matching funds are cash that come from an institution's operating budget, private donations, foundations, or other sources. Matching funds must be documented and auditable. Cost sharing made in a proposal becomes part of the award, whether or not the cost sharing was required.

Most government agencies provide standard forms for single-year and multi-year budgets. Experienced funding seekers supplement these forms with budget detail and narrative to provide a comprehensive description of project expenditures. Budget detail is a brief description of project expenditures (e.g., three computers @ $1,500 = $4,500). These parenthetical statements should explain each line item so calculations are clear to grant reviewers. Budget narrative provides a written explanation of complex or unusual project expenditures. Narrative is not necessary when project costs are straightforward. All budget detail and narrative must be clear, factual, and supportable.

At least two budget drafts should be developed and thoroughly checked by in-house reviewers. Reviewers should assess budgets in relationship to project objectives, activities, and solicitation requirements. Budgets must:

- provide appropriate personnel and sufficient resources necessary to complete the proposed project,

- include only allowable direct and indirect expenditures in the format requested by the government agency,

- provide detail and narrative so agency reviewers understand how expenditures were calculated,

- specify cost sharing (matching and in-kind) contributions, if applicable,

- consider salary and benefit raises and cost-of-living allowances when calculating multi-year projects, and

- present a plan for sustainability (to demonstrate long term financial viability of the project after depletion of grant funds).

Review Questions

(Answers to Review Questions are on p. 274.)

(Answers to Review Questions are on p. 274.)

Directions: For statements 1–15, circle "T" for True or "F" for False.

T F   1. Sound budgets identify realistic project expenditures.

T F   2. The Office of Management and Budget (OMB) circulars provide guidelines for determining allowable project costs.

T F   3. Direct costs are expenditures identified with a particular sponsored project or that can be directly assigned to such activities readily with a high degree of accuracy.

T F   4. Fringe benefits are indirect costs.

T F   5. Travel and per diem expenses are direct costs.

T F   6. Federally approved per diem rates for U.S. regions are established annually by the U.S. General Services Administration.

T F   7. Project supplies are reasonable consumable project items.

T F   8. Indirect costs are expenditures incurred for common objectives and therefore cannot be identified specifically with a sponsored project.

T F   9. Cost-sharing contributions are the difference between actual cost and the amount requested from the government agency.

T F   10. Matching funds are monies that come from the funding seeker's institutional general operating budget, private donations, etc.

T F   11. Budget detail is a brief parenthetical description of project expenditures.

T F   12. Budget narrative provides a thorough written explanation about complex or unusual project expenditures.

T F   13. Government agencies operate under the same fiscal budget terms and conditions.

T F   14. Grant application budgets are credibility statements.

T F   15. Arithmetic errors in subtotals and totals are common problems with grant applications submitted by funding seekers.

Exercise 6-1

Prepare a Proposal Budget (Information Technology)

(Answers to Exercise 6-1 are on p. 298.)

Directions: Prepare a budget for the grant application that you developed for Exercise 5-2 (p. 134) in response to the State Community College Board RFP SCCB 315 for a new special initiative grant program designed to increase the number of Information Technology (IT) graduates. Use the proposal outline and schedule developed in Exercise 4-2 (p. 91) and reread the memorandum (p. 92) and RFP (pp. 93–96) to develop your budget. The budget should follow the format sheet on p. 96 and include the following direct cost line items:

1. Personnel Salaries

2. Fringe Benefits

3. Travel and Per Diem

4. Equipment and Expendable Supplies

5. Contractual Services

6. Other Direct Costs

Exercise 6-2

Prepare a Proposal Budget (School-To-Work)

(Answers to Exercise 6-2 are on p. 299.)

Directions: Read the proposal narrative (pp. 159–161) and identify elements that have budget implications. Use the proposed budget form on p. 162 to prepare a line item budget that indicates direct costs requested from the (1) government agency and (2) cost sharing to be contributed by Anytown School District.

Assume the following information:

1. You are:

> Dr. John Ling, Superintendent of Schools
> Anytown School District (ASD) (Employer # 96-0065765)
> 1311 Northwest Main Street
> Anytown, USA 98765
> (555) 435-XXXX

2. ASD serves a population of 26,000 students.

3. You are submitting a grant application in response to a government agency solicitation.

4. Proposed project staff members and annual salaries are listed below.

Personnel	Annual Salary
• Project Oversight Manager	$85,010
• Project Administrator	$78,008
• Project Specialist #1	$40,996
• Project Specialist #2	$50,003
• Financial Manager	$85,010
• Document Preparation Specialist	$36,000

5. Other direct expenses associated with the proposed grant project are listed below:

   • 25% Staff Fringe Benefits

   • Travel and Per Diem
     - $100 travel for teachers, advisory board members, and students
     - $100 travel for specialists (when away from Anytown residence)
     - $800 travel for national speaker
     - $400 travel for each state speaker
     - $140 daily per diem for teachers, advisory board members, and speakers
     - $ 50 daily per diem for students
     - $ 35 daily per diem for specialists (when away from Anytown residence)

   • $1,000 for each curriculum package

   • $1,000 honorarium for national speaker and $500 for each state speaker

   • $1,000 per day rental fee for conference building

   • $50 per square foot per year for the Career Information Center space

6. No indirect (facility and administrative) costs are allowed.

Exercise 6-2 continues on the next page.

Anytown School District (ASD) Proposal Narrative

Read pp. 159–161 and use the proposed budget form on p. 162 to develop a line-item budget.
Assume that costs will be paid by the government agency unless otherwise noted.

The bulk of federal funding requested for the Anytown School District (ASD)
School-To-Work (S-T-W) Implementation Project will be used to hire two project
specialists for one year. Each project specialist will be responsible for working
with students, parents, teachers, and administrators in 22 ASD local schools for
three days. The remaining budget items include a S-T-W conference for local
teachers and area school board members, a student work experience program,
travel and per diem, and S-T-W curriculum materials.

School-To-Work Key Personnel
Successful implementation of the S-T-W program at ASD is directly related to the
quality of project staff. Much thought and effort was taken to identify key staff
members who would serve in leadership roles to ensure successful
implementation of the S-T-W project.

Project Oversight Manager—Dr. John Ling, superintendent of ASD, will take
responsibility for ensuring that the S-T-W project complies with federal
regulations. Salary and fringe benefits for Dr. Ling will be provided by ASD. The
project oversight manager's responsibilities include:
- serve as the S-T-W contact for federal officials,
- monitor and evaluate S-T-W implementation in ASD, and
- disseminate federal S-T-W information to state and regional representatives.

Project Administrator—Mr. James Schmidt will assume the role of project
administrator. Mr. Schmidt, working with the financial manager, will maintain
accurate and complete records, which will be reviewed by administrators and
auditors. Mr. Schmidt will work closely with the project specialists (Mr. Greg
Miroski and another project specialist to be hired) to implement S-T-W programs
in the ASD area. The project administrator's responsibilities include:
- serve as the S-T-W contact for state officials,
- monitor the implementation of S-T-W programs,
- assist in the development of S-T-W curriculum in response to students' needs,
- recruit business and industry leaders as S-T-W partners,
- monitor, assist, and evaluate the progress of S-T-W programs at ASD,
- work with ASD employers and advisory committees,
- disseminate information regarding current rules and trends in S-T-W,
- work cooperatively with education agencies in ASD,
- evaluate the development of S-T-W curriculum, and
- prepare S-T-W quarterly financial and progress reports.

Exercise 6-2 continues on the next page.

Project Specialists—Mr. Greg Miroski and one other project specialist to be hired will work in the local ASD area to implement the S-T-W program. The ASD program will comply fully with all federal, state, and local laws relating to equal employment opportunity and affirmative action when hiring the additional project specialist. In addition, minorities and women, and other underrepresented groups, will be encouraged to apply for this position. The project specialists' responsibilities include:

- design and implement S-T-W programs in local schools,
- disseminate S-T-W information to students, parents, and teachers,
- assist students with portfolio development,
- connect students with agencies/businesses,
- recruit outside business representatives for mentoring activities,
- establish work experiences and internships for students,
- coordinate with community agencies and businesses to promote S-T-W, employment opportunities for students,
- work with site administrators, counselors, teachers, and students to locate job training placement,
- maintain a systematic set of S-T-W monitoring and enrollment records, and
- assist the project administrator with other duties as required.

Project Financial Manager—Mr. David Black, financial manager for ASD, will be responsible for the management and control of all grant funds. Mr. Black will ensure that all expenditures occur within the regulations of the state and U.S. Departments of Education and Labor. Salary and fringe benefits for Mr. Black will be provided by ASD. The project financial manager's responsibilities include:

- maintain accurate financial records for S-T-W activities, which include staff labor and other direct expenses, and
- prepare and represent ASD in any S-T-W program audit.

S-T-W Document Preparation Specialist—Ms. Sharon Samuels will serve as the document preparation specialist and will handle all word processing and graphic design work for the S-T-W project. Salary and fringe benefits for Ms. Samuels will be provided by ASD. The document preparation specialist's responsibilities include:

- prepare all S-T-W documents,
- design final S-T-W reports,
- prepare tables, charts, and graphs for S-T-W presentations,
- schedule S-T-W meetings, conferences, etc., and
- assist the project administrator with other duties as required. **See Table 1**.

Exercise 6-2 continues on the next page.

Table 1

Time Commitment of S-T-W Project Personnel

Name	Position	Commitment
John Ling*	Project Oversight Manager	15%
James Schmidt	Project Administrator	25%
Greg Miroski	Project Specialist #1	100%
To be hired	Project Specialist #2	100%
David Black*	Financial Manager	10%
Sharon Samuels*	Document Preparation Specialist	25%

*Salary and fringe benefits provided by ASD

S-T-W Conference for Teachers and Area School Board Members

Project specialists (Anytown residents) will lead a two-day S-T-W conference in Anytown in the fall. The conference will serve as a public relations meeting for employers and community members, as well as an introduction meeting for 22 ASD teachers and 22 ASD Advisory School Board (ASB) members (ASD will pay travel and per diem for ASB members). The meeting will also serve as an orientation program for local employers and present such topics as the purpose of S-T-W programs, working with youth, job shadowing, and serving as a mentor.

One national and two state speakers will be invited to the conference to present innovative S-T-W activities. Speakers will be paid an honorarium and travel and per diem to attend this conference.

Student Work Experience Program

The student work experience program is for 20 students for 14 days at Anytown and covers six career pathways. Students will learn about technical and management positions; level of education needed for each position; local, state, and national job outlook for careers; and expected salaries.

A Career Information Center will be established in Anytown to furnish career and occupational information to students. ASD will provide 400 square feet of office space for the center. ASD will also donate $1,000 per year for student career occupational information packets that will be available at the center.

S-T-W Implementation Project in Local Schools

Both project specialists will travel to 22 schools in the state (spending three days per visit) and work directly with ASD teachers to implement S-T-W curriculum. Project specialists will introduce S-T-W to all students, parents, administrators, and employers in local schools through the use of S-T-W curriculum materials to be obtained from ABC Publishers, Inc. One set of curriculum materials will be obtained for each of the 22 schools.

Exercise 6-2 continues on the next page.

Proposed Budget Form			
Directions: Use this form to prepare a line-item budget that indicates direct costs requested from the government agency and cost sharing to be contributed by ASD.			
Budget Category	**Agency**	**ASD**	**Total**
Personnel Salaries and Fringe Benefits			
Travel and Per Diem			
S-T-W Conference			
Student Work Experience			
S-T-W Implementation Project in Schools			
Equipment and Expendable Supplies			
Contractual Services			
Total Project Costs*			

*Note: No indirect (facilities and administrative) costs are allowed.

Chapter 7

Produce, Assemble, and Submit the Grant Application

After the proposal narrative and budget have been developed, proposal directors must make sure the complete grant application is produced, assembled, and submitted to the government agency before the deadline. Grant proposal producing, assembling, and submitting tasks must not be taken lightly. Poor grant application producing and assembling can result in missing sections or pages, unsigned forms, as well as a host of other problems that can influence government agency reviewers' overall rating of the grant application. Grant applications submitted after the due date and time specified in the RFP/RFA are generally not considered for funding. **See Exhibit 7-1.**

Produce and Assemble the Grant Application

Grant proposal narrative must follow RFP/RFA content and format guidelines. Proposal directors should check and recheck grant applications against RFP/RFA requirements for compliance. Funding seekers must stay under any word count for abstracts, provide text in the desired format (required text spacing, page margins, etc.), use appropriate typeface and size asked for in the RFP/RFA, and stay under the total pages of narrative requested for grant applications (and do not reduce the font size or margins to accommodate additional pages). Funding seekers must provide exactly what is requested in the RFP/RFA to be considered a viable candidate for funding. **See Exhibit 7-2.**

Assemble the proposal cover sheet, table of contents (TOC), narrative, budget, application forms, and appendix materials in the exact manner specified in the RFP/RFA guidelines. Complete a quality control check of the TOC to ensure that major headings and page numbers used in the narrative are included in the TOC. Major headings should generally match the RFP/RFA evaluation criteria.

Résumés, letters of support and commitment, and other supplemental material should be organized in a logical manner in the proposal appendix. A TOC with descriptive headings and page numbers should precede appendix materials.

Exhibit 7-1

Produce, Assemble, and Submit the Grant Application

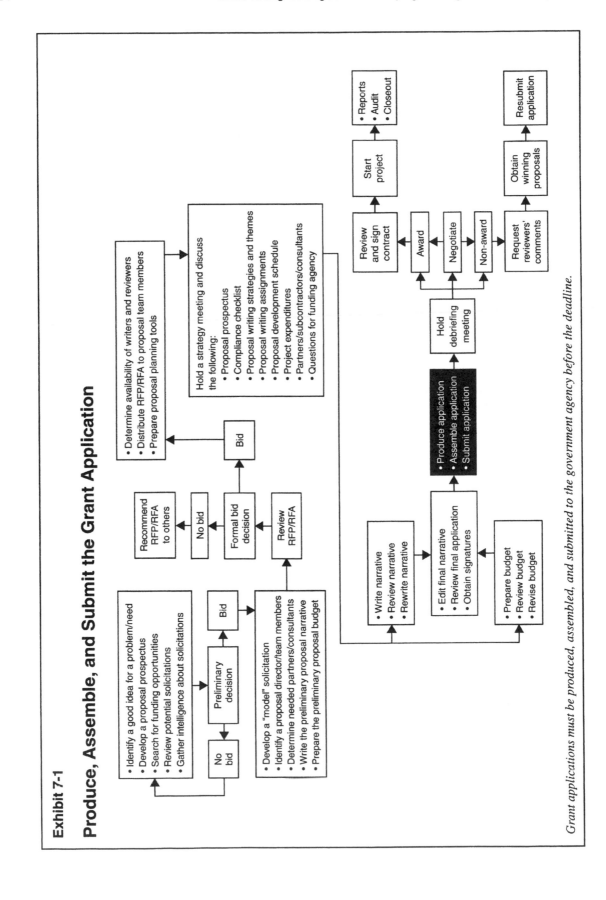

Grant applications must be produced, assembled, and submitted to the government agency before the deadline.

Exhibit 7-2

Sample Grant Application Format Guidelines

Funding seekers who win consistently pay special attention to content and format criteria before submitting the grant application to the funding agency.

Page Limit	Some government agencies limit the proposal narrative to a specific number of pages. The page limit may or may not apply to the cover sheet; budget, including the budget justification; assurances and certifications; abstract; or appendix materials. When submitting grant applications electronically, it is strongly recommended that funding seekers submit the narrative as a PDF to avoid formatting changes, which may alter the number of pages submitted to the agency. Charts, tables, figures, and illustrations in the application narrative will count toward the page limit.
Page Size/ Margins	Most government agencies define a "page" as 8.5" x 11" on one side only with 1" margins at the top, bottom, and both sides.
Text Spacing	Many government agencies request double-spaced text (no more than three lines per vertical inch) in the application narrative, including titles, headings, footnotes, quotations, references, and captions. Always follow the RFP/RFA formatting guidelines. Funding seekers may use single-spaced text in all charts, tables, figures, and illustrations.
Typeface and Font Size	Some government agencies specify the exact typeface (e.g., Times New Roman, Courier, Courier New, or Arial) and font size for grant applications. Most agencies request that funding seekers set their typeface at a size of 12 point. However, funding seekers may use a 10-point font in charts, tables, figures, and illustrations. Applications submitted in a typeface not explicitly recommended may be returned without review.

Note: Grant applications that do not follow prescribed RFP/RFA formatting standards may be returned to the funding seeker without being reviewed.

Funding seekers must adhere to all content and format standards presented in the RFP/RFA. Always consult with the POC about content and format questions.

A *quality control check* of the grant application from cover to cover should be completed after production/assembly and reproduction. If the grant application has numerous sections with a large appendix, the proposal director should develop a checklist to track proposal components. Some agencies provide a proposal checklist for funding seekers to use. **See Exhibits 7-3 and 7-4**.

Exhibit 7-3

Sample Funding Seeker Grant Application Checklist

Proposal Name: *Innovative Programs to Increase Information Technology*

CFDA/RFP/RFA#:   47202

Contact/Phone: David Johnson / 219-838-xxxx

Due Date/Time: March 15, 20xx / 4:00 p.m. CST

Proposal Component	Receive	Produce/ Assemble	Quality Control	Reproduce	Quality Control	Final Check/ Submit
Cover Sheet	✓	✓	✓			
Abstract	✓	✓	✓			
TOC	✓	✓	✓			
Introduction	✓	✓	✓			
Problem/Need	✓	✓	✓			
Goals/Objectives	✓	✓	✓			
Methods/Activities	✓	✓	✓			
Evaluation Plan	✓	✓	✓			
Budget	✓	✓	✓			
Appendix	✓	✓	✓			
Résumés	✓	✓	✓			
Support Letters	✓	✓	✓			
Mission Statement	✓	✓	✓			

A grant application checklist is used to track all proposal components after proposal production/assembly and reproduction.

Exhibit 7-4

Sample Government Agency Grant Application Checklist

Items Required in the Grant Application (Use this checklist to ensure that all required items are included in the grant application)	√
Application Cover Sheet	
Project Abstract (500 words or less)	
Project narrative • Relevant Organizational Experience • Problem/Need • Goals/Objectives • Methods/Activities • Evaluation Plans	
Budget • Direct Costs • Indirect (Facilities and Administrative) Costs • Matching Funds • Budget Detail and Narrative	
Agency Forms • Survey on ensuring equal opportunity for applicants • America's affordable communities initiative • Applicant/recipient disclosure/update report • Certification of consistency with strategic plan • Community outreach partnership • Verification of matching requirements • Client comments and suggestions	

Some Government agencies provide a checklist for funding seekers to follow when preparing a grant application to ensure submission of all required elements.

Submit the Grant Application

Government agencies may require a letter of intent prior to submitting a grant application. A *letter of intent* gives agency staff members an idea of the size and range of competition. The letter usually includes the names of key personnel and their institutions and a brief synopsis of the proposed project. Letters of intent are not externally evaluated and are not used in making the funding decision.

Some government agencies require that funding seekers submit preliminary proposals before the submission of a complete grant application. *Preliminary proposals* are used to screen project ideas, provide feedback to funding seekers, and invite or not invite funding seekers to submit a full proposal (typical grant application based on the RFP/RFA criteria).

Funding seekers may be required to submit grant applications electronically using Grants.gov or another electronic service (e.g., NSF's FastLane) or deliver the grant application via the U.S. Postal Service, by a commercial courier, or hand. Some agencies require both electronic and paper submissions.

Submit the Grant Application Through Electronic Means

Most federal agencies require that funding seekers submit grant applications electronically through the Grants.gov/"Apply" portal. Prior to submitting a grant application, funding seekers must register with Dun and Bradstreet Data Universal Numbering System (DUNS), the Central Contractor Registration (CCR), and Grants.gov. First time Grants.gov users should allow at least 30 days prior to the application deadline date to complete these requirements. To apply for a grant with Grants.gov, funding seekers must follow four steps:

Step 1—Download the appropriate grant application package and instructions.

Step 2—Complete the necessary grant application documents and forms offline, which gives you the flexibility to finish the application when and where you want.

Step 3—Upload all documents and forms and submit the application online. (Note: The time to upload a grant application will vary depending on the size of the file and Internet connection speed.) When applicable, funding seekers should submit proposal narrative as a PDF to avoid formatting problems. Grants.gov allows the funding seeker to attach files to the application, unless the agency has specific restrictions. When all application information is saved, Grants.gov will provide a "submit button." Only Authorized Organization Representatives (AORs) are able to submit applications to Grants.gov. Grants.gov will authenticate that you are the AOR before you can submit your application. Grants.gov automatically saves new information on the application when you close your document. The latest application will override earlier submissions.

After the application has been received, Grants.gov will send you e-mails about the progress of your submission. The first e-mail will confirm receipt of the application. A second e-mail will indicate that the application has been either successfully validated by the system prior to transmission to a specific government agency or has been rejected due to errors. An error message will appear if invalid or incomplete information is entered on the application form. If the application is rejected, you must address the errors and resubmit the application. The application is checked after submission by clicking "Check Application Status."

Step 4—Track the status of the completed grant application. After submission, the federal agency assigns a tracking number to your application, which is used to check the application status. In addition to electronic submission, the government agency may require funding seekers to submit a pre-specified number of paper copies of the grant application. **See Exhibit 7-5**.

Exhibit 7-5

Grant Application Submission Process Using Grants.Gov

Grant Application is Downloaded and Completed
Funding seekers download and complete the grant application offline
according to the government agency's instructions

Grant Application is Submitted to Grants.Gov
Grant application narrative, budget, and all necessary forms are
uploaded and submitted as PDF files to Grants.gov

Grant Application is Received by Grants.Gov
Grant application is date-and-time stamped. Grants.gov receives and
validates or rejects the grant application

Application is Validated
Grants.gov validates application—
available for agency to download

Application is Rejected
Grants.gov is unable to process
application because of errors

Grant Application is Received by Government Agency
Government agency confirms receipt of grant application via e-mail

Tracking Number is Assigned
Government agency assigns tracking number to grant application
(Note: Some agencies do not assign numbers)

Government Agency Reviews Grant Application
Agency reviewers read grant application and provide written comments
and recommendations to the government agency

*Many funding seekers submit proposal materials at the last minute and thus slow down the system.
Always plan ahead and submit grant applications early to avoid late submissions.*

Submit the Grant Application by Mail, Commercial Courier, or Hand Delivery
After proposal production and assembly, grant applications must be reproduced to provide sufficient copies for the government agency and proposal team members. Proposal directors must determine the (1) total number of proposal copies required by the government agency, (2) type of duplication (e.g., single-sided), (3) tabs needed, if any, and (4) binding type, if required by the agency. Tabs, if used, should be ordered prior to proposal reproduction and assembly. Proposal binding should consider the RFP/RFA specifications and cost and allow proposals to be easily reassembled and to lie flat when being read. After reproduction, another quality control check of each proposal copy should be made prior to submission to the government agency. Often, a "fresh pair of eyes" can spot overlooked mistakes. Don't allow reproduction errors to hurt your chances of delivering a winning proposal that you worked so hard to prepare. Always follow the specific RFP/RFA guidelines and provide exactly what the government agency requests. After sufficient copies of the grant application are reproduced, the proposal director must decide the most effective means to package and submit hardcopies of the grant application to the government agency via the U.S. Postal Service, commercial courier, or by hand delivery. **See Exhibit 7-6**.

Exhibit 7-6

Reproducing, Binding, Packaging, and Submitting Proposals

Reproducing (Number of grant applications needed.)

Government agency	_I_ original	_10_ copies	
Internal use	_—_ original	_6_ copies	
Total	_I_ original	_16_ copies	

Binding (Do not bind unless specifically required by the government agency.)

_____ Notebook	_X_ Staple	
_____ Plastic comb/wire	_____ Other: _____	

Transmittal Letter, Label(s), and Packaging

_X_ Transmittal letter   _J. Lebowski_

_X_ Label(s)   _R. King_

_X_ Packaging   _R. King_

Submitting (Always track the package delivery to the final destination.)

☐ U.S. Postal Service

☒ Commercial Courier

☐ Hand Delivery

Checklists are used to guide proposal directors in reproducing, binding, packaging, and submitting grant applications.

Proposals to be delivered by U.S. mail, commercial courier, or by hand must be carefully packaged to prevent damage. Follow exact packaging and submission specifications provided in the RFP/RFA guidelines and include any special markings (e.g., solicitation number) on the packaging. Finally, funding seekers should carefully recheck the delivery address for accuracy. **See Exhibit 7-7**.

Exhibit 7-7

Final Checklist Before Submitting the Grant Application

✓ **Due Date and Time**. Check and recheck the RFP/RFA guidelines concerning the date and time when the grant application is due and allow adequate time for delivering the application to the government agency. Note: Funding seekers submitting grant applications by mail should obtain appropriate proof of mailing.

✓ **Number of Copies**. Check the RFP/RFA guidelines to determine the number of proposal copies required by the government agency. The required number of copies will vary from agency to agency. Provide exactly what is requested in the RFP/RFA.

✓ **Government Agency Address**. Check and recheck the address where the grant application is to be submitted. Be sure to check spelling and zip code.

✓ **Authorized Signatures**. Check all grant application pages that require signatures. Most grant applications require an administrator's signature on assurance and certification forms. Some applications also require a signature on budget forms. Sign all forms in blue ink rather than photocopying signatures.

✓ **Packaging and Markings**. The length of the grant application and the number of copies required by the government agency will dictate if the submission will require an envelope, box, or multiple boxes. Use sturdy packaging that will protect your grant submission. Properly mark each envelope or box with the RFP/RFA number, project name, and quantity of proposals inside the package. If multiple boxes are submitted, indicate the number of boxes sent (e.g., 1 of 3 boxes, 2 of 3 boxes, and 3 of 3 boxes). Include a transmittal letter inside the packaging.

Funding seekers should complete a careful check of grant application requirements before submission.

Transmittal (Cover) Letter

A *transmittal (cover) letter* is not required by federal agencies that call for electronic submissions. However, transmittal letters with an authorized signature (e.g., CEO) are very appropriate for state agencies, non-government foundations, and when submitting government grant applications by U.S. mail, commercial courier, or delivering the application by hand. Prepare letters on organizational letterhead and address them to the POC identified in the RFP/RFA. Transmittal letters should include the RFP/RFA or *CFDA* number and identify the number of proposals included in the package as well as the contents of each proposal. In addition, letters should identify a knowledgeable contact person who can be reached for questions about the grant application. **See Exhibits 7-8 and 7-9**.

Exhibit 7-8

Sample Transmittal (Cover) Letter 1

March 15, 20XX

Anderson Health Trust
Carol Dean, Grant Coordinator
42nd Street and Elm
New York, NY 10014

Re: Grant Application in Response to RFP #0005321 ⟵ **RFP Number**

Dear Ms. Dean:

High Tower University (HTU) is pleased to submit three copies of our application to the ⟵ **Copies Required**
Anderson Health Trust to support the Nursing Education Wellness Service (NEWS) project.
This project will enhance the knowledge and clinical expertise of faculty members in the area
of community-based health and will also provide our students with clinical experiences that
will improve their ability to function in community healthcare settings.

The NEWS project planning has energized our nursing faculty members to look at new ways
to present the theoretical and clinical competencies necessary to prepare students for
community-based care. By developing a clinical setting on campus, students will be afforded
hands-on nursing experiences that have not been previously available. Additionally, nursing
students will have the opportunity to serve HTU faculty members, students, and staff in a
very meaningful way. ⟵ **Cost Sharing**

HTU is totally committed to assist in making NEWS a reality by contributing cost-sharing
funds in the amount of $63,800 for administrative personnel salaries, travel and per diem,
equipment and expendable supplies, and contractual services. Facility plans have been
altered to accommodate the required space necessary for the NEWS project.

HTU has administered more than 100 grants in a wide variety of educational and service
areas. If awarded, HTU will commit high-level administrators to the successful completion of
the NEWS project. If you have project oversight questions, please contact Patrick W. Smith,
Vice President of Academic Affairs, at (555) 312-3333 or e-mail: psmith@htu.edu. If you have
specific questions or concerns regarding implementation of the NEWS project, please contact
Ms. Gwen Olson, Chairperson of Nursing, at (555) 312-3344 or e-mail: golson@htu.edu.

Sincerely, ⟵ **Contact Person**

Abdul J. Kaakaji

Dr. Abdul J. Kaakaji, President ⟵ **Authorized Signature**

c: Dr. Patrick W. Smith
    Ms. Gwen Olson

*Transmittal (cover) letters should accompany grant applications submitted to state agencies, non-
government foundations, and when submitting government grant applications by U.S. mail,
commercial courier, or hand. Always place transmittal letters on official letterhead and identify a
knowledgeable contact person who can answer questions about the application.*

Exhibit 7-9

Sample Transmittal (Cover) Letter 2

March 11, 20XX

Buffalo Bill Historical Center
8845 Wilson Avenue
Capital City, UT 12345 ⟍— **RFP Number and Title**

RE: RFP #12237 New Initiatives in Farming and Ranching ⟍— **Number of Proposals**

The Old Ranchers Association is pleased to submit one original and four copies of our grant application in response to the above-referenced solicitation. Our proposal includes the following sections as specified in the solicitation for grant application:

- Abstract
- Project Narrative
- Budget } ⟍— **Proposal Contents**
- Certifications and Assurances
- Appendix

If you have questions or concerns, please do not hesitate to contact me.

Sincerely, ⟍— **Contact Person**

Charles Wagon

Dr. Charles Wagon
President
(555) 435-8400

Transmittal (cover) letters should be addressed to the specific agency, include the RFP/RFA number, identify the number of proposals included in the package, and list proposal contents.

Always deliver grant applications in a timely fashion. Many institutions spend a considerable amount of time and money developing grant applications, but do not allow sufficient time for submitting the grant application before the due date and time. For grant applications that are critical to your institution, hand delivery might be a viable consideration. When delivering in person, be sure to obtain a receipt from the government agency representative to verify the application was received before the deadline.

Some agencies allow proposals to be submitted by the U.S. Postal Service. Make sure all such deliveries are postmarked by the date specified in the RFP/RFA. It is also suggested that funding seekers obtain a certificate of mailing.

If the grant application cannot be submitted electronically and U.S. mail or hand delivery methods are not warranted, commercial couriers can provide a reasonably safe and cost effective way to deliver a grant application.

There are several reliable express commercial couriers that will deliver a grant application overnight to most U.S. cities for a relatively inexpensive rate. Most express commercial couriers provide delivery rates and shipping charges by delivery zone. Check the commercial courier's website to learn about delivery costs to the final destination. Example commercial couriers include:

- DHL (www.dhl.com),

- FedEx (www.fedex.com), and

- United Parcel Service (www.ups.com).

Before using a commercial courier, funding seekers should know the package dimensions (height, width, and length) and weight as well as the specific address where the package will be sent (including zip code). Commercial couriers cannot deliver to a P.O. box. Obtain a tracking number from the commercial courier representative for each package that is shipped. Use the Internet to track the package delivery to the final destination. Always obtain a delivery confirmation.

If you are running late or if unexpected circumstances (e.g., inclement weather) could delay the delivery of the grant application package, consider sending two complete application packages using two different couriers. Even though these commercial couriers guarantee "on time delivery or your money back," the financial courier's reimbursement will hardly compensate your institution for grant funds lost due to late delivery.

Always follow the government agency's guidelines for submitting the grant application to ensure compliance. Funding seekers should not arbitrarily submit the grant application via e-mail or fax.

Track Proposal Submissions

Organizations applying for multiple grants should use a spreadsheet or database to track submissions and create end-of-the-year reports. This spreadsheet or database should identify the:

- grant title,

- *CFDA* or RFP/RFA number,

- institutional (internal) proposal tracking number,

- PI/PD,

- government agency and POC,

- performance period,

- amount of funding requested,

- whether proposals were awarded, denied, or pending, and

- financial amounts awarded, if the grant was funded. **See Exhibit 7-10.**

Exhibit 7-10

Sample Proposal Tracking Spreadsheet

Title of Grant CFDA/RFP/RFA#	Internal Proposal Number	Department Contact/Phone	Agency/POC Performance Period	Amount Requested	Awarded Denied Pending	Amount Awarded
Early School Program RFP 203136	201	Social Science Brooks/5920	STATE / J. Marshal April 1, XX–June 30, XX	$16,201	Awarded	$16,201
Career Opportunities in Biology NSF 02-36	202	Science Ash/6489	NSF / M. James July 1, XX–June 30, XX	$208,500	Pending	0
Hispanic Serving Institutions RFP 14621	203	Social Science Richards/7090	HUD / K. Watkins July 1, XX–June 30, XX	$154,320	Denied	0
Excellence in Electronics NSF 03-27	204	Technology Howard/4452	NSF / M. Ellis July 1, XX–June 30, XX	$4,330,232	Pending	0
Work Study Program RFP 555102	205	Technology Wheeler/4487	HUD / D. Studdert July 1, XX–June 30, XX	$263,920	Awarded	$263,920
School-to-Work CFDA 84-2788	206	Technology Michaels/2732	EDUC / K. Addel July 1, XX–June 30, XX	$487,215	Awarded	$487,215
YouthNet Project RFP 454521	207	Social Science Collins/8816	DHS / L. Green July 1, XX–June 30, XX	$160,000	Awarded	$160,000
Community Development RFP 133421	208	Social Science Collins/8816	EDUC / T. Foreman July 1, XX–June 30, XX	$48,711	Awarded	$48,711

Funding seekers can use a spreadsheet or database to track multiple grant submissions.

Chapter Summary

After the proposal narrative and budget have been developed, proposal directors must make sure the complete grant application is produced, assembled, and submitted to the government agency before the deadline.

Proposal directors should check and recheck the grant application against RFP/RFA requirements for compliance. Funding seekers must provide exactly what is requested in the RFP/RFA to be considered for funding. A quality control check of the grant application from cover-to-cover should be done after proposal production/assembly and reproduction.

Grant applications are submitted electronically using Grants.gov, or submitted via the U.S. Postal Service, commercial courier, or hand delivery. Some agencies require both electronic and paper submissions. Check the proposal critically against the criteria in the RFP/RFA guidelines before submitting the grant application to the government agency.

Grant applications submitted electronically through the Grants.gov portal require that funding seekers complete the following four steps:

1. Download the appropriate grant application package and instructions.

2. Complete the necessary grant application documents and forms offline.

3. Upload all documents and forms and submit the grant application online.

4. Track the status of the completed grant application.

Grant applications submitted via the U.S. Postal Service, commercial courier, or hand delivery must be reproduced to provide sufficient copies for the government agency and proposal team members. Proposals to be delivered by non-electronic means must be carefully packaged to prevent damage. Follow exact packaging and submission specifications provided in the RFP/RFA guidelines. Funding seekers should always double check the delivery address for accuracy.

Grant applications should include a transmittal (cover) letter when submitted by U.S. mail, courier, or when delivering by hand. Transmittal letters are prepared on organizational letterhead and addressed to a specific agency POC. Transmittal letters should include the RFP/RFA number and identify the number of proposals included in the package as well as the contents of the proposal. In addition, letters should identify a knowledgeable contact person who can be reached for questions about the application.

Always deliver the grant application in a timely manner. Make sure that U.S. Postal Service packages are postmarked by the date specified in the RFP/RFA. It is also suggested that funding seekers obtain a certificate of mailing.

For grant applications that are critical to your institution, hand delivery might be a viable consideration. When delivering in person, be sure to obtain a receipt from the government agency representative to verify that the grant application was received before the deadline.

Commercial couriers can provide a reasonably safe and cost-effective way to deliver the grant application package overnight. Obtain a tracking number from the commercial courier representative and use the Internet to track the package delivery to the final destination.

Organizations applying for multiple grants should use a spreadsheet or database to track submissions and create end-of-the-year reports. This spreadsheet or database should include the following information:

- grant title,

- *CFDA* or RFP/RFA number,

- institutional (internal) proposal tracking number,

- PI/PD,

- government agency and POC,

- performance period,

- amount of funding requested,

- whether proposals were awarded, denied, or pending, and

- financial amounts awarded, if the grant was funded.

Review Questions

(Answers to Review Questions are on p. 274.)

T F   1. Grant applications submitted after the due date and time specified in the RFP/RFA are considered for funding.

T F   2. Grant proposal narrative must follow RFP/RFA content and format guidelines.

T F   3. A quality control check of the grant application from cover to cover is completed after production/assembly and reproduction.

T F   4. A checklist is used to track and assemble complex grant applications that have numerous sections and a large appendix.

T F   5. Most government agencies require that funding seekers submit grant applications electronically through the Grants.gov/"Apply" portal.

T F   6. Prior to submitting a grant application using Grants.gov, funding seekers must register with the Dun and Bradstreet Data Universal Numbering System.

T F   7. When using Grants.gov, funding seekers must download the appropriate grant application package and complete it offline.

T F   8. Funding seekers are advised to submit grant application narrative to Grants.gov as an HTML file.

T F   9. Only Authorized Organization Representatives are allowed to submit grant applications using Grants.gov.

T F   10. Funding seekers should submit two extra copies when submitting grant applications by U.S. mail or commercial courier.

T F   11. Transmittal (cover) letters are appropriate when submitting proposals to state agencies, non-government foundations, and when submitting applications by U.S. mail, commercial courier, or hand delivery.

T F   12. The PI/PD signs cover letters.

T F   13. Transmittal (cover) letters should include the RFP/RFA or *CFDA* number, and identify the number of proposal copies as well as the contents of each proposal.

T F   14. Funding seekers should always obtain a receipt when hand delivering a grant application.

T F   15. Considering today's technology, it is highly advisable to submit grant applications by fax or e-mail to ensure delivery on time.

Exercise 7-1

Write a Cover Letter and Determine Proposal Delivery Method

(Answers to Exercise 7-1 are on pp. 300–301.)

Directions: Write a grant application cover letter based on the situation below.

Situation: You are a senior faculty member at Sears Tower College, 233 South Wacker Drive, Chicago, Illinois 60606. You and a team of staff members in your department have been working on grant application *CFDA #255G* for the last month, and it must be delivered tomorrow to the U.S. Department of Education in Washington, D.C. The proposal is requesting $250,000 to enhance your current instructional programs, which may be eliminated due to insufficient college funds.

It is February and the temperature is below freezing. It is currently 5:10 p.m. CST and weather forecasters are predicting a snowstorm starting at 12:00 midnight with the accumulation of several inches. Grant applications are due tomorrow at 2:00 p.m. EST in Washington, D.C. You must submit the grant application via commercial courier or hand delivery.

The government agency requires 1 original and 11 copies of the proposal. After reproduction, the approximate weight of 12 proposals (225 pages each) is 27 pounds. The packing material and shipping box (approximate dimensions: 12" x 12" x 12") weigh an additional 3 pounds.

Proposals must be delivered to the following address:

U.S. Department of Education
CFDA #255G
Application Control Center
1990 K Street NW
Washington, DC 20202-4725
Attn: Ms. Pam Sarver, POC

You must deliver the grant application package before the due date and time specified above. The U.S. Department of Education is open from 9:00 a.m. to 4:30 p.m. EST Monday through Friday except for federal holidays. The agency will <u>not</u> accept electronic or fax submissions for this grant competition.

Exercise 7-1 continues on the next page.

Exercise 7-1 (Continued)

Write a Cover Letter and Determine Proposal Delivery Method

(Answers to Exercise 7-1 are on pp. 300–301.)

Directions: Based on the situation presented on p. 179, determine the delivery method you will use to ensure the grant application package is delivered in a timely manner. Indicate the approximate costs associated with the delivery method and identify the pros/cons associated with this delivery method considering the weather, deadline date, and time to deliver the package to Washington, D.C.

Delivery Method (Attach all delivery method documentation.)

Approximate Costs

Pros/Cons

Chapter 8

Perform Postsubmission Activities

After the grant application has been submitted to the government agency, proposal writers and reviewers should meet to debrief and discuss the proposal submission. Grant applications received by a government agency undergo a thorough review that may take several months before a funding outcome is determined. After the review process, government agencies make award decisions based on recommendations from agency reviewers. Government agencies may decide to (1) not fund the proposed project, (2) request clarifications about the proposal narrative and/or budget, or (3) fund all or part of the proposed project. **See Exhibit 8-1**.

Hold a Debriefing Meeting

Once the grant application has been submitted, there is a natural tendency to relax and go back to normal activities, but this is a mistake. Immediately after the grant application has been submitted, the proposal director should hold a debriefing meeting and organize and file all documents in anticipation of questions from the government agency. A debriefing meeting is held in an effort to identify proposal strengths and weaknesses. Prior to the debriefing meeting, proposal team members should review the entire grant application and identify potential problems and deficiencies while they are fresh in their minds, thus the rationale for having the debriefing meeting immediately after proposal submission. Proposal team members should focus on answers to the following questions when reviewing the grant application:

- Is the proposal compliant?
- Are project claims substantiated?
- Are project benefits emphasized?
- Are costs appropriate?

Strategies for improving the proposal narrative and budget should be noted at the debriefing meeting and used later to clarify any concerns voiced by the government agency. The primary outcome of a debriefing meeting is to ensure that key proposal team members are prepared to answer government agency questions about the grant application. The original RFP/RFA and grant application should be stored for safekeeping. Grant application narrative and budget computer files should be backed up and kept in a separate location.

Exhibit 8-1

Perform Postsubmission Activities

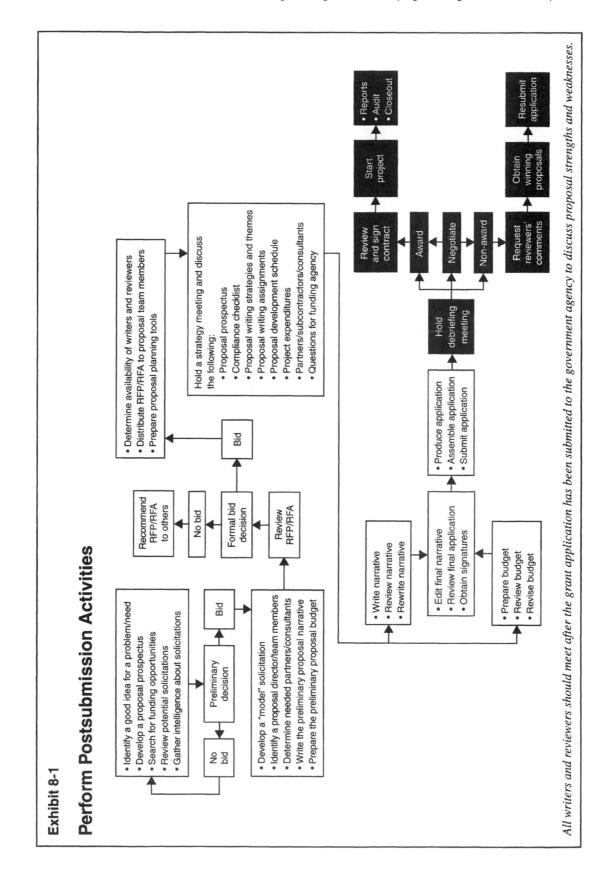

All writers and reviewers should meet after the grant application has been submitted to the government agency to discuss proposal strengths and weaknesses.

Government Agency Proposal Review Process

Government agencies are not obligated to review grant applications that (1) do not meet eligibility requirements, (2) fail to address review criteria, (3) are not responsive to proposal preparation guidelines, (4) exceed funding limits, or (5) are not submitted prior to the deadline. Applications that fail to meet requirements may be returned without review. Proposals that were previously declined and not substantially revised may also be returned without review. Proposals that meet the agency's requirements are evaluated and scored by agency reviewers with a cross-section of education, experience, and geographic representation. Agency reviewers are chosen from universities, colleges, secondary schools, business and industry, and professional associations, or may be selected from recommendations made by PIs/PDs or from other reviewers. Most government agencies welcome letters and résumés from potential readers interested in reviewing grant applications. Agency reviewers receive training from government agencies about specific responsibilities prior to evaluating proposals. **See Exhibit 8-2.**

Exhibit 8-2

Sample Government Agency Reviewers' Responsibilities

- Read the entire RFP/RFA.
- Evaluate each application based on rating criteria published in the RFP/RFA.
- Assign a numerical rating to each application section (based on criteria).
- Write detailed comments relating to the application's strengths and weaknesses.
  - Comments must be evaluative, not descriptive.
  - Comments must be directly tied to the rating criteria.
  - Comments must be thorough and objective since they are used in funding decisions and debriefing of unsuccessful grant applicants.
- Meet with other agency reviewers to discuss each application. The purpose of this meeting is to allow reviewers the opportunity to discuss application scores and provide justification of those scores. This is the only opportunity to revise scores if reviewers see differences based on ambiguous language within a proposal.
- Keep all review proceedings confidential. Reviewers are not permitted to discuss applicants, contents or scoring of applications, identity of other reviewers, or any other part of the review process with anyone—either during or after the review.

Agency reviewers must agree to specific responsibilities prior to evaluating grant applications.

Agency reviewers must sign an assurance form to ensure that they do not have a conflict of interest with respect to grant applications in the competition. A conflict of interest might include the reviewer's affiliation with the applicant's institution or personal or professional relationship with a PI/PD. Reviewers must safeguard the confidentiality of proposals and proposal reviews. The names of agency reviewers are generally not disclosed; however, anonymous copies of individual reviews are usually made available to grant applicants. **See Exhibit 8-3.**

Exhibit 8-3

Sample Government Agency Reviewers' Agreement

Freedom of Information Act

I understand that under the Freedom of Information Act, the government may release my reviews verbatim to the public. The government may also release individual reviewers' names in conformance with the government's disclosure policy, but generally will not identify an individual reviewer with a particular review. However, to avoid complicating the release of reviews, I agree not to make comments that could be seen as offensive or constitute an invasion of privacy.

Confidentiality of Documents and Restriction on Contact

I understand that applications are made available to agency reviewers solely for the purpose of reviewing against the selection criteria. I agree *not* to discuss the information contained in applications after the review process, and to discuss only with the agency reviewers and in the context of and under the procedures for application review. I agree to follow all written instructions provided by the government for the completion of review forms. I agree not to contact the originator of the application being reviewed concerning any aspects of its contents.

Conflict of Interest

I hereby certify that to the best of my knowledge I do not have a conflict of interest and that my particular circumstances are not likely to raise the appearance of a conflict of interest (or have received a waiver) with respect to any grant application in this competition. For purposes of this agreement I recognize that I will have a conflict of interest, if any of the following has a financial interest in an application:

- I, my spouse, minor child, or partner,
- a for-profit or nonprofit organization in which I serve as an officer, director, trustee, partner, or employee, or
- any person or organization with whom I am negotiating or have an arrangement concerning prospective employment.

I acknowledge that this agreement is in effect at all times until I have completed all work to be performed. If I discover that I might have a conflict of interest or the appearance of a conflict of interest with any grant application in the competition, I will inform the appropriate program official immediately.

Agreement on Scope of Work

Before reviewing and scoring grant applications, I will read all instructions, regulations, criteria, and review forms.

- I will read and score all grant applications.
- I will score each application solely on its content and the degree to which the application meets the appropriate priorities and criteria.
- I will sign and date a review form for each application and return it to the appropriate program official.

Agency reviewers must sign a government agency reviewer's agreement before reading grant applications.

Evaluation of grant applications will vary from agency to agency. Government agencies want to ensure that finances support project ideas that have a good possibility of successfully improving a problematic situation. Most government agencies include solicitation guidelines and expect funding seekers to follow them diligently. Funding seekers who consistently win, pay special attention to content and format criteria before submitting proposals. Content criteria identify the composition of components and subcomponents expected in grant applications. Normally, content criteria include the same "weighted" point system that government agency reviewers use to evaluate proposals. Format criteria identify the layout of content that is expected in grant submissions. Some solicitations specify the number of words or pages allowed for each narrative section (500 words or less for the abstract, problem/need must not exceed five pages, etc.). In other instances, government solicitations provide a specific outline of content and format guidelines for grant applications. Funding seekers must follow these guidelines if they expect to score high and be recommended for funding.

Grant applications are evaluated on the basis of how well applicants responded to criteria in the RFP/RFA and the quality and feasibility of proposed project ideas. Basic review questions include:

- Is the proposed project consistent with the agency's funding priorities?

- Were proposal guidelines followed?

- Is there a compelling problem/need statement for this project, and is it well documented?

- Is the project's purpose (goals and objectives) clearly identified?

- Do the methods/activities describe specific tasks to meet the project's goals/objectives? Do project personnel have the knowledge, skills, and commitment to carry out the project tasks within the period of performance?

- Will the proposed evaluation plans determine project effectiveness?

- Is the budget within the agency's funding range, well justified, and accurate?

- Is the grant proposal well written, logical, reasonable, and free from errors?

Government agency review panels consisting of at least three agency reviewers are selected to read grant applications. Agency reviewers use their professional judgment to rate each grant application using an assessment form based on criteria published in the RFP/RFA. Agency reviewers read each proposal independently and provide ratings and written recommendations about the submission. Agency reviewers' comments must address the strengths and weaknesses of the applicant's proposed project and must not include biases that jeopardize the integrity of the review process. **See Exhibit 8-4**.

Exhibit 8-4

Sample Grant Application Evaluation Form

Applicant: *Hoosier State College*

Reviewer Team #: *3*   **Points Awarded**

Criteria (Possible Points)

Problem/Need (30)

• Persuasive statement that describes the problem/need	12	12
• Recent and relevant citations document the problem/need	5	5
• Manageable problem of reasonable size	5	5
• Clear project idea for solving the problem	8	8

Goals/Objectives (10)

• Realistic and measurable (quantifiable) outcomes	5	5
• Manageable, ambitious, but attainable outcomes	5	5

Methods/Activities (45)

• Clear plan of work to be accomplished	10	10
• Experienced personnel with documented qualifications	10	10
• Clear project management plan with specific personnel duties	5	5
• Clear project organization and reporting lines of authority	10	9
• Realistic project timetable	10	9

Evaluation Plans (10)

• Clear data collection strategies	5	5
• Clear data analysis procedures	5	5

Budget (5)

• Necessary and reasonable project costs	5	5
Total	**100**	**98**

Government agency reviewers evaluate grant applications using a review form with the same weighted criteria that were published in the RFP/RFA.

Government agency reviewers may also use a rubric with specific criteria and a predetermined number of points to judge each section of the grant application. These criteria and point values are the same as what was published in the RFP/RFA. **See Exhibit 8-5.**

Exhibit 8-5

Sample Rubric Used to Evaluate Grant Applications

Quality of Key Personnel

To what extent are the past experiences and training of key professional personnel directly related to the stated activity objectives?

Excellent (7 points)	In all cases, the past experience and training of all proposed key professional personnel involved in the proposed project directly relate to the objectives stated. There is an extremely high likelihood that key personnel will be able to achieve the objectives.
Good (5–6 points)	In most cases, the past experience and training of all proposed key professional personnel involved in the proposed project directly relate to the objectives stated. There is a high likelihood that key personnel will be able to achieve the objectives.
Average (3–4 points)	In some cases, the past experience and training of all proposed key professional personnel involved in the proposed project directly relate to the objectives stated. There is some likelihood that key personnel will be able to achieve the objectives.
Minimal (1–2 points)	In a few cases, the past experience and training of all proposed key professional personnel involved in the proposed project directly relate to the objectives stated. There is a slight likelihood that key personnel will be able to achieve the objectives.
Not Addressed (0 points)	Applicant did not address these issues.

Government agencies may require reviewers to use a rubric to evaluate grant applications sections.

Reviewing grants is a human process and every member of an agency review panel can interpret a proposal differently. Consequently, in order to win, funding seekers must provide agency reviewers with a clear message that is innovative, easy to understand, and better than other grant applications. Funding seekers must provide themes that show a passion for the topic. Winning proposals make it easy for reviewers to identify and support persuasive ideas. Funding seekers must present information in such a manner that it will provide agency reviewers with a clear but comprehensive understanding of what they are proposing to do. Specifically, grant proposals should contain key themes that sell the strengths of the project and cause at least one member of the agency review panel to support the proposal as a winning application. To win, your proposal must excite agency reviewers about your ideas and make them think your application is better than other grant applications.

After evaluating proposals on an independent basis, agency reviewers meet via conference calls, Internet chat rooms, or in person and discuss the merit and rating of grant applications. The purpose of the panel discussion is to (1) share professional judgments and ratings, (2) assist agency reviewers in reevaluation of his/her ratings, if necessary, (3) clarify information in grant applications that may have been overlooked, and (4) eliminate, where possible, wide differences between the highest overall rating and the lowest rating where those differences result from lack of information, misinformation, or misunderstanding. While agency reviewers use this meeting time to discuss proposal deficiencies and variations in ratings, a consensus is not required by all government agencies. Reviewers may revise their ratings and comments if the panel discussion provides new insight and a different conclusion. If necessary, an arbitrator will intervene to resolve disagreements about grant application sections.

Agency reviewers must provide a fair, courteous, straightforward, and specific analysis that justifies their score for a particular proposal evaluation criterion. In addition, agency reviewers must be sure that points awarded correspond with narrative comments. Since the Freedom of Information Act (FOIA) allows all applicants the opportunity to request copies of reviewers' scores and comments about grant applications, agency reviewers must write substantive and analytical comments that directly relate to criteria published in the RFP/RFA. A video on peer review at the National Institutes of Health provides insight about how NIH applications are reviewed (see http://www.csr.nih.gov/video/video.asp).

Following panel discussions, written summary reports and ratings are submitted to the government agency for each grant application. The agency uses these reviews as a basis for funding the best-of-the-best applications. **See Exhibit 8-6**.

Exhibit 8-6

Sample Summary Report of Agency Reviewers' Scores

Applicant Name: <u>Chicago Community College, Chicago, Illinois 60606</u>

Reviewer Team #: <u> 17 </u>

⌐ **Score (100 Possible Points)**

1st Reviewer's Score: <u>98</u>   Name: <u>Tasha Spade</u>   Date: <u>1/15/20XX</u>

2nd Reviewer's Score: <u>100</u>   Name: <u>Burt Reagan</u>   Date: <u>1/15/20XX</u>

3rd Reviewer's Score: <u>96</u>   Name: <u>Robert Barker</u>   Date: <u>1/15/20XX</u>

Average Score: <u>98</u>   ⌐ **Signatures**

Three government agency reviewers complete independent reviews of each grant application. All agency reviewers meet and discuss the strengths and weaknesses of the application, and final scores are recorded. The highest-scoring applications are recommended to the agency for funding.

Losing Grant Applications

Reasons for losing grants will vary from proposal to proposal. Common causes for rejection include (1) lack of a good idea that addresses a problem/need; (2) superficial, unfocused, or unrealistic project methods; and (3) poor evaluation plans. Applications may not receive funding even though a tremendous amount of work went into developing the proposal. Even a "perfect" proposal might be rejected for a number of reasons. If you lose, it is important that you find out why you were denied funding. If your application was not funded, you should request (1) a debriefing meeting with the POC, (2) reviewers' comments (if none were received), and (3) copies of several winning applications. As Mike Ditka often said, "You never really lose until you quit trying." **See Exhibits 8-7 and 8-8**.

Request a Debriefing Meeting with the Point of Contact

If your organization was not selected to receive an award, a debriefing meeting should be set up with the POC immediately after grant award winners have been selected. Ask the POC to explain the basis for selecting grant recipients and discuss the shortcomings of your grant application. In the same conversation, ask the POC about specific suggestions to improve your proposal narrative and budget. Take careful meeting notes and discuss this feedback information with proposal writers and reviewers.

Exhibit 8-7

What to Do When Proposals Are Not Funded

If your application was not funded, you should find out the reasons behind the denial and then try again. By law, public agencies are required to provide adequate reasons for turning down a grant application (policies do not apply to private foundations).

Reapplication

Government agencies generally look favorably upon reapplications. Some agencies specifically state that reapplications are welcome and declare no bias against them. Many reapplications succeed because applicants had requested a "why not" letter and improved their proposals on the basis of reviewers' comments. In some cases you may need to file a FOIA request to receive a written response. Not every request for feedback produces improvement in proposals. And, no matter how persistent, not all applicants who reapply will win grant funding. Most agency representatives will tell you, unless the reapplication involves excessive labor, there is no harm in trying.

"Why Not" Requests

Some government agencies such as the Department of Health and Human Services inform all applicants automatically of reasons why grant applications are not funded. Other agencies, such as the National Endowment for the Humanities, respond to letters from funding seekers that request "why not" as a matter of courtesy. The letter need not be complex—a short written request is sufficient.

If grant funds are not awarded, it is important to find out why, make appropriate corrections, and reapply for the next round of grant competition.

Exhibit 8-8

"Why Not" Letter

AMERICAN COMMUNITY COLLEGE

July 15, 20XX

— RFP Number and Title

Re: RFP #200-189-02—Workforce Development Initiative

Dear Ms. Luttrell: *— Obtain Scoring Sheets*

While American Community College is disappointed in not being recommended for funding, we greatly appreciate your agency's efforts in reviewing our workforce development initiative grant application. In the interest of improving our grant application for the next round of competition, would it be possible to obtain the government agency reviewers' comments and scoring sheets or a written explanation of where our grant application was not fully persuasive?

If your schedule will allow, I would like to meet with you to discuss ways to strengthen our proposal for the next competition. I will call you next week to set up a meeting date and time that is mutually convenient. I look forward to meeting you.

Sincerely,   *— Administrator's Signature*

Juan Rodriguez

Juan Rodriguez

If your grant application is not funded, meet with the agency's POC and request copies of several winning proposals. Study the reviewers' concerns, decide if problems are repairable, and address each criticism carefully. Never accept rejection as the final step in the grant application process.

Request Reviewers' Comments

Always request reviewers' comments if they were not previously provided by the government agency. When reviewing grant proposal feedback, determine which criticisms are valid and make appropriate corrections. **See Exhibit 8-9**.

Based on an analysis of 700 proposals that were *not* funded from the U.S. Public Health Services, the following errors were the basis for rejection:

- Inadequate planning led to carelessly prepared applications (39%). Simple mistakes such as failure to follow agency guidelines or failure to specifically address funding priorities were apparent.

- Competency of applicants was not shown (38%). Note the problem was not applicant qualifications, but that qualifications were not clearly identified and tied to proposed projects.

- Unclear or incomplete presentation of ideas (18%). Most agencies receive more proposals with good ideas than they can fund; the difference between an accepted and rejected proposal is attention to detail and presentation of innovative project ideas. Plans must be focused and easy to understand.

Exhibit 8-9

Sample Proposal Debriefing Letter

Anytown
SCHOOL DISTRICT

July 15, 20XX — *CFDA* **Number and Title**

RE: *CFDA* #278C—S-T-W Application — **Cite FOIA, if Necessary**

Based on the Freedom of Information Act, Anytown School District requests a written debriefing of its School-To-Work (S-T-W) Implementation Project grant application submitted earlier this year. We would appreciate the scoring sheets and specific reviewers' comments to strengthen our proposal for the next round of applications. Please send the specified information to:

David Jackson
1311 Northwest Main Street
Anytown, USA 98765

Please contact me at (555) 435-8400 if you have questions. Thank you.

Sincerely, — **Contact Person**

David Jackson

Dr. David Jackson, Superintendent

Always request the government agency reviewers' comments if your grant application was not funded.

Request Winning Grant Applications

It is usually worthwhile to request the names and addresses of winning PIs/PDs and copies of several winning grant applications from the government agency POC. With some agencies, a telephone call or e-mail is all that is needed to obtain copies of winning proposals. Other agencies require a formal letter that references the FOIA before they will reply. Copies of winning proposals and other information received from the government agency may provide new insights and ideas that can be used to revise and improve your grant application. Government agencies are supposed to respond to FOIA letters within 10 working days of receipt. While some may delay, no agency can completely ignore a legitimate FOIA request. The best strategy to use with government agency staff members is to ask politely but immediately for everything related to funding competitions that will be helpful to you in resubmitting your grant application. However, note that government agencies can legally limit the number of pages sent to funding seekers without charging for clerical and/or reproduction costs. In addition, information about other applicants and internal agency memoranda or review materials is not covered by FOIA. Armed with copies of winning proposals and knowledge about the competition, consider resubmitting your grant application to the same agency or another potential funding source. Many grant awards are made to institutions that submit proposals that have been revised thoughtfully and resubmitted after having been declined initially.

Winning Grant Applications

Winning grant applications present new ideas, have clear project aims, provide detailed project methods, and propose staff members with appropriate experience. After grant applications have been reviewed, the agency will send notifications to funding seekers regarding proposal outcomes. If your proposed project was selected for funding, you or your institution will receive a grant award notification letter or a detailed contract that specifies the funding amount to complete the proposed work identified in the grant application. Grant award notification letters may also include attachments that delineate the terms and conditions of the award and provide further guidance about administrative procedures. **See Exhibit 8-10**.

Exhibit 8-10

Sample Grant Award Notification Letter

Title: Forging Connections between Business, Education, and Government for Strengthening Technological Skills Among Urban Students

Dear Dr. Brown: **Award Amount**

The National Science Association hereby awards a grant of $84,427 to Jackson University to support the project referenced above under the direction of Dr. Nancy Brown, PI. This award is effective July 1, 20XX and expires June 30, 20XX. Performance and financial reports are due on a quarterly basis.

Grant Period

This grant is awarded pursuant to the following NSA terms and conditions:

- The grantee agrees to provide cost sharing as specified in the referenced grant application in the amount of $56,162. No NSA funds may be used to meet the grantee's cost-sharing obligation.

Cost Sharing

The cognizant NSA program official for this grant is Ms. Janet Hall (703) 306-1100. Please contact Ms. Hall if you have questions.

Agency Contact

Sincerely,

Lynette Winterbaum

Lynette Winterbaum
NSA Grant Officer

c: Janet Hall

Grant award notification letters specify the awarding agency, funding amount, recipient (institution), reference to project title, name of PI/PD, period of performance, when progress and financial reports are due, and outline the terms and conditions of the award in attached documents or incorporated by reference.

Grant award conditions are binding and must be followed by the grantee. Some awards have relatively few conditions, while others are laden with significant limitations and extensive reporting requirements. Most grant awards require periodic progress and financial reports that provide detail about the completion and cost of proposed activities in relation to project objectives. Most grant award documents contain narrative regarding the (1) amount of funds awarded, (2) period of performance, (3) work to be done, (4) financial and performance reports and due dates, (5) contractual conditions, and (6) other documents incorporated by reference. Detailed contracts may contain clauses that should be reviewed by legal counsel prior to signing. By accepting an award, the grantee agrees to comply with all applicable federal requirements and the prudent management of project activities and expenditures. Always notify internal proposal team members and administrators, as well as partners, subcontractors, and consultants, about awards. After an official award notification has been *fully executed* (signed by the government agency and your organization), the PI/PD should work with post-award financial management staff members to establish an organizational funding account. After the account has been set up, the PI/PD should hire staff and purchase equipment and supplies necessary to start the project. The PI/PD must complete all appropriate written reports and adhere to the approved budget.

Proposal Negotiation and Clarification

In some cases, agencies reviewers may determine through cost analysis that certain project activities are unnecessary and recommend deleting them and their associated costs from the award. In other cases, government agencies might determine that amounts requested for particular items are excessive and will want to negotiate a lower funding amount with your organization. Any budget reduction should impact the proposed project's scope of work. Funding seekers should always prepare before negotiating with representatives from a government agency. Decide beforehand who will attend the negotiation session, what documents are necessary (proposal narrative, project expenditures and contributions as well as calculations to support budget items), and be prepared to both give and take. The government agency representative may ask questions that require funding seekers to clarify points, correct errors, or respond to suggestions made by agency reviewers. Questions may require written and/or oral responses. Potential award recipients must be responsive, yet not over-interpret questions. Asking questions about a grant submission is a positive sign and should be treated favorably, not defensively. The length of a negotiation session will depend on the number of fiscal or regulatory issues pertaining to the grant application and the proposal's complexity. Funding seekers should prepare written responses that (1) answer the questions succinctly, (2) eliminate deficiencies, (3) make appropriate changes, and (4) improve the proposal. A government agency representative may also believe your project can be completed for a smaller budget. Funding seekers should respond positively to such requests and scale the project wisely.

Funding seekers should never turn down funding (even if it is less than what was desired). Rather, funding seekers should prioritize the critical cost elements associated with the project, readjust the statement of work to compensate for fewer dollars, and respond quickly—but carefully. Keep in mind that during a negotiation session, proposal funding is still pending. An award is not official until an award notification is fully executed. An organization that makes financial commitments prior to a signed agreement does so at its own risk. If you receive an award amount that was less than what you proposed and there is no room for negotiating, it is strongly suggested that you reread the proposal narrative and make appropriate corrections to the proposed activities. A letter should then be sent to the POC explaining what activities have been changed to meet the financial limitations of the award. **See Exhibit 8-11**.

Exhibit 8-11

Sample Letter to POC After Receiving a Low-Budget Award

June 20, 20XX

```
                         ┌─ RFP Number/Title
Re:  RFP #42702 ✎
     Innovative Programs to Increase IT Graduates
```

HOOSIER STATE COLLEGE

Dear Dr. Thomas:

Thank you for your comments concerning our Information Technology (IT) Special Initiative Grant (SIG). Hoosier State College was very pleased to receive the Grant Award Notification indicating that we received $40,000 to implement the IT project.

We have altered several proposal tasks to account for the $10,000 difference between our $50,000 original budget request and the $40,000 award from your agency. Specifically, instead of sending IT faculty for out-of-state training, we were able to negotiate an understanding with 3-Com to have them come to Hoosier State College and train both college and high school instructors at a savings of $7,000.

Other funding will be used to provide outreach materials to local high schools, which will result in a $3,000 savings. Enclosed is a revised proposal and budget to reflect the $40,000 award. Specifically note the changes to proposal activity items 1.1a and 2.1d under measurable outcomes of the project overview and timeline.

Sincerely,   ┌─ **Contact Person/Phone Number**

Janet Passmore ✎

Dr. Janet J. Passmore, President
219-834-5555
E-mail: jpassmore@hoosierstate.edu

When awarded a budget amount less than requested, you should make appropriate corrections to the original proposal and write a letter to the POC explaining what activities have been changed to meet the financial limitations of the award. When making these changes, take care not to alter the purpose of the application. The government agency program officer must approve all changes.

Reports, Audits, and Closeout

If you have been awarded grant funding, your work has just begun. Now, you must complete the proposed project activities for the total costs identified in the budget. An award represents a binding contract that obligates your institution to complete the tasks identified in the narrative. Grant recipients must request approval from the awarding agency for any change in the scope of work or status of key personnel specified in the award document. (See OMB circular A-110.)

Successful grant projects require the PI/PD and grantee organization to:

- Begin the project on time.

- Complete all activities within the budget period and the funds authorized. Manage expenditures according to fiscal regulations specified by the agency.

- Schedule regular meetings with key project personnel to keep them informed.

- Keep in-house administration informed about the grant project.

- Complete the project evaluation plans as specified in the proposal. Report project failures as well as successes.

- Recognize project problems and develop solutions. Seek approval from the funding agency about any changes to the proposed project and expenditures.

- Prepare and submit timely project reports that include a summary of progress toward achieving the originally stated objectives.

- Prepare and submit accurate and timely performance and financial reports as required by the government agency. Auditors have the right to access and review all internal accounting records associated with a grant project. Always retain reports for three years after project completion. Incremental funding or future funding may depend upon receipt of these reports.

The PI/PD should never incur project expenditures before the official award date or after the termination date of the grant without official authorization from the government agency program officer. Grant budget deviations and reallocations are allowable only after receiving approval from the program officer. Ultimately, it is the responsibility of the PI/PD to prevent unallowable project expenditures.

Expenditure reports are required documentation based on official accounting records from the grantee's organization to indicate the financial status of the grant project. Financial reports are subject to audit requirements based on OMB circulars. Institutional financial management packages are used to track expenditures for most grant awards. Savvy grant award recipients will also maintain a separate spreadsheet or database that can track budget items and ascertain if the accounting process is error free. **See Exhibit 8-12**.

Exhibit 8-12

Sample Grant Expenditures Spreadsheet

Quarterly Expenditures					
Budget Items	1st Quarter 7/1–9/30	2nd Quarter 10/1–12/31	3rd Quarter 1/1–3/31	4th Quarter 4/1–6/30	Total
Personnel Salaries	3,525	3,525	3,525	3,525	14,100
Fringe Benefits	860	860	860	860	3,440
Travel and Per Diem	3,225	2,225	1,250	1,250	7,950
Equipment	5,856	5,777	6,435	6,555	24,623
Expendable Supplies	2,559	2,010	4,445	1,245	10,259
Contractual Services	3,660	3,660	3,660	3,660	14,640
Other	500	1,239	1,250	0	2,989
Total	$ 20,185	$ 19,296	$ 21,425	$ 17,095	$ 78,001

A spreadsheet or database can be used to track expenditures for small grant projects.

Project expenditures must be checked at regular intervals as mandated in the grant award notification for budget reports and final grant closeout activities (administrative and financial wrap-up tasks associated with completing a discretionary grant). Closeout activities should happen as soon as possible after expiration of the grant period of performance. Most institutions require grantees to submit final financial and progress reports within 90 days after the grant period of performance unless an extension is granted by the government agency.

Winning Strategies for Funding Seekers: Final Thoughts

Funding seekers must remember that patience, persistence, and a positive attitude are needed to win grant funding. Keep in mind these final thoughts:

- Identify a clear project idea that is innovative, creative, manageable, and cost effective. Discuss the project idea with knowledgeable colleagues.

- Use the Internet and register for e-mail notifications about grant opportunities with Grants.gov and get on free mailing lists to obtain early alerts about grant opportunities so you have time to prepare winning applications. Use the resources available from your office of sponsored programs to locate potential funding opportunities.

- Research potential government agencies thoroughly. Study the government agency's homepage and abstracts of winning proposals. Make sure your project idea matches the agency's mission (needs and wants).

- Read the RFP/RFA instructions carefully. Ask the POC about any ambiguities in the solicitation.

- Contact the agency's POC before and during the proposal development process. Ask the POC to provide feedback about your proposal prospectus or an initial draft.

- Attend pre-application or pre-proposal conferences and technical workshops offered by government agencies. Ask questions about your proposed project and take careful notes.

- Develop boilerplate materials that can be reused in grant applications.

- Secure collaborators for areas in which you lack experience. Submit signed partner, subcontractor, and/or consultant agreements as part of the grant application.

- Examine successful grant applications that are similar to your proposed project. Study the background and experience of successful PIs/PDs. You will obtain some good ideas and an understanding of the competition.

- Volunteer to serve as a grant reviewer for funding agencies. You will gain valuable information about the review process and see several competitors' grant applications.

- Always follow the government agency's directions and instructions. Address the specific selection criteria. Organize the proposal according to the agency's format.

- Be extremely choosy about the grants you go after. State funds are often the easiest to obtain; federal funds are more difficult. Partner with experienced PIs/PDs to gain experience.

- Prepare an extensive outline of the project idea before writing the narrative. Use headings and subheadings to present a clear presentation of ideas.

- Don't procrastinate about writing the proposal. There is never sufficient time to write the perfect grant application. Write a little each day until you finish the application.

- Prepare the grant application early. Use a proposal schedule to meet government agency deadlines. If you don't have time to do it right, don't compete for grant funds.

- Demonstrate the existence of a problem with recent and relevant statistics. Provide compelling evidence to demonstrate how the project idea will address a specific need.

- Write objectives that are quantifiable, realistic, and attainable considering your timeframe and budget.

- Describe in detail the proposed project activities. The methodology must be a compelling and convincing plan of work. Identify specific tasks to be completed by partners, subcontractors, and consultants.

- Demonstrate that personnel have appropriate management skills (especially grant management experience) and can complete successful projects on time. Describe key personnel qualifications and commitment to the project.

- Use rules of writing that make the proposal narrative shine.
    - Use current government agency language; write to express, not to impress.
    - Develop two to three proposal drafts.
    - Use headings and subheadings to make the narrative easier to read.
    - Use figures, tables, and charts to break up the monotony of the text.
    - Use in-house reviewers and editors to check and recheck all written work.

- Make budgets realistic and credible.
    - Check all calculations.
    - Keep a record of how specific costs were determined.
    - Don't ask for more than you need.
    - Keep budget detail and narrative clear, factual, and supportable.

- Develop an abstract that provides a brief but comprehensive overview of the proposed project.

- Complete and sign all necessary certification and assurance forms.

- Check the proposal against the criteria in the RFP/RFA guidelines before submitting the grant application to the government agency. Have in-house reviewers critically review the application prior to submitting it to the agency.

- Submit grant applications in a timely manner.

- Resubmit grant applications that were not funded. Use the agency reviewers' comments to revise and strengthen the proposal. Address all criticisms thoroughly and respond constructively. Applications that are revised and resubmitted have a higher acceptance rate than first-time applicants.

- Be realistic in what you propose to do. Remember that someone must actually execute what is proposed in the project narrative.

Chapter Summary

Immediately after the grant application has been submitted, the Proposal Director should hold a debriefing meeting to identify the proposal strengths and weaknesses in anticipation of questions from the government agency. Proposal team members should focus on answers to the following questions when reviewing the grant application:

- Is the grant application compliant?

- Are project claims substantiated?

- Are project benefits emphasized?

- Are project costs appropriate?

Strategies for improving the proposal narrative and budget should be noted at the debriefing meeting and used later to clarify any concerns voiced by the government agency program officer. The primary outcome of a debriefing meeting is to ensure that key proposal team members are prepared to answer government agency questions about the grant application.

After the grant application has been submitted to the government agency, the Proposal Director should organize and file all grant application documents and electronic files in a safe place. Backup copies of the narrative and budget should be stored in a separate location.

Grant applications received by government agencies undergo a thorough review that may take several months before a funding outcome is determined. Grant applications are evaluated and scored by agency reviewers with a cross-section of education, experience, and geographic representation.

Grant applications are evaluated on the basis of how well applicants respond to criteria in the RFP/RFA and the quality of the proposed project ideas. Most applications are read by at least three government agency reviewers that evaluate each proposal independently and provide ratings and written comments about the strengths and weaknesses of the grant application. After evaluating proposals on an independent basis, agency reviewers discuss grant application ratings. Reviewers may revise their ratings and comments if the discussion provides new insight and a different conclusion. If necessary, an arbitrator intervenes to resolve disagreements about grant applications. Following discussions, written summary reports and ratings are submitted to the government agency for each application. The agency uses these reviews as a basis for funding the best-of-the-best applications.

After the review process, government agencies make award decisions based on recommendations from agency-selected reviewers. Government agencies may decide to:

- not fund the proposed project,

- request clarifications about the proposal narrative and/or budget, or

- fund all or part of the proposed project.

If you lose, it is important that you find out why you were denied funding. If your grant application was not funded, you should request:

- a debriefing meeting with the POC,

- reviewers' comments (if none were received), and

- copies of several winning grant applications.

Use the reviewers' comments to revise the narrative and budget and resubmit the application. Grant applications that are revised and resubmitted have a higher acceptance rate than first-time applicants.

If your proposed project was selected for funding, you or your institution will receive a grant award notification letter or detailed contract that specifies the funding amount to complete the proposed work identified in the grant application. Grant award notification letters may also include attachments that delineate the conditions of the award and provide further guidance about administrative procedures. Grant award conditions are binding and must be followed by the grantee.

In some cases, government agencies may determine through cost analysis that certain proposal activities are unnecessary and recommend deleting them and their associated costs from the award. In other cases, government agencies might determine that amounts requested for particular cost items are excessive and will want to negotiate a lower funding amount with your organization. Any budget reduction should impact the proposed project's scope of work.

If you have been awarded grant funding, your work has just begun. A grant award represents a binding contract that obligates your institution to complete the tasks identified in the grant application. Any changes in the scope of work or status of key personnel during project performance must be immediately communicated to the government agency. Grant recipients must submit timely performance and expenditure reports as required by the government agency.

Review Questions

(Answers to Review Questions are on p. 274.)

Directions: For statements 1–15, circle "T" for True or "F" for False.

T F 1. Proposal writers and reviewers should discuss the application's strengths and weaknesses immediately after submission.

T F 2. Government agencies are not obligated to review grant applications that are not submitted prior to the deadline.

T F 3. Government agencies welcome letters of interest and résumés from potential grant application reviewers.

T F 4. The grant application review process is subjective.

T F 5. Agency reviewers must provide written comments about the strengths and weaknesses of grant applications.

T F 6. Agency reviewers must reach a consensus when scoring a grant application.

T F 7. Funding seekers should obtain agency reviewers' scores and written comments about a losing grant application.

T F 8. Government agencies are supposed to respond to FOIA letters within five working days of receipt.

T F 9. If your grant application did not receive funding, you should request several winning grant applications submitted by other organizations.

T F 10. Funding seekers should revise and resubmit grant applications that were not funded.

T F 11. Government agencies provide financial assistance to support grant projects through a grant award notification letter or a signed contract.

T F 12. Grant award conditions are binding and must be followed by grant recipients.

T F 13. Grant awards are not official until the grant award notification has been fully executed.

T F 14. If you receive a grant award for an amount that was less than what was proposed in the budget and there is no room for negotiating, it is strongly suggested that you make appropriate corrections to the proposed project to meet the financial limitations of the award.

T F 15. A spreadsheet or database is used to track costs for small grant awards.

Exercise 8-1

Evaluate Proposals in Response to Criteria

(Answers to Exercise 8-1 are on pp. 302–304.)

Directions: Read the situation below and evaluate the 10 responses to proposal criteria on pp. 203–212.

Situation: You are serving as a reviewer to evaluate proposals submitted in response to a solicitation to provide supervisory skills training to small business owners. The potential grant recipients have been narrowed to two organizations: Lincoln Department of Development and Jefferson Chamber of Commerce.

The following pages contain grant criteria with corresponding responses from the two organizations. Identify the strengths and weaknesses of each response and determine the lessons learned from each of the 10 proposal criteria.

Adapted from: *Writing Winning Grant Proposals: Simulation Learning Workshop for Non-Profit Organizations.* Westinghouse Electric Corporation, Carlsbad, New Mexico

Exercise 8-1 continues on the next page.

Criterion #1: The proposal must clearly describe the need for supervisory training for small business owners.

Lincoln Department of Development

Lincoln Department of Development conducted a survey of 120 small businesses in April 20XX. Ninety-two percent of small business owners indicated that they needed more supervisory skills to improve their business operations. Nearly 78 percent indicated that they would attend supervisory training if it were offered in the Lincoln community.

Strengths/Weaknesses:

Jefferson Chamber of Commerce

The primary reason for the proposed activities is that Jefferson Chamber of Commerce believes that education is a key element to continually improving economic development. Jefferson Chamber of Commerce is committed to use supervisory training to help all businesses in the Jefferson area.

Strengths/Weaknesses:

Lessons Learned:

Exercise 8-1 continues on the next page.

Criterion #2: The proposal must clearly describe a schedule for analyzing, designing, developing, implementing, and evaluating supervisory training.

Lincoln Department of Development

Lincoln Department of Development (LDD) will complete upfront analysis in an effort to design, develop, and implement supervisory training for small business owners. Specific testing methods will be developed and used to evaluate the effectiveness of the training program. LDD will adhere to the following schedule:

Task Name	JUN	3rd Quarter JUL	AUG	SEP	4th Quarter OCT	NOV	DEC	1st Quarter JAN	FEB	MAR	2nd Quarter APR	MAY
Receive Grant	▓											
Analyze Needs	██	██										
Job Analysis	▓											
Task Analysis		▓										
Design Training			██									
Curriculum Guide			▓									
Student Guide				▓								
Develop Training				████	████							
Lesson Plans				▓▓	▓							
Tests					▓							
Implement Training						▓▓▓▓▓▓▓▓▓▓▓▓▓▓▓▓▓▓▓▓▓						
Evaluate Training												▓

TASK ▓▓▓▓▓▓   SUMMARY ██████

Strengths/Weaknesses:

Jefferson Chamber of Commerce

Upon receipt of grant funds, Jefferson Chamber of Commerce will develop a schedule for the project. We plan to hire a consultant to assist us in developing the schedule and training. Be assured that Jefferson Chamber of Commerce recognizes the importance of having a detailed project schedule.

Strengths/Weaknesses:

Lessons Learned:

Exercise 8-1 continues on the next page.

Criterion #3: The proposal must clearly describe the time commitments of key personnel who will be responsible for completing the proposed activities.

Lincoln Department of Development

Table 1 shows key personnel, position, and time commitments for completing the proposed activities.

Table 1: Time Commitments of Key Personnel

Key Personnel	Position	Hours/Week
John Stanko	Executive Director	5
Sharon Cox	Administrative Assistant	10
Andrew Rodriguez	Executive Board Representative	5
Rachel McEwing	Small Business Owner	4
David Shields	University Liaison	4
Janice Hivar	Training Consultant	20

Strengths/Weaknesses:

Jefferson Chamber of Commerce

Key personnel who will be responsible for carrying out the proposed activities have committed a considerable amount of time for the project duration: the Executive Director will commit five hours per week, the Administrative Assistant will commit ten hours per week, the Executive Board Representative will commit two hours per week, the Small Business Owner Representative will commit one hour per week, the University Liaison will commit one hour per week, and the Training Consultant will commit twenty hours per week.

Strengths/Weaknesses:

Lessons Learned:

Exercise 8-1 continues on the next page.

Criterion #4: The proposal must clearly describe the involvement that stakeholder groups (administration, board members, small business owners, and the educational community) will have in training.

Lincoln Department of Development

All stakeholder groups will participate in the supervisory skills training project. The Executive Director will coordinate the project, ensuring it stays on schedule and produces desired deliverables and outcomes. The administrative assistant will provide desktop publishing support for material development. Board members, small business owners, and educational representatives will meet weekly as a steering group to guide the project through five phases: (1) analysis, (2) design, (3) development, (4) implementation, and (5) evaluation.

Strengths/Weaknesses:

Jefferson Chamber of Commerce

All stakeholder groups will participate in the training project. Coordination of the project to ensure that it stays on schedule and produces desired deliverables and outcomes will be the responsibility of the Executive Director. Desktop publishing will be the responsibility of the administrative assistant. Guidance of the project through the five phases—analysis, design, development, implementation, and evaluation—will be ensured by a steering group. Weekly steering group meetings will be attended by board members, small business owners, and educational representatives.

Strengths/Weaknesses:

Lessons Learned:

Exercise 8-1 continues on the next page.

Criterion #5: The proposal must clearly describe the proposal director's experience and training in strategic planning.

Lincoln Department of Development

The Lincoln Department of Development Executive Director has more than 20 years of on-the-job experience in developing long-range (5–10 year) plans, helping more than 100 small businesses. His planning contributions helped him earn a quality contributor award from the State Association of Chambers of Commerce last year. See the Executive Director's résumé in the appendix.

Strengths/Weaknesses:

Jefferson Chamber of Commerce

The Executive Director has a vast amount of experience in strategic planning, from designing the department's calendar to scheduling daily activities for staff members. The Executive Director was involved in the project, which, of course, was a huge success. The Executive Director has also been involved in other plans, and is recognized as one of the best planners in the field of economic development.

Strengths/Weaknesses:

Lessons Learned:

Exercise 8-1 continues on the next page.

Criterion #6: The proposal must provide evidence of commitment to the project that indicates the training program will be successful.

Lincoln Department of Development

The amount of time and money donated by the Department of Development, small businesses, and community representatives provides evidence of dedication to the project. We have raised more than $45,000 in contributions from the community to be used for the project. Community volunteers have agreed to donate more than 2,000 hours to this project.

Strengths/Weaknesses:

Jefferson Chamber of Commerce

Jefferson Chamber of Commerce personnel have read and heard quite a bit about the benefits of supervisory skill training and find the concept to be interesting. The grant will allow Jefferson Chamber of Commerce to offer training that could be valuable in the future.

Strengths/Weaknesses:

Lessons Learned:

Exercise 8-1 continues on the next page.

Criterion #7: In a single sentence, the proposal must clearly describe the project mission.

Lincoln Department of Development

The supervisory skills training program will help small businesses in Lincoln grow and improve by providing small business owners with knowledge, skills, and abilities to effectively manage their employees.

Strengths/Weaknesses:

Jefferson Chamber of Commerce

Jefferson Chamber of Commerce will develop a world-class training program. The program will be viewed as one of the best plans ever developed. Jefferson Chamber of Commerce will receive awards and national recognition for the training program.

Strengths/Weaknesses:

Lessons Learned:

Exercise 8-1 continues on the next page.

Criterion #8: In 30 pages or less, the proposal must address the following: (1) problem/need, (2) proposed activities, (3) key personnel, (4) commitment to broad-based participation, (5) evaluation plans, and (6) budget.

Lincoln Department of Development

Proposal Table of Contents

1. Problem/need   1
2. Proposed activities   3
3. Key personnel   15
4. Commitment to broad-based participation   21
5. Evaluation plans   23
6. Budget   26

Strengths/Weaknesses:

Jefferson Chamber of Commerce

Proposal Table of Contents

1. Needs analysis   1
2. Finance   7
3. Activities   11
4. Assessment plan   25
5. Commitment   27
6. People   33
7. Certification forms   36

Strengths/Weaknesses:

Lessons Learned:

Exercise 8-1 continues on the next page.

Criterion #9: The proposal must clearly describe what materials will be produced during the development phase of the project.

Lincoln Department of Development

During the development phase, the Lincoln Department of Development team will produce the following materials:

- 20 lesson plans (one per training session)
- 60 case studies (three per training session)
- 20 student handouts (one per training session)
- 40 examinations (two per training session)
- 2 course evaluation forms

Strengths/Weaknesses:

Jefferson Chamber of Commerce

The Jefferson team will coordinate activities to ensure that all required training materials are produced on schedule. The consultant will focus on lesson and examination development. The educational representative and small business representative will work on case studies. The administrative assistant will work on student handouts.

Strengths/Weaknesses:

Lessons Learned:

Exercise 8-1 continues on the next page.

Criterion #10: The proposal must clearly describe what performance indicators will be used to monitor the effectiveness of the program.

Lincoln Department of Development

The Lincoln Department of Development team has identified the following performance indicators to monitor program effectiveness:

- Sales volume/income
- Employee turnover rate
- Employee absenteeism rate
- Customer satisfaction rate

Strengths/Weaknesses:

Jefferson Chamber of Commerce

With the benefit of a practiced statistician, the Jefferson Chamber of Commerce will determine absenteeism, turnover, sales, and customer satisfaction parameters. We really think it's important to do this. State-of-the-art analytical engines will be utilized to originate key data. This should give us some neat numbers to crunch.

Strengths/Weaknesses:

Lessons Learned:

Exercise 8-1 continues on the next page.

Exercise 8-2

EagleEye Analysts

Evaluate Two Proposals

(Answers to Exercise 8-2 are on pp. 305–306.)

Directions: You work for EagleEye Analysts. Your company specializes in aerial/ satellite photograph analysis. You employ many technicians to analyze photographs for a variety of purposes, and you need a training program in aerial/satellite photograph analysis for entry- and mid-level employees.

EagleEye Analysts has received two proposals in response to a Request for Proposal (RFP). One proposal is from Instructors, Inc. (pp. 214–224), and the other is from Technical Trainers, Inc. (pp. 225–240). You know little about either firm, but have been assigned to an evaluation panel to read and score the two proposals. Your specific assignment is to evaluate the part of each proposal that addresses the firms' training philosophy and approach.

You will not have access to other parts of the proposals or to budget information. At this point you will not be able to ask questions of either training firm. Your evaluation must be made strictly on the basis of information contained in the proposals.

Proposal Preparation Instructions

The RFP provided the following proposal preparation information to all firms:

1. Describe your training philosophy and the principles your firm considers important in the development of training programs.

2. Describe your firm's approach to training program development and instruction.

3. Provide a detailed project plan for the development of a training program that includes (1) methods and time schedules for delivering the training, and (2) a comprehensive description of the experience and role of key members of the project team.

Evaluation Criteria

1. Does the firm's training philosophy seem appropriate to EagleEye Analysts' needs?

2. Does the firm present a sound training program based on a clear understanding of recent evidence from the literature?

3. Are proposed deliverables clearly described, and do they appear to be adequate?

4. Has the firm proposed an appropriately organized project team?

5. Are you persuaded that this firm has a sound approach overall?

Adapted from The Winning Proposal Student Workbook, ESI. Used with permission.

Exercise 8-2 continues on the next page.

Exercise 8-2

Evaluate Two Proposals

Use this form to evaluate Instructors Inc.'s proposal on pp. 215–224.

Proposal Scoring Sheet for Instructors, Inc.

Ratings

Superior	I am convinced that this is a capable training firm. They have a sound philosophy and approach.
Good	I think this training firm might be able to do the job, but I would not select them without asking more questions.
Marginal	I am not persuaded that this training firm could do the job. Their plan is unclear and lacking in important details.
Poor	I am convinced that this training firm cannot do the job.

Evaluation Criteria

Directions: Evaluate the proposal on the following criteria.

1. Does the firm's training philosophy seem appropriate to EagleEye Analysts' needs?

    Rating:_____

2. Does the firm present a sound training program based on a clear understanding of recent evidence from the literature?

    Rating:_____

3. Are proposed deliverables clearly described, and do they appear to be adequate?

    Rating:_____

4. Has the firm proposed an appropriately organized project team?

    Rating:_____

5. Are you persuaded that this firm has a sound approach overall?

    Rating:_____

Recommendation: Yes   No

Evaluator's name: _____

Exercise 8-2 continues on the next page.

Exercise 8-2 Evaluating Two Proposals

Instructors, Inc.'s Proposal

Training Philosophy

> Aerial photography analysis is a skill that must be learned by doing. Instructors, Inc. devotes at least half of class time to practical exercises. As a result, EagleEye Analysts' employees will return from our courses able to perform tasks, not just describe them.

Training experts agree: The best way to teach someone how to do a job is to show them how, let them try, and give them feedback.[1] A lecture may provide an informative and engaging account of how to analyze a satellite image, but will employees remember the lecture's instructions back at the workbench? Will employees be able to actually identify terrain and manmade features based on that memory? Experience has taught us that the answer is no.

Aerial/satellite photography analysis traditionally has been taught by lecture, with an occasional case study, demonstration, or practical exercise thrown in for variety. Instructors, Inc. has learned from a sampling of courses on aerial/satellite photography analysis that other training companies devote an average of 75 percent of class time to lecture.[2] Figure 1 contrasts our use of class time with that of our competitors.

Most competitors we observed use lecture to emphasize concepts and theory. They described procedures but provided participants with few opportunities to practice them. We suspect that, back at their workbenches, employees from those classes stared at their notes, tried to remember the lecturer's instructions, and found applying what they "learned" harder than anticipated.

Figure 1
Use of Class Time: Instructors, Inc. vs. Competitors

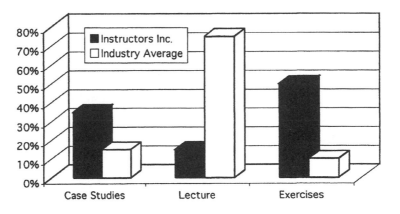

Instructors Inc., unlike most of its competitors, devotes at least 50% of class time to practical exercises, rather than lecture. Instructors, Inc. usually allocates at least 30% of class time to demonstrations and case studies.

Exercise 8-2 continues on the next page.

Instructors, Inc. training is task-oriented. Our philosophy is that aerial/satellite photography analysis training should teach participants how to perform workday tasks. Some lecture about concepts and theories is necessary, but even the most entertaining lecturer can become tiresome after a while. Research has shown that after an hour or so the average participant's attention span deteriorates.[3] Exercises, case studies, and demonstrations are keys to cost-effective training and on-the-job performance. Instructors, Inc. guarantees that EagleEye Analysts' training dollars will pay for experience, not just information.

Instructors, Inc. devotes no less than 50% of class time to realistic practical exercises in on-the-job tasks. The remaining time is allocated to demonstration, case studies, and lecture in that order of priority. Our market research indicates that no other trainer we studied devoted as much time to practice of work tasks.

Instructors, Inc.'s approach means that when EagleEye Analysts' employees attend our classes they will spend most of their time *doing*, instead of just listening and trying to memorize. In the five-day, seven-hour-a-day aerial photography analysis courses we developed for Orbitronics, participants spent no less than 18 hours doing procedures they had come to learn. Orbitronics' training dollars bought experience under the eye of skilled instructor-practitioners.

Supervised practice is the key to effective on-the-job performance and it is the philosophy underlying the approach we offer to EagleEye Analysts.

Instructors, Inc.'s Approach: Systematic, Phased, and Thorough

> Instructors, Inc. will confirm EagleEye Analysts' needs, specify what employees will be able to do after training, and develop a means of testing the training program *before* we design courses.
>
> Thus, Instructors, Inc. will design a training program to well-defined objectives. And we will have clear standards and methods for evaluating the program's effectiveness.

Instructors, Inc. uses a proven instructional systems development approach to training design and presentation based on a systems engineering approach to project management.[4] The key to our success has been the concentration of effort in upfront analysis, specification of objectives, and test development before beginning detailed program design. This approach helps us avoid costly mistakes and extra work during training.

Figure 2 shows our work breakdown structure for the EagleEye Analysts Training Program Development Project, which provides specific details about the training program.

Exercise 8-2 continues on the next page.

Figure 2
EagleEye Analysts' Training Program Development Project
Work Breakdown Structure

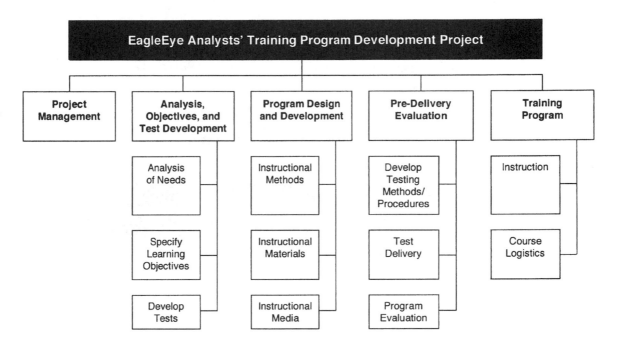

Instructors, Inc. training program provides a breakdown of the major project tasks. The proposal narrative addresses each task in detail, describing levels of effort and products.

We have broken the project down into five major elements or tasks: (1) project management; (2) analysis, objectives, and test development; (3) program design and development; (4) pre-delivery evaluation; and (5) training. These tasks are divided into subtasks as shown in Figure 2. This work breakdown structure is the foundation for our project planning, scheduling, and controlling, and is the basis for our project organization.

Approximately 30 percent of our effort will consist of upfront analysis and specification of objectives. We will dedicate an aerial/satellite photography analysis expert and program design specialist[5] to this phase of the training.

Exercise 8-2 continues on the next page.

Upfront analysis is important, because it reduces the risk of unnecessary and costly rework during the design and development and program evaluation phases.

Figure 3 shows our schedule for completing each phase of the project.

Note that the program design and development work of Phase II will not commence until the needs assessment, specification of learning objectives, and test development (Phase I) has been approved. Training (Phase IV) will not commence until we have established the validity of our program design through pre-delivery evaluation (Phase III).

Figure 3
Program Schedule

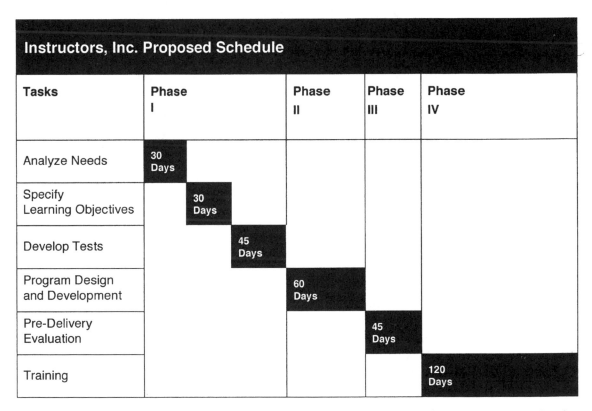

Instructors, Inc. Proposed Schedule					
Tasks	**Phase I**		**Phase II**	**Phase III**	**Phase IV**
Analyze Needs	30 Days				
Specify Learning Objectives		30 Days			
Develop Tests			45 Days		
Program Design and Development			60 Days		
Pre-Delivery Evaluation				45 Days	
Training					120 Days

Instructors, Inc. will proceed with the work in four phases. We will proceed with each phase only after EagleEye Analysts' representatives have approved the work of the preceding phase. EagleEye Analysts will be assured that training is proceeding toward the achievement of clearly defined objectives.

Exercise 8-2 continues on the next page.

Phase I: Analysis, Objectives, and Test Development

Phase 1 has three stages. First, we assess EagleEye's training needs. Our aerial/satellite photography analysis experts will interview managers, supervisors, and employees and observe them at work in order to understand their tasks and problems.

We will be especially concerned with distinguishing the differing needs of entry- and mid-level analysts. We will discuss with EagleEye management the knowledge and skills that should be taught. In this way, we will confirm the learning objectives for the training program.

Second, we will specify the learning objectives. Our aerial/satellite photography analysis experts and program design specialists will write a clear and detailed *Specification of Learning Objectives*—a description of what EagleEye's employees will be able to do after they have attended the training.[6] This document will be available for EagleEye's review and approval before Phase II. EagleEye's approval will ensure that our design efforts will address employees' needs.

Third, we will develop testing methods. Our test development specialists, working from the *Specification of Learning Objectives*, will design written and performance tests to measure the level of participants' analytical skills after training. These tests will be described in a *Student Achievement and Program*

Evaluation Test Specifications. This document will be available for EagleEye's review and approval upon completion.

Approved *Specification of Learning Objectives* and *Student Achievement and Program Evaluation Test Specifications* will be used as the baseline during Phase II: Program Design and Development.

Phase II: Program Design and Development

Only after approval of the learning objectives and testing methods will we design and develop training methods and media. Products of this phase will be an *Instructor's Statement of Work and Methods* and workbooks and media that will be used in the classroom.

Instructors, Inc. will allocate at least 50 percent of class time to skills practice. Demonstrations and discussions of sample analyses will consume at least another 30 percent. We will use lecture to present only those concepts, theories, and facts essential to achieve the learning objectives. As a result, employees sent to classes will return with actual analytical experiences.

Our program design specialists and instructors will work with the documentation developed during Phase I: Analysis, Objectives, and Test Development. Our design specialists will develop practical exercises in aerial/satellite photography analysis that give employees feedback on their learning and performance progress.

Exercise 8-2 continues on the next page.

They will also develop a participant workbook and sample analyses that will provide useful reference material back on the job. Finally, they will develop instructional materials: videos, DVDs, PowerPoint presentations, and demonstration handouts.

Instructors, Inc. will complete phase II in 60 days. The *Instructor's Statement of Work and Methods* and the course media will be made available for EagleEye's review.

We will develop instructional methods and media based on clearly specified learning objectives that EagleEye Analysts has reviewed and approved. Our design effort will focus on EagleEye's training needs. The development of testing methods and procedures will give EagleEye a way to evaluate the effectiveness of our program design. Our task-oriented design will ensure that EagleEye employees will learn not only what to do, but how to perform the necessary tasks to be effective workers.

Phase III: Pre-Delivery Evaluation

With clearly defined learning objectives, course methods and media, and evaluation methods and procedures in hand, we will test the program. Instructors, Inc. will conduct a demonstration training session for a group of employees selected by EagleEye Analysts. At the conclusion of the demonstration training, we will test participants to determine the effectiveness of our instructional methods and media in achieving the specified learning objectives.

Exercise 8-2 continues on the next page.

Two weeks later, after employees have had an opportunity to apply their skills on the job, our aerial/satellite photography analysis experts and program development specialists will interview them. They will determine whether the results of the earlier tests are confirmed by actual work experiences. We will provide a complete post-training debriefing for EagleEye's management to review.

Instructors, Inc. will use the testing results and post-training debriefings to evaluate program effectiveness. We will provide EagleEye Analysts with the results of our analysis and findings.

If necessary, we will modify the course design. If modifications are required, we will provide EagleEye Analysts with modification plans. We will complete any necessary redesign and submit the final design for EagleEye's approval.

We will deliver the following after EagleEye Analysts approves the training design:

• Specification of learning objectives

• Student achievement and program evaluation test specifications

• Instructor's statement of work and methods

• Course workbook and instructional media

Our systematic approach assures you of program effectiveness before we deliver any training. EagleEye will know that precious training dollars are being used to purchase results.

Phase IV: Training Program

After the proposed instructional program has been approved, we will conduct training in accordance with EagleEye Analysts' schedule, at the specified site(s). Our staff will handle the logistics of facility arrangements and shipment of materials to the site. A list of all training seminars we have managed in the past (which provides detailed information about our training and logistical experiences) is presented in the appendix.

All our instructors have had hands-on experience in aerial/satellite photography analysis, meet all requirements in the RFP, and are skilled trainers. Comprehensive résumés of all key staff proposed for this project are located in the appendix.

Phase IV will continuously evaluate the effectiveness of the training program and seek recommended improvements.

EagleEye Analysts' management staff will always know what employees are supposed to be able to do after training and whether objectives are being met.

Instructors, Inc.'s Key Project Staff are Skilled, Experienced, and Responsive

Colby Haverstock will manage this project on a full-time basis. He will have complete authority over all project controls—quality, schedule, and cost. He will also be our principal liaison with EagleEye Analysts. Mr. Haverstock is a training development specialist and instructor with more than 25 years of industrial training experience.

Pamela Keaton will work full-time on this project and will manage the needs analysis, specification of objectives, and program design and development under Mr. Haverstock's direction. Ms. Keaton has designed 12 programs for Instructors, Inc. and has 10 years of training development experience.

Regina Clark, a U.S. Navy–trained expert with 20 years of experience in aerial/satellite photography analysis, will assist Ms. Keaton in needs analysis and program development.

Mary Gutierrez, Director of Program Evaluation for Instructors, Inc., will manage program test development and pre-delivery evaluation. Although her staff will support Mr. Haverstock, Ms. Gutierrez will report independently to corporate management and EagleEye Analysts. Ms. Gutierrez has been evaluating industrial training programs for 16 years and is the author of several articles on the subject.

Exercise 8-2 continues on the next page.

Richard McMahon will be chief instructor for the program. Mr. McMahon will teach the initial courses, and he will train and supervise all other course instructors. Mr. McMahon has been lead instructor for several technical training programs and was a cartographer and photographic analyst for the Defense Mapping Service for 25 years before joining Instructors, Inc.

Albert Cabriales, Instructors, Inc.'s Chief of Administration, will be in charge of course logistics. He will report to Mr. Haverstock. Mr. Cabriales has managed the administrative aspects of Instructors, Inc. programs throughout the United States and in foreign countries for seven years. See Figure 4.

Figure 4
Project Organization for EagleEye Training Program Development

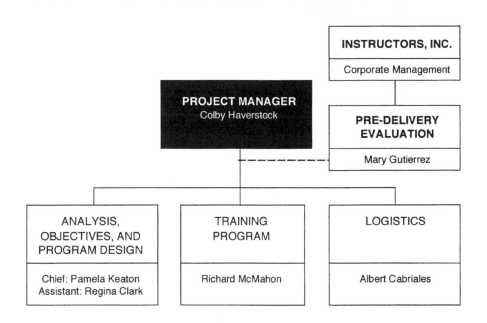

Instructors, Inc.'s project organization is led by a team with a combined total of more than 103 years of experience in technical training, program development, and delivery. The project manager has full authority over project control and contractual relations and will deal directly with EagleEye's representatives. Résumés of key personnel are located in the appendix.

Exercise 8-2 continues on the next page.

Conclusion

Instructors, Inc. will provide EagleEye Analysts' employees with on-the-job skills necessary for effective analysis of aerial/satellite photographs. We will achieve results through a systematic phased approach that specifies program learning objectives and evaluation criteria before program design begins. Throughout the design process EagleEye Analysts will have opportunities to check and evaluate the progress toward clearly defined goals. We will conduct no scheduled training until EagleEye Analysts has had a chance to verify our ability to achieve the results desired.

Figure 5 shows the program deliverables. Our record of past performance with other aerial/satellite photography clients is located in the appendix.

Figure 5
Deliverables for EagleEye Analysts Training Program

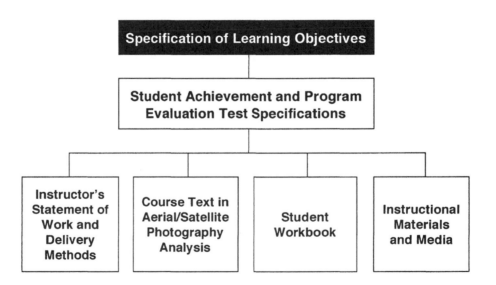

After program objectives and evaluation criteria have been clearly described and approved by representatives from EagleEye Analysts, we will design course methods and media. Scheduled training will not begin until deliverables have been inspected and accepted. EagleEye Analysts can be assured that the design is objective-driven and effective.

Exercise 8-2 continues on the next page.

References

1. Gagne, R.M. (20XX). *Designing Instructional Programs.* Hillsdale, NJ: Capital Publishing.

   Earl, C.M. (20XX). *Instruction in Action.* Hillsdale, NJ: Capital Publishing.

2. Miller, D.D. (20XX). *Training Designed for Aerial/ Satellite Photography Analysis.* (In the appendix of this proposal.)

3. Wilson, B.G. (20XX). Techniques for Teaching Technical Subjects. *Journal of Training and Development,* (18)1, 2–5.

4. Kemp, J. (20XX). Instructional Design Process. NY: Harper Publishing.

   Schiff, S. (20XX). Instructional Systems Design. *Journal of Instructional Development,* (19)2, 14–21.

5. Position titles and comprehensive responsibilities of all project staff are provided in the appendix.

6. Specific examples of program documents to be used in this project as well as materials developed for other satellite photography analysis clients are provided in the appendix.

Exercise 8-2 continues on the next page.

Exercise 8-2

EagleEye Analysts

Evaluate Two Proposals

Use this form to evaluate Technical Trainers, Inc.'s proposal on pp. 226–240.

Proposal Scoring Sheet for Technical Trainers, Inc.

Ratings

Superior	I am convinced that this is a capable training firm. They have a sound philosophy and approach.
Good	I think this training firm might be able to do the job, but I would not select them without asking more questions.
Marginal	I am not persuaded that this training firm could do the job. Their plan is unclear and lacking in important details.
Poor	I am convinced that this training firm cannot do the job.

Evaluation Criteria

Directions: Evaluate the proposal on the following criteria.

1. Does the firm's training philosophy seem appropriate to EagleEye Analysts' needs?

   Rating:_____

2. Does the firm present a sound training program based on a clear understanding of recent evidence from the literature?

   Rating:_____

3. Are proposed deliverables clearly described, and do they appear to be adequate?

   Rating:_____

4. Has the firm proposed an appropriately organized project team?

   Rating:_____

5. Are you persuaded that this firm has a sound approach overall?

   Rating:_____

Recommendation: Yes   No

Evaluator's name: _____

Exercise 8-2 continues on the next page.

Exercise 8-2: Evaluating Two Proposals

Technical Trainers, Inc.'s Proposal

The focus of Technical Trainers, Inc.'s business since 1991 has been developing and conducting training courses in aerial/satellite photography analysis addressing the needs of both industry and government for audiences reflecting a wide range of professional orientation and experience. This section of our proposal describes the teaching philosophy, capabilities, techniques, and modes of instruction employed by Technical Trainers, Inc. in presenting training courses.

Instructional Methodology

Technical Trainers, Inc.'s Approach

Aerial/satellite photography has traditionally been taught in lecture format, with the occasional use of samples, films, or case studies to retain student interest and illustrate practical applications. Technical Trainers, Inc., on the other hand, has designed training courses that emphasize experiential learning and effectively use instructional techniques and media. To ensure effective implementation, we have retained individuals who are comfortable in leading dynamic participant-oriented, rather than passive instructor-oriented, training sessions.

Technical Trainers, Inc. favors the use of case studies, simulations, and other practical exercises. Such exercises can be used effectively to "break up" or "wrap up" instructor presentations and class discussions: first, participants are presented with concepts, policies, and procedures; then, an exercise is used to illustrate application. However, it is a mistake to employ practical exercises solely in this manner. We have found that participants need opportunities to learn by doing—that is, opportunities to identify, through experience, the problems that arise in the course of a certain task and then reflect on the experience and arrive at key learning points. When used in this way, exercises challenge and strengthen the ability of participants to exercise judgment in coping with situations they face on the job. Exercises provide practice in identifying and using resources, developing and weighing alternatives, and reaching and implementing decisions.

All courses presented by Technical Trainers, Inc:

- Present aerial/satellite photography analysis as a process with successive, interrelated steps.
- Devote an appropriate portion of class time to learning experiences in which participants encounter situations that typically arise on the job and in which they learn by doing.
- Use instructional techniques appropriate to the knowledge/skills being taught.
- Convey basic principles or needed guidance through introductory or summary lectures, coupled with visual aids to increase retention.
- Demonstrate procedures, such as completion of forms and other "paper skills," using step-by-step visual aids.

Exercise 8-2 continues on the next page.

- Simulate actual tasks to develop skills.
- Hone issue identification and decision-making abilities through recorded simulations and other activities based on actual cases.
- Improve research skills by providing, in the classroom, a comprehensive library of resource documents—all the references normally available in an aerial/satellite photography analysis office—which participants use in completing case studies and other activities.
- Develop communication skills through the use of role-playing.
- Use exercises as both skill-building and diagnostic tools.
- Use quizzes so participants can assess their own comprehension.
- Stress learning competencies that participants need to attain for successful workplace performance.
- Use the space and equipment provided by the instructional facility.

Variation in Approach from Course to Course

We believe that the interplay of four primary factors—(1) course length, (2) subject matter, (3) training objectives, and (4) class composition—shape the approach to be taken in designing and presenting a given course.

A one-day session aimed at orienting aerial/satellite photography analysts to their role and responsibility, for example, would necessarily rely on lecture/discussion, with ample opportunity for question-and-answer periods, and a limited number of exercises illustrating practical applications. A two-week course on basic aerial/satellite photography analysis principles and practices, however, would need to be highly experiential, taking participants through their responsibilities from A to Z, with a large amount of hands-on practice and substantial variety in instructional methods. An intensive case study and discussion approach, on the other hand, would be suitable for a one-week course in the subject for legal and management personnel.

The level of coverage that is intended—basic and advanced—is a critical aspect of the training objectives. The challenge of a basic-level course is "begin at the beginning"—ensuring that those who truly need a thorough, ground-level introduction to the subject matter get one—while at the same time maintaining a pace that challenges those with some knowledge and experience. Well-structured and skillfully led lecture/discussion/question-and-answer sessions are critical. So are exercises and quizzes that give participants frequent feedback. Group exercises tend to work better than individual exercises, in that less-experienced participants can work along with those who have more experience.

Even when all participants have been carefully screened or required to complete a basic course or courses as a prerequisite, the challenge of addressing varying levels of knowledge, experience, and interest inevitably arise in presenting an advanced course. Instructors must take care in establishing baseline information from which to launch into more sophisticated or complex treatments.

Exercise 8-2 continues on the next page.

Instructors must be clear in adhering to objectives and at the same time be flexible in working with individuals who need help in mastering the basics. Lectures/discussions can be faster-paced in basic courses. A greater proportion of coursework can be done on an individual basis and more responsibility given for homework assignments. Whatever the methods used, participants' knowledge, experience, and expertise must be acknowledged and respected.

Handling of Practical Exercises

Technical Trainers, Inc. sees the use of practical exercises as essential. To enhance interest and retention, such exercises should be used in all courses, even those of only one or two days' duration. Small exercise groups are usually best, as participants can learn much from their interaction with one another.

To be effective, exercises must be introduced properly. Participants must understand the purpose of the exercise and how it fits in with the overall learning objectives. Participants must also understand precisely what is expected from them, and the time frame in which they must work. Written instructions should be provided, but instructions should also be communicated by the instructor, with opportunities to ask questions before starting and while doing exercises. Instructors should be active observers while exercises are being done so as to become better acquainted with stumbling blocks and intervene to keep participants from going off in a totally nonproductive direction.

"Processing" of participants' solutions to problems posed by exercises is also critical. All Technical Trainers, Inc. instructors are skilled in encouraging participants to present outcomes of their work. They know how to question why each step presented was taken, reinforce creative thinking and good judgment, and allot adequate, but not excessive, time for discussion of each exercise.

Instructor's Skill and Style

We have found that no factor is as critical to the success of a training course as a skilled instructor. Further, we have discovered that the best instructors are those individuals who know their subject, know their audience, and have the ability to convey that they both know and care about each.

Technical Trainers, Inc. uses instructors who possess both technical expertise and highly developed instructional skills. Personal style is critical and each person's style is different. We have found, however, that the best instructors have certain characteristics and competencies in common:

- Ability to convey that, for the duration of the course, they are fully committed to helping participants master the subject at hand, however that can best be accomplished.

- Ability to help participants see specifically "what's in it for them"—how it will make them better at what they do, make their job easier for them, improve their work product, and the like.

Exercise 8-2 continues on the next page.

- Ability to perceive, as the class progresses, where participants' on-the-job problems actually lie and where reinforcement of information and skills is most critically needed—as well as flexibility in adapting the agenda and approach to meet those needs.

- Ability to capture interest and increase understanding by providing pertinent, realistic examples and illustrations.

- Ability to engender a classroom atmosphere of camaraderie and collaboration—despite the inevitably wide range of skill and interest levels that participants bring to the learning experience.

- Ability to make the learning process an active one, even when participants are in a listening mode (by raising thought-provoking questions and pausing to allow for participant responses).

It is these abilities, along with instructional format variations, that keep a class of adult participants interested, whether for one day or three weeks.

Skillful fielding of questions is another facet of an instructor's capability that both sustains class interest and enhances learning. Our instructors believe that asking questions is a vital element of the learning process—a class that raises questions is much to be preferred over one that sits back passively.

All Technical Trainers, Inc. instructors are adept at fielding questions:

- Creating an atmosphere where participants feel comfortable asking questions.

- Repeating/paraphrasing the question to make sure that all other participants hear it and, as necessary, to make sure that the instructor himself or herself understands its nature and purpose.

- Saying, "I don't know, but I'll get the answer and get back to you," when necessary, and then taking steps to get the information as promptly as possible (with assistance as needed from staff at the Technical Trainers, Inc. office).

- Achieving the appropriate balance between responsiveness to a given individual's often limited or tangential concerns and adherence to the overall class objectives and agenda.

Other Training Elements

Class Discussion

Class discussion plays a central role in Technical Trainers, Inc.'s approach to training. As we see it, all lectures should actually be lectures/discussions. As they present their material, our instructors elicit comments and questions from participants. Also, they are mindful of the fact that participants can often learn as much from one another as they can from the instructor. In processing the results of practical exercises, they encourage an interplay of ideas and approaches among the participants, intervening only as warranted to keep the discussion constructive and on track.

Exercise 8-2 continues on the next page.

Visual Aids

Our experience has shown that visual aids should be of two kinds: pre-prepared and generated-in-process. Pre-prepared visual aids include PowerPoint presentations, DVDs, and demonstration equipment. Through experience, we have developed the following guidelines concerning the use of visual aids:

- Visual aids must track the instructor's lesson plan and course materials.

- Their most effective use is generally in providing a coherent overview of coverage and highlighting key points.

- Overuse of visuals is just as much to be avoided as underuse.

- Participants may be given handouts mirroring visual aids for note-taking purposes, but only in instances where complex information (math needed in price analysis or cost analysis, for example) is being conveyed.

- Any DVD or video used must be relevant and current.

- All visual aids must be interesting to every participant.

Technical Trainers, Inc.'s design staff members use the most recent software to produce attractive, legible, and professional-quality instructional materials. We generally prefer to develop PowerPoint presentations because it is easy to change material quickly.

All Technical Trainers, Inc. instructors are adept not only at using pre-prepared visual aids but also at generating visual aids spontaneously during the instructional process. They frequently make flip charts for noting key points raised by class members and outlining examples; these aids are very useful in focusing attention and enhancing comprehension during class discussion. Technical Trainers, Inc. instructors are skilled in using recording equipment to record and play back class participant role-plays—an invaluable way of reinforcing interactive communication skills, especially negotiation techniques.

Pretests, Quizzes, and Examinations

Technical Trainers, Inc. endorses the use of pretests. Preliminary testing can provide the instructor with a valuable indicator of participants' initial knowledge levels. Pretests also alert participants to the course content and to inadequacies in their own mastery of it, thereby heightening their interest and participation. On the other hand, they can threaten, discourage, and "turn off" participants. To be effective, pretests must (1) represent course content, (2) be aimed at "middle-level" difficulty, and (3) be presented in a non-threatening manner. Instructors must explain the purpose of pretests from both the participants' and instructors' points of view. Pretest scores should be between the instructor and participant, not put on record, and should be provided to participants the first day of class. To make this possible, participants may be allowed to grade their own tests as the instructor reviews the answers; then, tests should be collected for verification of scores and reviewed by the instructor.

Exercise 8-2 continues on the next page.

We also favor the use of periodic quizzes, both written and oral, to reinforce key learning points and give participants needed feedback on their progress.

Technical Trainers, Inc. is experienced in constructing course examinations that are fair and valid indicators of both how well an individual has comprehended and retained the information conveyed in a course, and how well prepared he or she is to apply that information on the job. A well-designed examination is an outgrowth of a well-designed course: accurate analysis of the on-the-job competencies (knowledge, skills, and abilities) needed in a given subject area lays the groundwork for realistic learning objectives. Those learning objectives are, in turn, the basis for both sound lesson plans and valid tests of what has been learned. Technical Trainers, Inc. favors the use of multiple-choice test questions over true-false test questions, as they provide participants with greater direction, less chance of guessing correctly, and when devised with care, a more thought-provoking task. We employ the services of an expert in test construction who carefully screens question terminology and format.

Tailoring Teaching Methods to Learning Objectives

Instructional design experts, whether in public or private sectors, agree that there are three cardinal rules for successful course development and instruction and, consequently, good training.

1. *Establish learning objectives.* It must be clear, from the outset, what participants are expected to know at the conclusion of the course.

2. *Teach to reach the learning objectives.* The plans the instructor develops or uses during the course must be sufficiently flexible that the style of teaching can be tailored to suit participants who constitute a particular class and learning experience.

3. *Test for achievement of the learning objectives.* Test results must demonstrate that participants have acquired the skills and knowledge they need to operate competently within the course area.

Technical Trainers, Inc. instructors use various techniques to ensure participant and instructor success in any class situation. These techniques are not, of course, used wholesale in every teaching situation. Rather, a skillful instructor will use a combination of those techniques to ensure a learning environment that accomplishes the course learning objectives.

<u>Motivation</u>

Students must enter the course emotionally prepared to learn, or the teacher must stimulate the desire to learn. Participants can be warmed up for a lesson by doing an activity that starts them thinking in the way that they will be asked to think during the course. The Technical Trainers, Inc. instructor will use this method to determine the participants' backgrounds, positions and organizational affiliations, individual strengths and weaknesses, and the like. The instructor will then adjust lesson plans to meet the needs of participants.

Exercise 8-2 continues on the next page.

Application and Participation

The more relevant a task is to the participants' world, the easier it is to learn. Based on information obtained about participants at the beginning of the first day of class, the instructor will make explicit references to participants' work experiences as a way of connecting content with participants' experience, or in some other way embed the content in the participants' framework of meaning. It is critical that students operate, respond, move about, and talk during the course of the learning experiences embodied in the principle of active participation.

Goal Setting

The Technical Trainers, Inc. instructor may involve students in goal setting; the instructor could ask them what they expect to get from the course and what they plan to do with what they learn. When students become involved in goal setting for their learning, they learn more, and both their motivation to accomplish and their ability to self-evaluate increase.

Role-Playing

Students should practice new skills in the setting and manner in which they will be used in real life. The instructor may divide the class into small groups to enable them to participate in simulations of specific tasks that arise on the job. The use of recording is encouraged during these sessions. It is important that instructors provide detailed guidance in learning new tasks and withdraw such guidance gradually with demonstrated student proficiency.

Feedback and Self-Critiquing

Feedback to students on their work should be given as rapidly as possible after completion. Playing the recording of a practice session immediately after the experience and involving students in critiquing it is an example of immediate feedback. The instructor will ask questions throughout the session to see whether students understand the process, to correct errors in the process, and so on. At the conclusion of small-group problem-solving sessions, a useful approach is to have a representative from one the groups present the group's response to the problem. The instructor will ask questions and review key points of the lesson.

Positive Reinforcement

It is important during any question-and-answer session that the instructor never says, "That's wrong." Students get powerful messages from our responses to their answers, and it is these messages that influence the way they participate. As influential as an instructor's questions may be in getting students interested, in stretching their thinking, and in guiding discussions, the questions alone do not account for the quality of the discourse. The instructor must respond in a way that keeps students open and thinking rather than shut down and afraid.

Whatever the mix of instructional techniques, they must always be directed toward achieving the established learning objectives.

Exercise 8-2 continues on the next page.

Project Plan and Project Controls

Phase I: Training Materials Development

Our approach to completing Phase I—Training Materials Development—involves the following steps:

- Confirmation of objectives
- Development
- Review and finalization
- Production

Confirmation of Objectives

During a post-award meeting, we will meet with EagleEye personnel to:

- Establish and confirm detailed requirements and schedule Phase I tasks.
- Identify and obtain all published policy and procedural guidance applicable to the course material to be developed.
- Identify EagleEye personnel to be interviewed in developing course materials.
- Establish criteria for editorial style and format.
- Establish procedures for communications between Technical Trainers, Inc. and EagleEye analysts.

Development

A draft of each course manual will be developed by researchers/writers working closely with the Technical Trainers, Inc. Project Manager.

The Project Manager will meet with EagleEye personnel to define the outline, scope, and coverage of the course material and the course length.

The Project Manager will be cognizant of the current status and extent of completion of each objective and will report promptly to the Technical Trainers, Inc. Officer-in-Charge concerning any problems encountered or anticipated, with their proposed resolution, obtaining guidance from EagleEye as needed.

Review and Finalization

Complete drafts of each course manual will be submitted to EagleEye for review. Course manuals will be revised as necessary to incorporate any changes or additions requested by EagleEye and resubmitted in final form.

Production

Upon receipt from EagleEye that a draft is final and that no other changes need to be made, Technical Trainers, Inc. will produce the course material in final form, and deliver printed copies and computer files as called for by the contract.

Exercise 8-2 continues on the next page.

Time-Based Planning Chart

Attached, as Exhibit 1, is a time-based planning chart representing actions to complete the training materials.

Progress Reporting

All project staff members will be required to report the status of their assigned projects to the Project Manager on a weekly basis. In addition, any unforeseen developments that might impact the completion of a task will be reported to the Project Manager immediately.

Phase II: Conducting the Training Program

Our approach to performance of Phase II—Conducting the Training Program—is based on these proven principles:

- An in-place, dedicated organization of professional and support resources is the key to effective management of a training program.

- Effective administration and review are critical to program success.

- Continuity in instructors is vital to maintaining consistency and quality of classroom presentations.

- Production processes must be available to support the preparation, production, and distribution of course materials.

Orientation of Instructors

The Project Manager together with a team of researchers/writers, will conduct an orientation briefing for all instructors. The briefing will cover an overview of:

- EagleEye's mission, organization, and operating environment.

- Training curriculum and specific materials for each course.

- Issues of critical concern to EagleEye management.

The Highest Level of Teaching Skills

Technical Trainers, Inc. employs only instructors of proven quality and dynamism. Students evaluate the class and instructor at the conclusion of each course. The Project Manager "sits in" on courses and reviews all instructor evaluation forms and student test results; based on this first-hand observation and student feedback, instructors are given specific directions and advice as to what might be needed to improve their performance. Any instructor receiving an average evaluation score of less than 8 (on a scale of 1 to 10) receives counseling to improve performance. Any instructor receiving less than an average rating of 7 on two occasions, or 5 on one occasion is immediately replaced. Technical Trainers, Inc.'s instructors, over a period of years, have consistently achieved course evaluation ratings averaging 9 and above. Student comments have consistently demonstrated enthusiasm for courses presented by Technical Trainers, Inc.'s instructors.

Exercise 8-2 continues on the next page.

<u>Timely Production of Course Materials</u>

Technical Trainers, Inc. publishes its own course materials and produces online courses for a number of customers.

Technical Trainers, Inc. will provide all services and materials, including tabbed binders with a complete set of course materials for each student scheduled to attend a particular course. Specifically, Technical Trainers, Inc. will take responsibility for:

- Assembling all materials for reproduction. Technical Trainers, Inc. will assure that all course materials are current and that all approved changes and updates have been incorporated into the package.

- Reproducing and assembling course materials (including printing, collating, and binding).

- Assuring quality. The Project Manager will perform a quality review of course material to ensure the highest standards of workmanship. Course material will also be inspected after production and before shipment.

- Packing and appropriate labeling of boxes before shipment.

- Storing all course materials at Technical Trainers, Inc. until the appropriate time for shipment.

- Shipment of course materials to the training site.

Technical Trainers, Inc. has a full-scale in-house production facility that can easily accommodate these requirements. Each month, Technical Trainers, Inc. runs 500,000 or more copies and produces hundreds of course packages.

Project Staffing

Phase I: Training Materials Development

For Phase I—Training Materials Development—we have proposed a core staff of researchers/writers selected on the basis of their previous successful experience on similar projects for Technical Trainers, Inc. Core staff will be available for the duration of the assignment. Additional fully qualified personnel may supplement core staff, if needed to complete several tasks concurrently.

Janice Esposito, Corporate Officer-in-Charge of Phase I, and Tim Reed, the Project Manager, have proven credentials and extensive experience on similar projects, as have the assigned researchers/writers. All these personnel have worked together on previous projects and have proven their ability to work together as a team.

Exercise 8-2 continues on the next page.

Phase II: Conducting the Training Program

For Phase II—Conducting the Training Program—we have assembled an experienced management and teaching team. Technical Trainers, Inc.'s president, Janice Esposito, will serve as Corporate Officer-in-Charge and will be fully accessible to the Project Manager, Guadalupe Sanchez. Reflecting the importance of this project to both Technical Trainers, Inc. and EagleEye, Ms. Esposito will also serve as a course instructor. Ms. Esposito's experience as Officer-in-Charge of the course materials development effort will greatly enhance her management of the teaching effort and will enable her to provide substantive guidance.

We have selected a core group of instructors who are subject-matter experts as well as seasoned teachers; they have consistently received outstanding ratings from their students and will bring a wealth of experience to the program. They will be available for the duration of the training program and will be supplemented by equally qualified teachers if needed to meet the requirements of multiple, simultaneous, or overlapping course presentations.

Course Administration

Technical Trainers, Inc.'s administrative staff is thoroughly experienced in all tasks associated with effective course administration, such as processing student enrollment forms, preparing class rosters, making travel arrangements for instructors, tabulating test and evaluation results, preparing and mailing course completion certificates, and getting the proper course materials to the place of instruction on time.

Staffing Plan

Exhibits 2 and 3 are our staffing charts for Phase I: Training Materials Development and Phase II: Conducting the Training Program. Résumés for project personnel and references for previous similar projects are located in the appendix.

Exercise 8-2 continues on the next page.

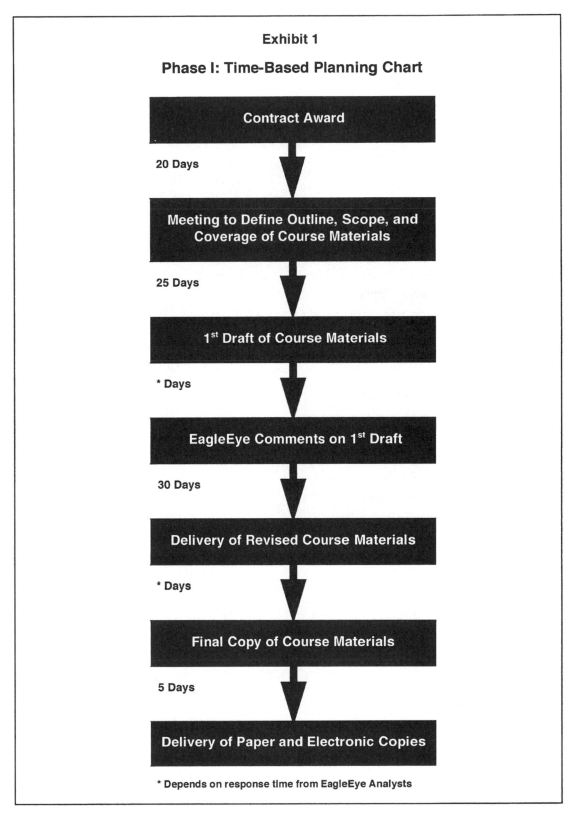

Exhibit 1

Phase I: Time-Based Planning Chart

Contract Award

20 Days

Meeting to Define Outline, Scope, and Coverage of Course Materials

25 Days

1st Draft of Course Materials

* Days

EagleEye Comments on 1st Draft

30 Days

Delivery of Revised Course Materials

* Days

Final Copy of Course Materials

5 Days

Delivery of Paper and Electronic Copies

* Depends on response time from EagleEye Analysts

Exercise 8-2 continues on the next page.

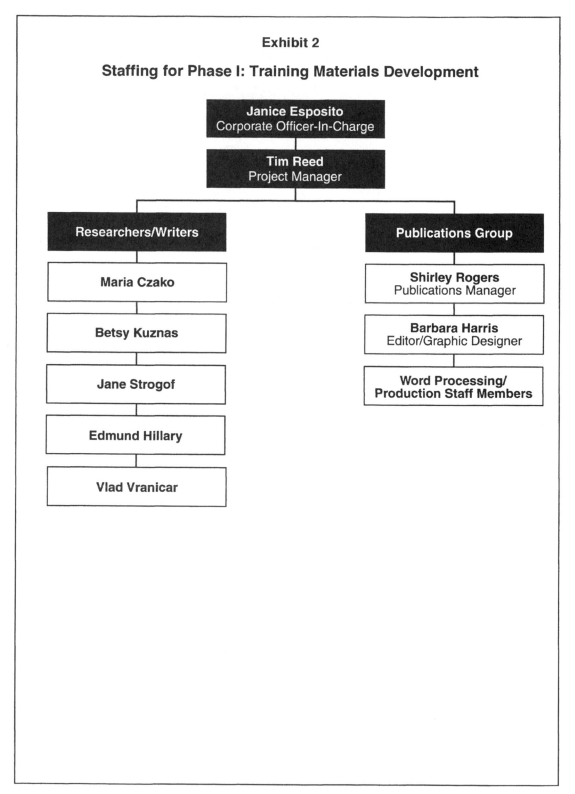

Exercise 8-2 continues on the next page.

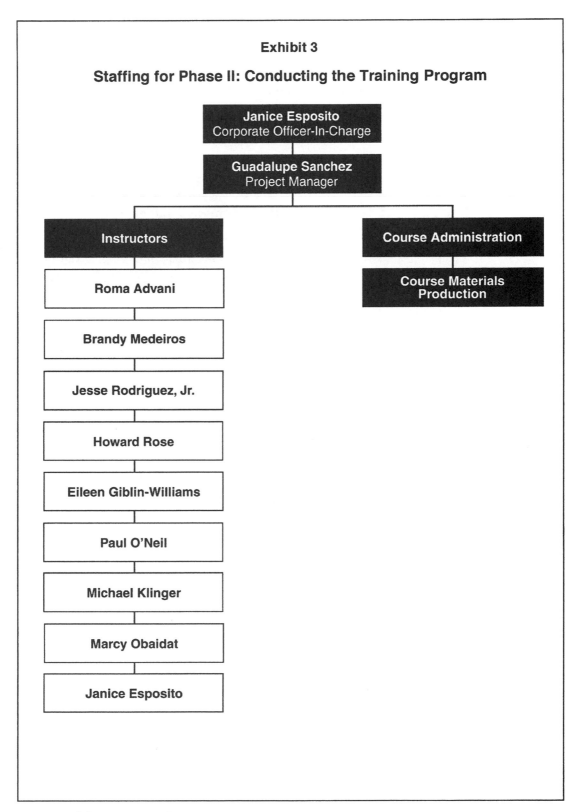

Exhibit 3

Staffing for Phase II: Conducting the Training Program

Janice Esposito
Corporate Officer-In-Charge

Guadalupe Sanchez
Project Manager

Instructors

Roma Advani

Brandy Medeiros

Jesse Rodriguez, Jr.

Howard Rose

Eileen Giblin-Williams

Paul O'Neil

Michael Klinger

Marcy Obaidat

Janice Esposito

Course Administration

Course Materials Production

Exercise 8-2 continues on the next page.

Bibliography

Baker, B. & Thomas, J.J. (20XX). *Evaluation and Assessment of Technical Training*. Chicago, IL: G. Disc Worldwide.

Lebec, L. (20XX). *Training for Entry-Level Employees in Technical Subjects*. Alexandria, VA: Capitol Publications.

Perez, M. (20XX). *Contemporary Aerial/Satellite Photography for Professionals*. Atlanta, GA: Get Smart Book Company.

Wilson, B.G. (20XX). *Industrial and Business Training*. New York: Springer Publishing.

Yu, P. (20XX). *Aerial/Satellite Photography for Professionals*. San Francisco: Browning Press.

Glossary

This glossary of terms is intended to help grant seekers understand basic terminology associated with grants, cooperative agreements, and procurement contracts. This glossary is not intended to override agency-specific definitions provided in federal and state guidelines.

Abstract—One-page proposal summary that highlights the features and benefits of the grant project.

Acquisition—Procurement function to fulfill a government agency's needs.

Allowable Costs—Project expenditures that are reasonable, allocable, and handled in a consistent manner according to the Office of Management and Budget circulars.

Amendment—Modification or change to a solicitation.

Appendix—Back section of a grant proposal that contains supplemental information too detailed to include in the main body of the application.

Application—Request for financial support of a project or activity that is submitted to a government agency.

Application Notice—Grant notice published in the *Federal Register* that includes (1) program rules and regulations, (2) guidelines for proposal development, (3) application forms, and (4) submission instructions. See Request for Proposal (RFP)/Request for Application (RFA).

Application Package—Complete solicitation (includes forms and other documents) used to develop a grant application.

Application Package Template—One or more forms that can be reused with multiple grant application packages.

Appropriation—Funds authorized by Congress that are provided to a federal agency to support grant awards.

Assurances and Certifications—Government agency conditions agreed to by an organization when submitting a prospective grant proposal. These may include antidiscrimination requirements; drug-free workplace requirements; lobbying restrictions; environmental protection assurances; public employee standards; health, safety, and welfare of human subjects; and other assurances and certifications that must be met by the organization responding to solicitations.

Audit—Systematic review of internal grant accounting practices to determine if financial reports are accurate, reasonable, and fair.

Authorized Organization Representative (AOR)—Individual who has the authority to sign required forms and submit grant applications to a government agency.

Boilerplate—Generic narrative and budget materials used and reused in preparation of grant application drafts.

Broad Agency Announcement (BAA)—Federal agency announcement or competitive solicitation that invites proposals from funding seekers.

Budget—Estimated costs to complete a grant project. Budgets include direct and indirect (facilities and administrative) costs, if allowed. Budgets generally consist of an itemized list of expenses and a justification of why the expenses are necessary.

Budget Detail—Brief parenthetical explanation used to clarify project expenditures (e.g., three computers @ $1,500 = $4,500).

Budget Narrative—Thorough written explanation and justification of unusual or complex cost expenditures for a proposed grant project.

Catalog of Federal Domestic Assistance (CFDA)—Publication and online database that lists the domestic assistance programs of all federal agencies. The *CFDA* provides information about the program's authorization, eligibility requirements, fiscal details, regulations, and award process. The *CFDA* uses a federal identification number that consists of a two-digit prefix that indicates the agency and a three-digit code for the authorized program.

Central Contractor Registration (CCR)—Primary vendor database for the U.S. federal government, which validates applicant information and electronically shares the secure and encrypted data with the federal agencies' finance offices to facilitate paperless payments through electronic funds transfer (EFT). The CCR stores the grant applicant's organizational information, allowing Grants.gov to verify identity and to pre-fill organizational information on grant applications.

Clinical Trial—Study designed to answer specific questions about the effects of specific biomedical or behavioral interventions on human subjects or animals.

Closeout—Administrative and financial wrap-up tasks associated with completing a discretionary grant or cooperative agreement.

Code of Federal Regulations (CFR)—Document published by the National Archives and Records Administration that includes a collection of general and permanent rules for agencies of the federal government.

Cognizant Agency—Federal agency responsible for negotiating and approving indirect cost rates for institutions on behalf of all federal agencies. Cognizance is assigned to the agency that provided the most funds to the institution over the past three years.

Community of Science (COS)—Information database designed to help grant seekers identify appropriate funding sources.

Compliance Checklist—List of requirements obtained from a solicitation that is used as a guide in developing a grant application.

Conflict of Interest—Situation in which a grant reviewer (or a relative or partner, etc.) has an interest, or appears to have an interest, in the funding of a grant application, or in which a grant reviewer has an affiliation with a grant applicant or other conflict that may lead to or suggest influence in the government agency's decision.

Consultant—Outside professional expert hired to provide advice or to assist fund-seeking institutions in completing specific project tasks for a fee.

Continuation Grant—Funding awarded to a grant recipient beyond the initial budget period of a multi-year discretionary grant or cooperative agreement.

Contract—Legal document indicating the amount as well as the conditions of an award for a grant or cooperative agreement. A fully executed contract is signed by the appropriate government agency's representative and the grantee's institutional representative.

Contractual Services—Direct costs that include consultant fees, rentals, tuition, service contracts, equipment repairs, and other purchased services.

Cooperative Agreement—Financial assistance awarded to a recipient to accomplish a proposed project where substantial involvement is expected between the federal agency and recipient during the performance period.

Cost-Plus-Fixed-Fee Contract—Contract where the funding seeker has minimal responsibility for performance costs and the negotiated fee (profit) is fixed.

Cost-Reimbursement Contract—Contract that provides payment of allowable incurred costs to the extent prescribed in the contract.

Cost Sharing—Project costs not borne by the federal government. Cost sharing is the difference between the actual cost and amount requested from the government agency. Cost sharing may be mandatory as part of the eligibility requirement for proposal submission or voluntarily done by the grant-seeking institution. Cost sharing includes matching and in-kind contributions that are documented and auditable.

Data Universal Numbering System (DUNS)—Unique nine-character identifying number issued by Dun and Bradstreet and used as an identification and tracking number often required on the cover sheet of grant applications.

Date of Completion—Date when all work under an award is completed, or the date on the award letter or amended document that indicates when the awarding agency sponsorship ends.

Direct Costs—Specific costs necessary to complete a proposed sponsored project (e.g., personnel salaries and fringe benefits, travel and per diem, equipment and expendable supplies, contractual services, and other direct costs).

Disallowable Costs—Charges to an award that agency reviewers determine are unallowable in accordance with applicable federal cost principles or other award terms and conditions.

Equipment—Tangible nonexpendable items having an expected service life of two or more years and costs at least $5,000 per unit.

Evaluation Plans—Procedures used to measure the success of a grant project's goals/objectives.

Facilities and Administrative (F&A) or Indirect Costs—Costs that cannot be identified with or charged to a specific project. F&A expenditures include facility operation and maintenance costs; utility costs; general administrative costs (e.g., accounting, payroll, and purchasing); library costs; office of sponsored programs administration costs; and department administrative costs associated with grant projects. Typically, indirect costs are calculated as a fixed percentage rate of the total direct costs or modified total direct costs.

FedBizOpps.gov (FBO)—Single point of electronic public access to government-wide procurement contract opportunities.

Federal Acquisition Regulations (FAR)—Document used by federal agencies that contains uniform policies and procedures for governing acquisition activity.

Federal Register (FR)—Daily publication by the National Archives and Records Administration that lists all federal agency regulations and legal notices, including details about grant competitions.

Field Readers—Agency reviewers or peer reviewers who evaluate discretionary grant applications. Readers are selected based on education, experience, and geographic representation.

Financial Report—Report by the grant recipient that indicates the amount of expenditures made during a budget period. Quarterly and annual expenditure reports are often required by government agencies.

Firm-Fixed-Price Contract—Contract where the recipient has full responsibility for performance costs and resulting profit or loss.

Fixed-Price Contract—Contract that provides a firm, predetermined (fixed) price for work specified in the proposal.

Formative Evaluation—Monitoring the initial and ongoing progress of a grant project.

Freedom of Information Act (FOIA)—Administrative procedures act that allows the public to have access to agency records maintained by the government.

Fringe Benefits—Part of personnel costs that include medical and dental coverage, life insurance, workman's compensation and unemployment, Medicare, and retirement pension.

Full-Time Equivalent (FTE)—Cost to replace faculty or staff members. One full-time equivalent is one person working eight hours per day, five days per week, for the entire year.

Funding Opportunity Announcement—Government agency announcement to award discretionary grants or cooperative agreements, usually as a result of competition for funds. Funding opportunity announcements are also known as program announcements, notices of funding availability, solicitations, or other names depending on the agency. Funding opportunity announcements can be found at Grants.gov and at the government agency's website.

Gantt Chart—Project planning chart often used by experienced grant writers to indicate specific tasks to be accomplished within a time frame.

Gift—Voluntary transfer of property to another made gratuitously and without consideration.

Goals/Objectives—Measurable project outcomes that relate to the government agency's wants and needs. Goals/objectives indicate what will be done, under what conditions, and how the target population will be affected as a result of the proposed activities.

Grant—Financial assistance to an eligible recipient to accomplish a proposed project where there is no substantial involvement between the federal agency and recipient during the performance period. Grant notices inviting applications are published in the *Federal Register*.

Grant (Continuation)—Additional funding awarded to a recipient for a specific time after the initial budget year of a multi-year grant.

Grant (Discretionary)—Competitive grant where a government agency has the discretion to determine the recipients and award amounts. Awards are made to those institutions whose applications ranked the highest based on review criteria published in the *Federal Register*. Award decisions are based on a peer review process.

Grant (Mandatory, Entitlement, or Formula)—General revenue or federal pass-through funds allocated by state agencies to institutions based on a predetermined formula. Agencies make awards so long as regulatory conditions are met.

Grant Award Notification (GAN)—Official notification of award signed by a program official who is authorized to obligate funds on behalf of the government agency. The GAN states the amount of the award, contact information, and the conditions of the award for a discretionary grant or cooperative agreement.

Grantee—Individual or organization that has been awarded financial assistance under an agency's discretionary grant program.

Grants.gov—Web portal that provides free online service to find and apply for federal grants from 26 grant-making agencies.

Human Subjects—Living individuals about whom an investigator collects data through intervention or personal interaction.

In-House Reviewers—In-house staff members who review each proposal draft to ensure that writers have addressed the evaluation criteria in the RFP/RFA and present a comprehensive, coherent, and persuasively written document. In-house reviewers must make sure the proposal is compliant and that all information required by the government agency is included in the grant narrative and budget.

In-Kind Contribution—Non-financial donations (equipment, materials, or services of recognized value) that are offered to the proposed project from the grant-seeking institution, partners, and/or local business and industry.

Indirect Costs—See Facilities and Administrative costs.

Indirect Cost-Rate Agreement—Organizational indirect cost rate percentage negotiated with a cognizant government agency (as prescribed in OMB Circular A-21) and used with other government agencies when applying for grants. This established indirect cost rate percentage is honored by other agencies when organizations apply for grants.

Informed Consent—Participants have been adequately informed about the research effort and participate willingly.

Institutional Review Board (IRB)—Institutional committee that is responsible for reviewing grant proposals to ensure that no harm will come to human subjects in sponsored research efforts.

Key Personnel—Primary personnel (e.g., project director or principal investigator and other senior project staff members) who are responsible for the successful completion of a proposed grant project.

Letter of Commitment—Letter from individuals or organizations that will be actively involved in the proposed project. The letter should document specific financial and non-financial commitments (personnel time, office equipment, materials, supplies, building space, etc.) to the grant project.

Letter of Intent—Letter required by some government agencies prior to submission of a full proposal so agency staff can gauge the size and range of the competition. The letter usually asks for the names of key personnel and institutions and a brief synopsis of the proposed project.

Letter of Support—Letter from individuals or organizations within or outside the institution applying for the grant that are not actively involved in the proposed project. The letter should endorse the merit of the proposed grant project.

Matching Funds—Possible government agency requirement that obligates the grant-seeking institution to make a financial commitment to the proposed project.

Methods/Activities—Specific tasks and procedures to be completed to meet proposed project goals and objectives. Methods/activities are a project means to meet the goals/objectives (project ends).

Model Solicitation—Preliminary solicitation developed by a funding seeker that is based on information obtained from intelligence-gathering activities and an analysis of similar solicitations. The "model" solicitation is used as a proposal guide until the government agency's RFP/RFA is released.

Modified Total Direct Costs (MTDC)—Total direct costs that are modified by excluding equipment and capital expenditures, patient care, tuition remission, rental costs, scholarships, fellowships, and subawards in excess of $25,000 for purposes of calculating indirect costs.

Negotiation—Discussion about a grant proposal prior to a funding decision. Negotiation may involve answering questions to clarify points in a proposal, to correct errors, or to respond to changes suggested by the government agency. Negotiation may require written and/or oral responses.

Office of Management and Budget (OMB) Circulars—Policy guidelines that provide instructions about the administration of federal grants and cooperative agreements.

Partners—Other institutions, business and industry, and/or local community organizations that have made financial and/or in-kind commitments to assist with the proposed grant project.

Peer Review—Objective review of grant applications by professional peers.

Per Diem—Cost per day that an organization allows an individual to spend on meals and incidental expenses during travel. The U.S. General Service Administration establishes per diem rates for most U.S. cities on an annual basis.

Performance Period—Amount of time authorized by a government agency to complete a grant project. Also referred to as the project period.

Performance Report—Report of activities performed during a specified budget period.

Person Hours—Total number of hours an individual will dedicate to a funded grant project.

Point of Contact (POC)—Government agency staff member to be contacted for questions about a specific grant solicitation.

Postsubmission Activities—Activities that occur after the grant application is submitted to the government agency.

Pre-application Conference—Conference held by government agency personnel to answer questions and provide explanations regarding a solicitation. Information provided at the conference is usually published and disseminated to all RFP/RFA recipients. The pre-application conference may also be referred to as a bidder's conference or technical workshop.

Preliminary Budget—Grant proposal budget that is based on a "model" solicitation and other intelligence gathering activities and is prepared prior to the release of the RFP/RFA.

Preliminary Proposal (Developed by the Funding Seeker)—Grant proposal narrative that is based on a "model" solicitation and other intelligence-gathering activities and is prepared prior to release of the RFP/RFA.

Preliminary Proposal (Required by a Government Agency)—Proposal required by an agency prior to submission of a full grant application. The content of the preliminary proposal will vary from agency to agency. The decision about a preliminary proposal will determine the principal investigator's eligibility to submit a full grant application. Only individuals who submitted favorable preliminary submissions are invited to submit full grant applications

Principal Investigator—Key staff member who will manage the grant project and is responsible for ensuring that all conditions of the agreement are met. See Project Director.

Problem/Need Statement—Persuasive essay that convinces agency reviewers that a problem exists that needs to be resolved or improved. A problem/need statement must establish the importance of the problem and identify the individuals to be served by the proposed project.

Procurement Contract—Legal instrument for acquiring products or services governed by the Federal Acquisition Regulations (FAR) for the direct benefit of or use by the government.

Program Announcement—Government agency's announcement or solicitation used to announce funding opportunities for a specific program area.

Program or Project Officer—Designated government agency officer responsible for the technical and programmatic aspects of a specific grant, cooperative agreement, or procurement contract.

Project Costs—Allowable costs incurred by a recipient to accomplish the objectives of grant award during the project period.

Project Director— Key staff member who will manage the grant project and is responsible for ensuring that all conditions of the agreement are met. See Principal Investigator

Project Period—Period established in the grant award notification letter, which indicates when the approved government agency support begins and ends.

Proposal—Grant application developed in response to a government solicitation. Proposals usually include information about the problem/need, goals/objectives, methods/activities, evaluation plans, and budget.

Proposal Director—Person chosen to lead the development of a grant proposal in response to a specific government agency solicitation.

Proposal Outline—Outline of the grant proposal narrative to be completed by writers. Proposal outlines should correspond with RFP/RFA requirements and identify the proposal authors for each narrative section to be written.

Proposal Prospectus—Planning tool used to communicate basic grant project ideas developed before proposal writing.

Proposal Review Process—Process where agency reviewers evaluate proposals and make recommendations to a government agency about which grant applications should receive funding.

Proposal Schedule—Schedule used in grant development to determine when proposal writing, reviewing, and rewriting as well as budgeting, reviewing, and rebudgeting will take place. Schedules must also consider the time for producing, assembling, and submitting grant applications.

Proprietary Information—Confidential or privileged information used in grant applications. This information must be clearly labeled "proprietary" to maintain unauthorized access to such confidential material.

Quality Control Checks—Checks after the grant application has been produced/assembled and reproduced to ensure a complete and error-free submission.

Reasonable—Reflects the action of a prudent person.

Recipient—Individual or organization that receives financial assistance from a government agency to complete a sponsored project or program.

Request for Proposal (RFP) / Request for Application (RFA)—Solicitation used to obtain grant applications from prospective organizations.

Solicitation—Request for Proposal (RFP) or Request for Application (RFA) that invites organizations to submit grant proposals in response to the government agency requirements and conditions.

Sponsored Project—Project or activity funded from a government or non-government source.

Standard Forms—Standard government forms that are completed and submitted as part of a grant application.

Strategy Meeting—Initial meeting of grant proposal writers and reviewers that serves as a strategy session for responding to a solicitation. Discussion should focus on writing assignments and other responsibilities, adhering to a proposal schedule, questions to the government agency, and the formulation of budget assumptions.

Style Sheet—Format and style guidelines that writers and editors follow in preparing a grant proposal. A style sheets usually includes guidelines for text, levels of headings, references, illustrations, and terminology specific to a solicitation.

Subcontract—Written agreement that transfers a portion of funds from a grant or contract to another institution or organization in exchange for specific services.

Subcontractor—Outside organizations or personnel that agree to work with the funding seeker to complete part of the project, if the grant is awarded.

Submission Window—Designated periods of time during which grant applications are accepted for review.

Summative Evaluation—Process of judging the overall quality or worth of a grant at the end of a defined project period.

Suspension—Post-award action by a government agency that temporarily withdraws the agency's financial assistance under an award, pending corrective action by the recipient or pending a decision to terminate the award.

Synopsis of Funding Opportunity Announcement—Summary information extracted from or based on a funding opportunity announcement that is electronically posted at Grants.gov. The Grants.gov synopsis includes a direct link to the full grant opportunity announcement.

Teaming Agreement—Written document that identifies the conditions between two or more organizations that plan to respond to a solicitation.

Technical Report—Narrative report on the progress and/or status of a government-funded project. May also be referred to as a project report.

Termination—Cancellation of government agency sponsorship, in whole or in part, under an agreement at any time prior to the date of completion.

Total Direct Costs (TDC)—All direct costs charged to a project.

Total Project Costs (TPC)—Total allowable direct and indirect costs to complete an approved project.

Trading Partner Identification Number (TPIN)—Restricted access number assigned by the Central Contractor Registry (CCR).

Transmittal (Cover) Letter—Cover letter (signed by an upper-level administrator) that is included with a grant application sent to a government agency. Transmittal (cover) letters should include the RFP/RFA or *CFDA* number and identify the contents of each proposal. In addition, the transmittal (cover) letter should identify a knowledgeable contact person who can be reached for possible questions.

Unallowable Costs—Costs determined to be unallowable in accordance with the cost principles or other conditions identified in the grant award.

Uniform Contract Format—Organizational format (parts and sections) for a procurement contract solicitation.

Unsolicited Proposal—Proposal submitted to a government or non-government sponsor that is not in response to a agency solicitation.

Work Breakdown Structure—Hierarchical analysis of RFP/RFA requirements into basic components. Work breakdown structures provide an understanding of the underlying nature of the government agency's needs as well as the relationship among RFP/RFA parts.

Acronyms

A-21	OMB Circular 21	**FAR**	Federal Acquisition Regulations
A-110	OMB Circular 110	**FBO**	Federal Business Opportunities
A-133	OMB Circular 133	**FEDIX**	Federal Information Exchange
ADA	American Disabilities Act	**FOA**	Funding Opportunity Announcement
AOR	Authorized Organization Representative	**FOIA**	Freedom of Information Act
BAA	Broad Agency Announcement	*FR*	*Federal Register*
CAS	Cost Accounting Standards	**FTE**	Full-Time Equivalent
CBD	Commerce Business Daily	**FY**	Fiscal Year
CCR	Central Contractor Registration	**F&A**	Facilities and Administrative
CEO	Chief Executive Officer	**GAN**	Grant Award Notification
CFDA	*Catalog of Federal Domestic Assistance*	**GMO**	Grants Management Office
CFO	Chief Financial Officer	**GPO**	Government Printing Office
CFR	Code of Federal Regulations	**GPRA**	Government Performance and Results Act
CO	Contracting Officer	**GSA**	General Services Administration
COLA	Cost-of-Living Allowance	**HBCU**	Historically Black College and University
COS	Community of Science	**IDC**	Indirect Costs
DC	Direct Costs	**IFB**	Invitation for Bid
DUNS	Data Universal Numbering System	**IRB**	Institutional Review Board
EFT	Electronic Funds Transfer	**MOU**	Memorandum of Understanding
EOE	Equal Opportunity Employer	**MTDC**	Modified Total Direct Costs

NAICS North American Industry
Classification System

NARA National Archives and Records
Administration

OMB Office of Management and Budget

ORC Operational Research Consultants

OSP Office of Sponsored Programs

PA Program Application

PD Project Director

PDF Portable Document Format

PI Principal Investigator

POC Point of Contact

RFA Request for Application

RFC Request for Comment

RFP Request for Proposal

RFQ Request for Quotation

SF Standard Form

SGA Solicitation for Grant Application

SOW Statement of Work

TDC Total Direct Costs

TPC Total Project Costs

TPIN Trading Partner Identification
Number

TOC Table of Contents

URL Universal Resource Locator

WBS Work Breakdown Structure

Resources

Books

Bauer, D.G. (2003). *The "How To" Grants Manual: Successful Grantseeking Techniques for Obtaining Public and Private Grants*. Westport, CT: Praeger Publishers.

Brewer, E.W. & Achilles, C.M. (2008). *Finding Funding: Grantwriting From Start to Finish, Including Project Management and Internet Use*. Thousand Oaks, CA: Corwin.

Browning, B. (2005). *Grant Writing for Dummies, 2nd Edition*. Hoboken, NJ: Wiley Publishing.

Browning, B. (2008). *Perfect Phrases for Writing Grant Proposals*. New York: McGraw-Hill.

Carlson, M. (2002). *Winning Grants Step by Step: The Complete Workbook for Planning, Developing and Writing Successful Proposals, 2nd Edition*. San Francisco, CA: Jossey-Bass.

Carter-Black, A. (2006). *Getting Grants: The Complete Manual of Proposal Development and Administration*. Canada: Self-Counsel Press, Inc.

Coley, S. M. & Scheinberg, C.A. (2008). *Proposal Writing: Effective Grantsmanship, 3rd Edition*. Thousand Oaks, CA: Sage.

Council for the Advancement and Support of Education. (2004). *Management and Reporting Standards for Annual Giving and Campaigns in Educational Fund Raising, 3rd Edition*. Washington, DC: CASE.

Council for Resource Development. (2007). *Federal Funding to Two-Year Colleges Report 2007–2008*. Washington, DC: Council for Resource Development.

DuBose, M., Davis, M. & Black, A. (2005). *Developing Successful Grants: How to Turn Your Ideas into Reality*. Columbia, SC: Research Associates, Inc.

Gerin, W. (2006). *Writing the NIH Grant Proposal: A Step-by-Step Guide*. Thousand Oaks, CA: Sage.

Hall, M.S. & Howlett, S. (2003). *Getting Funded: The Complete Guide to Writing Grant Proposals*. Portland, OR: Portland State University.

Harris, D. (2007). *The Complete Guide to Writing Effective and Award-Winning Grants.* Ocala, FL: Atlantic Publishing Group, Inc.

Henson, K.T. (2003). *Grant Writing in Higher Education: A Step-by-Step Guide.* Boston: Allyn & Bacon.

Karsh, E. & Fox, A.S. (2006). *The Only Grant Writing Book You'll Ever Need: An Insider's Guide.* New York: Carroll & Graf Publishes.

Knowles, C. (2002). *The First-Time Grantwriters Guide to Success.* Thousand Oaks, CA: Corwin.

Kulakowski, E.C. & Chronister, L.U. (2006). *Research Administration and Management.* Sudbury, MA: Jones and Bartlett.

Locke, L.F., Spirduso, W.W., & Silverman, S.J. (2007). *Proposals That Work: A Guide for Planning Dissertations and Grant Proposals.* Thousand Oaks, CA: Sage.

Miner, L.E. & Miner, J.T. (2003). *Proposal Planning and Writing, Third Edition.* Westport, CT: Greenwood Publishing.

Miner, T.J. & Miner, L.E. (2005). *Models of Proposal Planning and Writing* Westport, CT: Praeger Publishers.

New Carter, C. & Quick, J.A. (2003). *How to Write a Grant Proposal.* New York: John Wiley.

Reif-Lehrer, L. (2004). *Grant Application Writers Handbook, 4th Edition.* Boston: Jones and Bartlett.

Scheir, L.M. & Dewey, W.L. (2007). *The complete writing guide to NIH Behavioral Science Grants.* London: Oxford University.

Seligman, R.P. (2008). *Sponsored Research Administration: A Guide to Effective Strategies and Recommended Practices.* Washington DC: Atlantic Information Services and National Council of University Research Administrators.

Slocum, J.M. (2006). Federal Research Contracts. In E.C. Kulakowski & L.U. Chronister (Eds.), *Research Administration and Management.* (pp. 325-353). Sudbury, MA: Jones and Bartlett Publishers.

Thomson, W. (2007). *Complete Idiot's Guide to Grant Writing, 2nd Edition.* New York: Alpha.

Ward, D. (2006). *Writing Grant Proposals that Win.* Sudbury, MA: Jones and Bartlett.

Funding Source Publications

Aid for Education Report
CD Publications
8204 Fenton Street
Silver Spring, MD 20910-9935
Phone: 301-588-6380 or 800-666-6380
Fax: 301-588-6385
http://www.cdpublications.com

Education Grants Alert
LRP Publications
360 Hiatt Drive
Palm Beach Gardens, FL 33418
Phone: 561-622-6520
Fax: 561-662-9060
http://www.shoplrp.com

Federal Assistance Monitor
CD Publications
8204 Fenton Street
Silver Spring, MD 20910-9935
Phone: 301-588-6380 or 800-666-6380
Fax: 301-588-6385
http://www.cdpublications.com

Federal Grants and Contracts Weekly
LRP Publications
360 Hiatt Drive
Palm Beach Gardens, FL 33418
Phone: 561-622-6520
Fax: 561-662-9060
http://www.shoplrp.com

Federal Register
U.S. Government Printing Office
Superintendent of Documents
P.O. Box 371954
Pittsburgh, PA 15250-7954
Phone: 202-512-1800
Fax: 202-512-2250
http://www.archives.gov/federal-register/the-federal-register/about.html

The Grantsmanship Center Magazine
1125 W. Sixth Street, Fifth Floor
P.O. Box 17220
Los Angeles, CA 90017
Phone: 213-482-9860
Fax: 213-482-9863
http://www.tgci.com

Note: Every effort has been made to provide accurate website information. All website URLs were checked and accurate at the time of publication.

Funding Source Search Engines

Community of Science (COS)
http://www.cos.com

Catalog of Federal Domestic Assistance (CFDA)
http://www.cfda.gov

FedBizOpps
http://www.fedbizopps.gov

Federal Register
http://www.gpoaccess.gov/fr/index.html

Grants.gov
http://www.grants.gov

Illinois Research Information System (IRIS)
http://www.library.uiuc.edu/iris/

Sponsored Programs Information Network (SPIN)
http://www.infoed.org

Grant Writing Guides/Services/Tips

CFDA Developing and Writing Grant Proposals
http://12.46.245.173/pls/portal30/CATALOG.GRANT_PROPOSAL_DYN.show

Grant Proposal Writing Tips
http://www.grantproposal.com/

GrantProposal.com
http://www.cpb.org/grants/grantwriting.html

Grantsmanship Tutorial
http://www.aecom.yu.edu/ogs/Guide/Guide.htm

Guide for Writing a Funding Proposal
http://www.learnerassociates.net/proposal/

Proposal Writer's Guide (University of Michigan)
http://www.research.umich.edu/proposals/pwg/pwgcomplete.html

Proposal Writing Websites (University of Pittsburgh)
http://www.pitt.edu/~offres/propwriting.html

School Grants
http://www.schoolgrants.org/

U.S. Government Agencies

Department of Agriculture (USDA)
http://www.usda.gov

Department of Commerce (DOC)
http://www.doc.gov

Department of Defense (DOD)
http://www.defenselink.mil/

Department of Education (USDE)
http://www.ed.gov

Department of Energy (DOE)
http://www.energy.gov

Department of Health and Human Services (DHHS)
http://www.dhhs.gov

Department of Homeland Security (DHS)
http://www.dhs.gov

Department of Housing and Urban Development (HUD)
http://www.hud.gov

Department of the Interior (DOI)
http://www.doi.gov

Department of Justice (DOJ)
http://www.usdoj.gov

Department of Labor (DOL)
http://www.dol.gov

Department of State (DOS)
http://www.state.gov

Department of Transportation (DOT)
http://www.dot.gov

Department of the Treasury
http://www.ustreas.gov

Department of Veteran Affairs
http://www.va.gov

Environmental Protection Agency (EPA)
http://www.epa.gov

Food and Drug Administration (FDA)
http://www.fda.gov

National Aeronautics and Space Administration (NASA)
http://www.nasa.gov

National Endowment for the Arts (NEA)
http://www.arts.gov

National Endowment for the Humanities (NEH)
http://www.neh.gov

National Institutes of Health (NIH)
http://www.nih.gov

National Institute for Standards and Technology (NIST)
http://www.nist.gov

National Science Foundation (NSF)
http://www.nsf.gov

Professional Organizations

Council for Resource Development
http://www.crdnet.org

National Council of University Research Administrators
http://www.ncura.edu

Society of Research Administrators International (SRA)
http://www.srainternational.org

Other Resources

A Video on Peer Review at NIH
http://www.csr.nih.gov/video/video.asp

Code of Federal Regulations (CFR)
http://www.gpoaccess.gov/cfr

Federal Acquisition Regulations (FAR)
http://www.arnet.gov/far

Office of Management and Budget (OMB) Circulars
http://www.whitehouse.gov/omb/circulars/index.html

U.S. Government Printing Office (GPO)
http://www.access.gpo.gov

Comprehensive Review Questions

(Answers to Comprehensive Review Questions are on pp. 307–319.)

Directions: *For items 1–60, write your response below each question in the space provided.*

1. What are the primary sources for government (public) and non-government (private) funding?

2. What are three types of government funding?

3. What is the purpose of a government grant?

4. What is the difference between a discretionary grant and a mandatory grant?

5. What is the purpose of a cooperative agreement?

6. What is meant by substantial involvement?

7. What is the purpose of a procurement contract?

Comprehensive Review Questions continue on the next page.

8. What are two broad groupings of procurement contracts?

9. What is the primary search engine used by funding seekers to locate procurement contract solicitations over $25,000?

10. What are the major differences between assistance agreements (grants and cooperative agreements) and procurement contracts?

11. What are the differences between a restricted and an unrestricted gift?

12. What are the differences between government and non-government funding?

13. What are the six distinct proposal development phases that funding seekers must go through to prepare a winning grant application?

14. What are the steps involved in the grant process from legislation and acquisition to award?

15. What five activities should funding seekers complete before making a *preliminary* bid/no-bid decision?

Comprehensive Review Questions continue on the next page.

16. If the *preliminary* decision is to bid, what activities should funding seekers complete prior to release of a government solicitation?

17. What is a proposal prospectus?

18. What sources are used to locate grant opportunities?

19. What six components should funding seekers consider when reviewing a potential solicitation?

20. Who should funding seekers contact before making a preliminary bid/no-bid decision to submit a grant application?

21. What questions should funding seekers ask a Point of Contact before the RFP/RFA is released to the general public?

22. What questions should funding seekers ask past award winners?

23. What is a "model" solicitation?

Comprehensive Review Questions continue on the next page.

24. Who are the key staff members of a proposal development team?

25. What are the pros and cons of using external grant writers to develop a grant application?

26. What major activities should grant seekers complete the first day after the release of a government solicitation?

27. What questions should funding seekers answer before making a *formal* bid/no-bid decision about developing a grant application?

28. What proposal planning tools should funding seekers develop prior to holding a proposal strategy meeting?

29. What major topics should be discussed at a grant proposal strategy meeting?

30. What four skills should proposal writers possess?

31. What are the five "C's" of good proposal writing?

Comprehensive Review Questions continue on the next page.

32. What major narrative sections are contained in most grant applications?

33. What are the guidelines for writing a good problem/need statement?

34. What are the guidelines for developing good goals/objectives?

35. What major topics are discussed in a good methods/activities section of a grant application?

36. What are two forms of evaluation used in grant applications?

37. What documents are commonly found in a grant application appendix?

38. What is the difference between a "letter of support" and a "letter of commitment?"

39. What is the purpose of an Institutional Review Board (IRB)?

Comprehensive Review Questions continue on the next page.

40. What government agency certifications or assurances are often included in a grant application?

41. What are two types of proposal editing?

42. What "boilerplate" documents are often used to prepare a grant proposal?

43. What five *direct* cost items are used in grant budgets?

44. According to Office of Management and Budget Circular A-21, what four criteria are used to judge "allowable" costs for sponsored projects?

45. What six *indirect* (facilities and administrative) cost items are used in grant budgets?

46. What is an indirect cost-rate agreement?

47. What are total direct costs and modified total direct costs?

Comprehensive Review Questions continue on the next page.

48. What are two cost-sharing categories used in grant proposals?

49. What are budget detail and budget narrative?

50. What are three common budget problems with grant applications?

51. What four steps should funding seekers follow when submitting grant applications electronically through the Grants.gov portal?

52. What three components are found in a good proposal transmittal (cover) letter?

53. What are two reasons to hold a debriefing meeting with writers and reviewers after the grant application has been submitted?

54. What questions should proposal team members attempt to answer at the debriefing meeting?

55. When are government agencies not obligated to review grant applications?

Comprehensive Review Questions continue on the next page.

56. What basic questions do agency reviewers answer when evaluating grant applications?

57. What are three reasons why grant proposals are not funded?

58. What three activities should be completed if your grant proposal is not funded?

59. What information is included in most grant award documents?

60. What are three characteristics of successful grant projects?

Comprehensive Review Exercise

(The Evaluation Rubric for the Comprehensive Review Exercise is on p. 320.)

> *Directions: Read the memorandum and Request for Proposal (RFP) on pp. 269–272 and develop a grant application. No indirect costs are allowed.*

Memorandum

Date: June 1, 20XX

To: Funding Seekers

From: R.W. Chance, POC *RWC*
National Government Agency
101 Independence Blvd.
Washington, D.C. 20006
E-mail: rwchance@nga.gov

Subject: Call for Grant Applications
RFP#: NGA 5551212

The National Government Agency (NGA) will fund 15 projects with budgets of $25,000–$50,000 that directly relate to your proposed project idea. No indirect (facilities and administrative) costs are allowed. Each applicant is required to contribute a 25 percent cash match of the total amount requested from the NGA. For example, if an application requests $40,000, the applicant must contribute a cash match of $10,000. Consortia of two or more applicants are encouraged to apply.

The grant application must include the following components:

1. Transmittal (cover) letter
2. Grant application cover sheet and project abstract (see p. 271)
3. Proposal narrative (maximum five pages)
4. Budget (see p. 272)
5. References
6. Appendix

Proposals are due July 1, 20XX before 4:00 p.m. Assume that grant recipients will be notified before September 15. The period of performance is October 1 through September 30, 20XX. If you have questions, please do not hesitate to contact me at rwchance@nga.gov.

Request for Proposal (RFP#: NGA 5551212)

Grant Application Requirements and Point Values

Grant applications must include a detailed description of project activities and costs. Include the following information in your grant application (note point values in brackets):

- Transmittal (cover) letter (5 points)
- Grant application cover sheet and project abstract (10 points)
- Project narrative (60 points)
    - Problem/Need (15 points)
    - Goals/Objectives (10 points)
    - Methods/Activities (25 points) (plan of work, key personnel, management plan, and timeline)
    - Evaluation plans (10 points)
- Budget (20 points)
- References (2 point)
- Appendix (3 points)

Selection Criteria

- Does the cover letter conform to the textbook guidelines? See pp. 171–173.
- Does the abstract present a comprehensive 200-word summary of the project?
- Is the problem/need supported by recent and relevant citations?
- Do goals and objectives identify measurable project outcomes?
- Is there a logical and detailed plan of work to accomplish the proposed objectives?
- Are personnel qualification, responsibilities, and time commitments identified?
- Is there a management plan that shows the organizational structure of the project?
- Is there a reasonable timeline for completing the major project activities within the agency's period of performance?
- Do evaluation plans describe formative and summative procedures to measure the project's objectives?
- Is the budget reasonable and include 25 percent matching funds?
- Do the references include recent and relevant citations?
- Do the appendix items include materials that support the proposed project?

Submission Procedures

E-mail your grant application to:

> rwchance@nga.gov

Applications must be received no later than 4:00 p.m. EST on July 1, 20XX. The government agency will acknowledge all grant applications.

Grant Application Cover Sheet and Project Abstract **RFP#: NGA 5551212**
Name of organization: **Contact person**: **Office address**: **Telephone**: **Fax**: **E-mail**:
Descriptive title of application
Abstract (no more than 200 words)

Grant Budget
RFP#: NGA 5551212

Name of organization:

CFO name:

CFO signature:

Budget Items with Detail	Grant Funds	Matching Funds	Total Amount
Personnel			
_____	____	____	____
_____	____	____	____
_____	____	____	____
_____	____	____	____
Fringe Benefits			
_____	____	____	____
_____	____	____	____
_____	____	____	____
_____	____	____	____
Travel and Per Diem			
_____	____	____	____
_____	____	____	____
_____	____	____	____
Equipment and Supplies			
_____	____	____	____
_____	____	____	____
_____	____	____	____
Contractual Services			
_____	____	____	____
_____	____	____	____
_____	____	____	____
Other Direct Costs			
_____	____	____	____
_____	____	____	____
_____	____	____	____
Total Project Costs*	____	____	____

Note: No indirect (facilities and administrative) costs are allowed.

Appendix A

Answers to Chapter Review Questions

Chapter 1 (p. 9)					
Answer	Page	Answer	Page	Answer	Page
1. True	1	6. True	2	11. True	4
2. True	1	7. True	3	12. False	5
3. True	1	8. True	3	13. True	6
4. False	1	9. True	4	14. True	7
5. True	2	10. False	4	15. True	7

Chapter 2 (p. 21)					
Answer	Page	Answer	Page	Answer	Page
1. True	11	6. False	14	11. True	15
2. True	12	7. True	14	12. True	16
3. True	14	8. True	14	13. True	17
4. True	14	9. False	14	14. True	17
5. True	14	10. True	14	15. True	17

Chapter 3 (p. 52)					
Answer	Page	Answer	Page	Answer	Page
1. True	23	6. True	32	11. False	40
2. True	25	7. True	35	12. True	42
3. True	26	8. True	36	13. False	44
4. True	29	9. True	38	14. False	46
5. True	32	10. True	38	15. True	48

Chapter 4 (p. 84)					
Answer	Page	Answer	Page	Answer	Page
1. True	71	6. True	74	11. True	77
2. False	71	7. True	74	12. True	79
3. False	71	8. True	76	13. True	81
4. True	71	9. True	77	14. True	81
5. True	74	10. True	77	15. True	81

Answers to Chapter Review Questions continue on the next page.

Answers to Chapter Review Questions (Continued)

Chapter 5 (p. 132)					
Answer	Page	Answer	Page	Answer	Page
1. True	97	6. True	101	11. True	116
2. True	97	7. True	106	12. False	117
3. True	97	8. True	107	13. True	124
4. True	100	9. False	113	14. True	126
5. False	100	10. True	115	15. False	126

Chapter 6 (p. 156)					
Answer	Page	Answer	Page	Answer	Page
1. True	137	6. True	140	11. True	146
2. True	137	7. True	140	12. True	146
3. True	137	8. True	140	13. False	149
4. False	139	9. True	143	14. True	153
5. True	139	10. True	144	15. True	153

Chapter 7 (p. 178)					
Answer	Page	Answer	Page	Answer	Page
1. False	163	6. True	168	11. True	171
2. True	163	7. True	168	12. False	171
3. True	166	8. False	168	13. True	171
4. True	167	9. True	168	14. True	173
5. True	168	10. False	170	15. False	174

Chapter 8 (p. 201)					
Answer	Page	Answer	Page	Answer	Page
1. True	181	6. False	188	11. True	192
2. True	183	7. True	189	12. True	193
3. True	183	8. False	191	13. True	193
4. False	185	9. True	191	14. True	194
5. True	185	10. True	191	15. True	195

Appendix B

Answers to Chapter Exercises

Author's Note

Exercise answers have been field-tested with hundreds of workshop participants over the past 15 years. While the answers represent a sample of participants' responses, they do not represent all possible answers. Some exercises are based on individual grant interest, and thus no response is provided in this book.

Exercise 1-1: Describe Government and Non-Government Funding Sources
(Chapter 1, p. 10)

Directions: Describe the major characteristics of government and non-government funding sources.

Grants

- Government grants transfer money, property, or services to eligible recipients in order to accomplish a public purpose where no substantial involvement is anticipated between the funding agency and recipient during performance.

- Grants come from federal and state agencies where funding seekers write proposals or grant applications in response to a solicitation.

- Grants are grouped into two broad categories: (1) discretionary and (2) mandatory, entitlement, or formula.

Cooperative Agreements

- Cooperative agreements transfer money, property, or services to recipients to accomplish a public purpose where substantial involvement is anticipated between the funding agency and recipient during the performance period.

- A cooperative agreement involves a partnership-type relationship between agency staff members and the funding recipient to achieve project goals.

- Cooperative agreements are often used in large clinical research trails.

Procurement Contracts

- Procurement contracts acquire property or services for the direct benefit of or use by the federal government.

- Procurement contracts are grouped into two broad categories: (1) fixed-price contracts and (2) cost-reimbursement contracts.

- Procurement contracts usually require two separate proposals: (1) a technical proposal (or narrative) and (2) a cost proposal.

Gifts

- A gift is a voluntary transfer of property to another made gratuitously and without consideration.

- Gifts come from individuals, corporations, or philanthropic foundations.

- A gift may be either restricted or unrestricted. A restricted gift is targeted for a particular use; an unrestricted gift is donated to an organization without contingencies.

Exercise 2-1: Determine Winning Grant Proposal Characteristics
(Chapter 2, p. 22)

Compliant with RFP/RFA Requirements

The first and most important characteristic of any winning grant proposal is that it must follow the RFP/RFA directions and guidelines and meet specific criteria identified in the solicitation. Organizations must provide exactly what the government agency requires. If the proposal fails to include specific requirements or is not organized in the manner specified in the solicitation, the agency may consider the proposal noncompliant and refuse to consider it for funding. At the very least, agency reviewers may subtract points for missing proposal components or lack of proper organization.

Good Project Idea that Addresses a Problem/Need

The problem/need statement is a persuasively written essay that convinces agency reviewers a problem exists. Problem/need statements must be compelling and establish the significance and timeliness of the proposed project. This section should use test results, local statistics, feedback from questionnaires, and various database reports and records to justify the problem and support the project needs.

The problem/need is followed by the proposed project idea that will correct, resolve, or reduce the problem. Winning proposals must present project ideas that are innovative, original, and/or unique. Good ideas are measurable, provide useful knowledge, are feasible, understandable, and have widespread beneficial effects on larger groups or organizations.

Measurable Goals and Objectives

The primary purpose of the goals and objectives section is to provide agency reviewers with a better understanding of the proposed project's intended outcomes. Goals and objectives must be clear and quantifiable statements that are realistic and responsive to the government agency's wants and needs.

Clear Project Activities/Procedures

Proposals should describe the activities that will be accomplished to achieve the proposed goals and objectives. The methods/procedures section should indicate the "how," "who," "where," and "when," of the project. Good project activities include a timetable and indicate what will be done and by whom. Project activities must be realistic and reasonable; remember someone must complete what is being proposed. This section should also address collaborations with partners from business and industry, subcontracts with other institutions, and consultants.

Strength and Expertise of Personnel

The proposed project should include information about the role and responsibilities of key personnel. Résumés should be included in the appendix and indicate the expertise, education, and previous grant management experience of proposed personnel. This section should also identify the project management structure and reporting lines within the grant-seeking organization.

Answers to Exercise 2-1 continue on the next page.

Exercise 2-1: Determine Winning Grant Proposal Characteristics (continued)
(Chapter 2, p. 22)

Strong Evaluation Plans

Evaluation plans should include formative and summative measures that detail how the project goals and objectives will be assessed. Plans should indicate procedures to collect and analyze data in an effort to demonstrate what has been achieved. In addition, plans should indicate how the project would continue after grant funding ends.

Appropriate and Reasonable Cost

Budgets are fundamental components of all grant applications and should indicate financial responsibility. Budgets must include accurate and reasonable costs to complete the proposed project activities. Proposal reviewers assess budgets in relationship to project objectives, proposed activities, and RFP/RFA requirements. Incomplete budgets signal poor preparation; inflated budgets indicate waste, and low budgets cast doubt on the planning ability of applicants. All project expenditures must be justified. Do not assume project costs will be obvious to government agency reviewers. Always use agency budget worksheets and include budget detail and narrative to provide explanation. Provide direct costs, indirect (facilities and administrative) costs, and cost-sharing funds, if applicable. Be prepared to prioritize budget needs if the government agency provides only partial financial support for the proposed grant project. In addition, the funding seeker should provide a discussion of the project's financial sustainability after grant funds are depleted.

Comprehensive Abstract, Strong Appendix items, and Complete Application Forms

Abstracts are usually the last proposal section written, but the first document seen by grant reviewers. Abstracts must represent a cogent summary of the proposed project, emphasize key proposal components, and comply with length restrictions.

Appendix items should include documentation to support the proposal narrative. Typical appendix components include (1) the institution's mission statement; (2) résumés of key personnel; (3) letters of support and commitment from partners, subcontractors, and consultants; (4) lengthy reports and papers; and (5) other documents too bulky for inclusion in the main body of the proposal narrative.

Grant proposals must follow all instructions when completing application materials. Funding seekers must check all standard forms for completeness and accuracy. All forms and application materials (e.g., assurance and certification forms) must be signed by appropriate institutional administrators/managers.

Professional Appearance

Proposal applications must have a professional appearance. Proposals should use headings and subheadings to provide a neat and organized presentation of material requested in the solicitation. Integrate tables, figures, and charts into the narrative to summarize and illustrate key project points. Check and recheck grammar, spelling, and punctuation before final submission.

Exercise 3-4: Review a National Science Foundation (NSF) RFP
(Chapter 3, pp. 58–70)

1. **What is the purpose of the NSF?**

   The purpose of the NSF is "to promote the progress of science, [and] to advance the national health, prosperity, and welfare by supporting research and education in all fields of science and engineering." **(See p. 70.)**

2. **What is the purpose of the Course, Curriculum, and Laboratory Improvement program?**

   The Course, Curriculum, and Laboratory Improvement (CCLI) program seeks to improve the quality of science, technology, engineering, and mathematics (STEM) education for all undergraduate students. The program supports efforts to create new learning materials and teaching strategies, develop faculty expertise, implement educational innovations, assess learning and evaluate innovations, and conduct research on STEM teaching and learning. The program supports three types of projects representing three different phases of development, ranging from small, exploratory investigations to large, comprehensive projects. **(See p. 60.)**

3. **Who is eligible to apply for funding?**

   None specified. **(See p. 65.)**

4. **Who should be contacted regarding general inquiries about this program?**

   General inquiries regarding this program should be made to:

   - Cameron Wiley, lead program director, telephone: (703) 292-XXXX, e-mail: cwiley@nsf.gov

   - Matt Clark, lead program director, telephone: (703) 292-XXXX, e-mail: mclark@nsf.gov

   - Amy Polk, lead program director, telephone: (703) 292-XXXX, e-mail: apolk@nsf.gov. **(See p. 70.)**

5. **How much funding is available for Phase 1, 2, and 3 projects? How long is the period of performance for Phase 1, 2, and 3 projects?**

   The funding amount and period of performance for project phases are:

   - Phase 1: Projects total budget up to $150,000 ($200,000 when four-year colleges or universities collaborate with two-year colleges) for one to three years.

   - Phase 2: Projects total budget up to $500,000 for two to four years.

   - Phase 3: Projects total budget up to $2,000,000 for three to five years. **(See pp. 62–63.)**

Answers to Exercise 3-4 continue on the next page.

Exercise 3-4: Review a National Science Foundation (NSF) RFP (continued)
(Chapter 3, pp. 58–70)

6. **What is the total anticipated funding amount for new and ongoing awards? How many estimated Phase 1, 2, and 3 awards will be made?**

    NSF anticipates having $34 million for new and ongoing CCLI awards, pending the availability of funds. The awards will be made as standard or continuing grants. The number and size of awards will depend on the quality of the proposals received and the availability of funds. NSF expects to make the following number of awards:

    - *Phase 1: Exploratory Projects*—70–90 awards expected.

    - *Phase 2: Expansion Projects*—20–30 awards expected.

    - *Phase 3: Comprehensive Projects*—2–5 awards expected.
    (See p. 65.)

7. **In addition to the *Grant Proposal Guide* and *A Guide for the Preparation and Submission of NSF Applications,* what other information should be read before submitting a proposal?**

    The "Guide for Proposal Writing" and the Grant Proposal Guide on "Proposals Involving Human Subjects." **(See p. 66.)**

8   **What project components should be included in the proposal?**

    Proposals may focus on one or more of the following project components:
    - Creating learning materials and teaching strategies
    - Developing faculty expertise
    - Implementing educational innovations
    - Assessing student achievement
    - Conducting research on undergraduate STEM education
    (See pp. 61–62.)

9. **What important features should be included in the project proposal?**

    All promising projects should include the following features:
    - Quality, relevance, and impact
    - Student focus
    - Use of and contribution to knowledge about STEM education
    - STEM education community-building
    - Expected measurable outcomes
    - Project evaluation
    (See pp. 63–64.)

10. **Who can submit grant applications?**

    The Authorized Organization Representative (AOR) must submit the application to Grants.gov. **(See p. 67.)**

Answers to Exercise 3-4 continue on the next page.

Exercise 3-4: Review a National Science Foundation (NSF) RFP (continued)
(Chapter 3, pp. 58–70)

11. What two NSF *criteria* are used to evaluate grant applications?

- *What is the intellectual merit of the proposed activity?*
  How important is the proposed activity to advancing knowledge and understanding within its own field or across different fields? How well qualified is the proposer (individual or team) to conduct the project? (If appropriate, the reviewer will comment on the quality of the prior work.) To what extent does the proposed activity suggest and explore creative and original concepts? How well conceived and organized is the proposed activity? Is there sufficient access to resources?

- *What are the broader impacts of the proposed activity?*
  How well does the activity advance discovery and understanding while promoting teaching, training, and learning? How well does the proposed activity broaden the participation of underrepresented groups (e.g., gender, ethnicity, disability, geographic)? To what extent will it enhance the infrastructure for research and education, such as facilities, instrumentation, networks, and partnerships? Will the results be disseminated broadly to enhance scientific and technological understanding? What may be the benefits of the proposed activity to society? **(See p. 67.)**

12. Who will review grant applications?

A scientist, engineer, or educator serving as an NSF program officer, and usually three to ten other persons outside NSF who are experts in the particular fields represented by the proposal, will carefully review proposals. These reviewers are selected by program officers charged with the oversight of the review process. A panel of experts will review proposals submitted in response to this program solicitation. Reviewers will be asked to formulate a recommendation to either support or decline each proposal. The program officer assigned to manage the proposal's review will consider the advice of reviewers and will formulate a recommendation. **(See pp. 67 and 68.)**

13. If awarded funding, what information will be included in the award letter?

An NSF award consists of (1) the award letter, which includes any special provisions applicable to the award and any number of amendments thereto; (2) the budget, which indicates the amounts, by categories of expense, on which NSF has based its support (or otherwise communicates any specific approvals or disapprovals of proposed expenditures); (3) the proposal referenced in the award letter; (4) the applicable award conditions, such as Grant General Conditions (GC-1) or Federal Demonstration Partnership (FDP) Terms and Conditions; and (5) any announcement or other NSF issuance that may be incorporated by reference in the award letter. **(See p. 69.)**

Answers to Exercise 3-4 continue on the next page.

Exercise 3-4: Review a National Science Foundation (NSF) RFP (continued)
(Chapter 3, pp. 58–70)

14. **If awarded, what project reporting is required?**

    For all multi-year grants, the principal investigator must submit an annual project report to the cognizant program officer at least 90 days before the end of the current budget period. (Some programs or awards require more frequent project reports.) Within 90 days after expiration of a grant, the PI also is required to submit a final project report. Failure to provide the required annual or final project reports will delay NSF review and processing of any future funding increments as well as any pending proposals for that PI. PIs should examine the formats of the required reports in advance to assure availability of required data. **(See p. 69.)**

15. **How many proposals are submitted to NSF each year? How many are funded?**

    NSF receives approximately 40,000 proposals each year for research, education and training projects, of which approximately 11,000 are funded. **(See p. 70.)**

Exercise 4-1: Prepare a Compliance Checklist
(Chapter 4, pp. 85–90)

RFP/RFA Requirements	Location in RFP/RFA	√	Location in Proposal	√
Include background statement about the offeror's experience and qualifications to perform the contract.	L-1-D			
Include résumés of all principal staff and consultants involved in tasks under the RFP as well as the primary contact for inquiries relating to contract compliance issues. Résumés shall include technical qualifications, such as duties, education, and experience.	L-1-D			
List recent private and government clients (contract names and numbers, client name, address, phone number, and contact person).	L-1-E			
Describe the quality control procedures that will be followed for data entry, data prep, data editing, site training, editing, and graphics.	L-1-F			
Present a detailed management and staffing plan, including hours or percentage of time for each individual or position.	L-1-G			
List all equipment used in accomplishing the work in the RFP.	L-1-H			
Present a plan to accomplish project objectives.	L-1-I-1			
Demonstrate a detailed understanding of pertinent problems and methods for overcoming them.	L-1-I-1			
Address each of the specific tasks in the statement of work, specifying methodology/approach for accomplishing each task. Indicate the number of person hours estimated for each task.	L-1-I-2			
Provide an approach to tasks including procedures, format, and designs to indicate how they will meet requirements.	L-1-I-2			
Show expertise in SPSS or SPSSPC and ability to modify data entry programs and log programs.	L-2-A-2			
Describe procedures to ensure quality and demonstrate experience in maintaining data integrity during data entry, multi-source data merging, and data reporting.	L-2-A-3			
Identify other problems that may occur in completing tasks specified in this RFP and recommend procedures to prevent or resolve them.	L-2-A-3			
Show an understanding and mastery of the complex practical issues involved in organizing, tracking, processing, and reporting results from a national multi-site data collection program.	L-2-A-3-a			
Demonstrate successful implementation of quality control measures and availability of personnel to respond to quality control issues.	L-2-A-3-b			

Answers to Exercise 4-1 continue on the next page.

Exercise 4-1: Prepare a Compliance Checklist (continued)
(Chapter 4, pp. 85–90)

RFP/RFA Requirements	Location in RFP/RFA	√	Location in Proposal	√
Propose procedures for attaining the following goals and cite recent experience in successfully accomplishing similar goals on projects involving collection of data from multiple independent sites:	L-2-A-3-b			
(1) Ensure that the total number of interviews per gender/age group received from a site is processed.	L-2-A-3-b-(1)			
(2) Ensure that all interview data are reported.	L-2-A-3-b-(2)			
(3) Ensure that the total number of specimen results received from the laboratory is processed.	L-2-A-3-b-(3)			
(4) Ensure that the total number of specimen results received from the laboratory is reported.	L-2-A-3-b-(4)			
(5) Ensure that data are reported separately for each site and quarter.	L-2-A-3-b-(5)			
(6) Ensure that data are reported separately for gender/age groups.	L-2-A-3-b-(6)			
(7) Ensure that data are entered accurately.	L-2-A-3-b-(7)			
(8) Ensure contract compliance with schedules outlined in the RFP.	L-2-A-3-b-(8)			
(9) Ensure confidentiality of site results.	L-2-A-3-b-(9)			
(10) Ensure confidentiality of Drug Use Forecasting (DUF) data (DUF data cannot be released without written approval).	L-2-A-3-b-(10)			
(11) Ensure accuracy in matching interview data and urine data when merging files.	L-2-A-3-b-(11)			
(12) Ensure that data sets are free from errors for all files (e.g., data files, systems files, and merged files).	L-2-A-3-b-(12)			
Enforce quality control issues concerning editing, graphics, and layout of DUF publications.	L-2-B-1			
Suggest problems that may occur in the publication tasks specified in the RFP and propose solutions or procedures to prevent them.	L-2-B-1			
Propose new graphic formats.	L-2-B-2-a			
Propose procedures to ensure high-quality presentation of data.	L-2-B-2-b			
Demonstrate experience in accurately representing quantitative data and provide points of contact for substantiation.	L-2-B-2-b			
Demonstrate an understanding of issues involved in publishing results from a national program under tight time schedules.	L-2-B-3-a			

Answers to Exercise 4-1 continue on the next page.

Exercise 4-1: Prepare a Compliance Checklist (continued)
(Chapter 4, pp. 85–90)

RFP/RFA Requirements	Location in RFP/RFA	√	Location in Proposal	√
Demonstrate experience in graphic design, editing, and report development.	L-2-B-3-b			
Demonstrate that sufficient quality control measures are in place and that personnel are available to respond to diverse quality control issues.	L-2-B-3-b			
Propose procedures for attaining the following goals and cite recent experience in successfully accomplishing similar goals on projects involving quantitative information for publication:	L-2-B-3-b			
(1) Ensure that data received from the National Institute of Justice (NIJ) are accurately transposed into graphic layouts.	L-2-B-3-b-(1)			
(2) Ensure that all materials are presented according to NIJ specifications.	L-2-B-3-b-(2)			
(3) Ensure that data presented in tables, graphs, or charts are consistent with corresponding text.	L-2-B-3-b-(3)			
(4) Ensure that a final review of the entire publication is conducted with emphasis on accuracy.	L-2-B-3-b-(4)			
(5) Ensure contract compliance with respect to timelines in the RFP.	L-2-B-3-b-(5)			
(6) Ensure confidentiality of data until the publication is released.	L-2-B-3-b-(6)			
Submit samples of weekly, monthly, and quarterly reports.	L-2-C-2			
Meet with the Contracting Office Technical Representative (COTR) in Washington, D.C. on a regular basis and sometimes on short notice. Enter into an agreement with a pool of consultants to provide a number of diverse tasks.	L-2-C-3			
Describe managerial staff.	L-3-A			
Demonstrate the degree of importance attached to projects of this nature.	L-3-A			
Include "organizational structure" as part of the management plan.	L-3-B			
Include résumés of key personnel.	L-3-C			

Exercise 4-2: Prepare a Proposal Outline and Schedule
(Chapter 4, pp. 91–96)

RFP: Innovative Programs to Increase Information Technology Graduates

1. Application Cover Sheet and Project Abstract *(P. Smith)*

2. Problem/Need *(P. Smith)*
   2.1   Critical shortage of qualified information technology (IT) workers
   2.2   Lack of Hoosier State College students preparing for IT jobs
   2.3   High school students not prepared for IT curriculum

3. Project Goals and Objectives *(P. Smith)*
   3.1   Increase awareness about IT career opportunities at local high schools
   3.2   Establish IT dual credit program for high school juniors and seniors
   3.3   Increase partnerships with business, industry, and IT professional groups

4. Project Activities and Timeline *(P. Smith and D. Johnson)*
   4.1   Develop marketing program for high school students and parents
   4.2   Develop IT curriculum
   4.3   Train IT community college and high school instructors
   4.4   Expand the number of IT internships for students
   4.5   Establish working relationships with IT professional organizations

5. Project Leadership and Partners *(D. Johnson)*
   5.1   Community college administrative leadership
   5.2   High school partners
   5.3   Local business and industry partners
   5.4   IT professional organizations

6. Budget *(P. Smith and D. Johnson)*
   6.1   Direct costs
         6.1.1   Personnel salaries and fringe benefits
         6.1.2   Travel and per diem
         6.1.3   Equipment and expendable supplies
         6.1.4   Contractual services
         6.1.5   Other direct costs
   6.2   Cash match of at least 25 percent

7. Appendix *(S. Gorbitz)*
   7.1   Résumés
   7.2   Organizational chart
   7.3   Letters of support
   7.4   Proposed training curriculum

(Indicates staff member responsible for proposal section.)

Answers to Exercise 4-2 continue on the next page.

Exercise 4-2: Prepare a Proposal Outline and Schedule (continued)
(Chapter 4, pp. 91–96)

RFP#:   SCCB 315

RFP Title: Innovative Programs to Increase Information Technology Graduates

Distribution: March 15, 20XX

Agency: State Community College Board (SCCB)

Issue Date: March 15, 20XX

Due Date: April 15, 20XX

Tentative Schedule

Activity	Date	Time	Place or Person
Strategy meeting ·	3/18	10:00 a.m.	Conference Rm. 210
1st draft to reviewers	3/24	5:00 p.m.	A. Turner
Reviewers' meeting	3/26	11:00 a.m.	Conference Rm. 210
2nd draft to reviewers	4/5	5:00 p.m.	A. Turner
Reviewers' meeting	4/8	1:00 p.m.	Conference Rm. 210
Edit final draft	4/11	flow basis	A. Turner
Production and assembly	4/13	1:00 p.m.	A. Turner and J. Rice
Submit application to SCCB	4/13	5:00 p.m.	P. Smith and D. Johnson
Grant application is due	4/15	4:00 p.m.	—

Writers

S. Gorbitz, D. Johnson, and P. Smith [1,2]

Reviewers

T. Baker, D. Johnson, J. Passmore,[2] and P. Smith[1,2]

Support Staff

A. Turner, J. Rice

[1] Proposal director
[2] Final review team member

Exercise 5-2: Prepare a Grant Application
(Chapter 5, p. 134)

Sample Transmittal (Cover) Letter

April 13, 20XX ⟵ **Agency and POC**

State Community College Board
Attention: Dr. Jean E. Thomas, CFO
401 East Highway Road
Capital City, IN 58765-1234 ⟵ **RFP Number/Title**

HOOSIER STATE COLLEGE

Re: RFP# SCCB 315/Innovative Programs to Increase Information Technology Graduates

Dear Dr. Thomas:

Hoosier State College (HSC) is pleased to submit our grant application *Information Technology: Program Linkages Between Hoosier State College and District High Schools* in response to the above-referenced solicitation. Our proposal addresses the categories of recruitment, high school/college program linkages, and employer linkages. The grant proposal includes the following sections:

- Grant Application and Project Abstract
- Problem/Need
- Project Goals and Objectives   } ⟵ **Proposal Contents**
- Project Activities, Outcomes, and Timeline
- Project Leadership and Partners
- Budget (See p. 298)
- Appendix

HSC is totally committed to assist in making the Information technology proposed project a reality by contributing matching funds of $12,575 for this project.

HSC has administered more than 100 grants in a wide variety of education and service areas. If you have oversight questions, please contact Dr. Patrick Smith, associate vice president of academic affairs, at (219) 834-5554 or psmith@hoosierstate.edu. If you have specific questions or concerns regarding the implementation of the information technology project, please contact Mr. David Johnson, project coordinator at (219) 834-5553 or djohnson@hoosierstate.edu.

Sincerely, ⟵ **Contact Person**

Janet Passmore

Dr. Janet J. Passmore
President

c: Dr. Patrick Smith
    Mr. David Johnson

Hoosier State College • 1001 Main Street • Hoosierville, Indiana 65432 • 219-838-3599

Answers to Exercise 5-2 continue on the next page.

Exercise 5-2: Prepare a Grant Application (continued)
(Chapter 5, p. 134)

Sample Grant Application and Project Abstract

Name of College: Hoosier State College

Contact Person: Dr. Patrick W. Smith

Office Address: 1001 Main Street, Hoosierville, IN 65432-8226

Telephone: 219-838-3536

Fax: 219-838-3774

E-mail: psmith@hoosierstate.edu

Descriptive Title of Application:

Information Technology: Program Linkages Between Hoosier State College and District High Schools

Abstract (no more than 200 words):

Hoosier State College's project will (1) increase awareness among high school students about career opportunities in Information Technology, (2) enhance our existing Tech Prep program that provide hands-on employability for our students, and (3) add local IT business partners to our internship pool. Hoosier State College, four local high schools (Eastland, Hoosierville North, Hoosierville South, and Richton Fields), the Career Preparation Network, 3Com Corporation, and local businesses will provide students with IT experiences to meet the current and future IT workforce needs. We will complete a marketing plan to disseminate information about IT courses available for high school and college students, which will include hosting informational meetings and visitation programs for high school students in the area. From this plan, we anticipate 150 students will be enrolled in the IT program in fall 20XX. To increase high school and college linkages, we will develop four dual credit courses, send eight instructors to Westnet training, and develop advanced IT courses. We will also provide 60 high school students with IT workplace experiences. During this same time, we will establish an Information Technology club on campus that will involve students and community business leaders.

Answers to Exercise 5-2 continue on the next page.

Exercise 5-2: Prepare a Grant Application (continued)
(Chapter 5, p. 134)

Sample Cover Sheet (Optional)

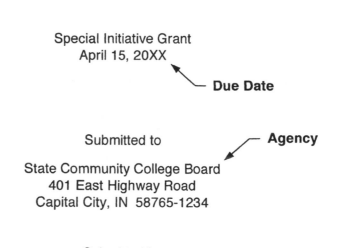

Proposal Title

Information Technology: Program Linkages Between Hoosier State College and District High Schools

Special Initiative Grant
April 15, 20XX

Due Date

Submitted to

Agency

State Community College Board
401 East Highway Road
Capital City, IN 58765-1234

Submitted by

Funding Seeker

Hoosier State College
1001 Main Street
Hoosierville, IN 65432-8226

Answers to Exercise 5-2 continue on the next page.

Exercise 5-2: Prepare a Grant Application (continued)

(Chapter 5, p. 134)

Sample Proposal Narrative (maximum five pages)

Introduction

Hoosier State College (HSC) is a publicly supported, comprehensive community college located in Northwest Indiana approximately 25 miles southeast of Chicago. The college's student population is culturally diverse with more than 52 percent of the population either African American or Hispanic. The economic strata of the college are equally distinct, with the district

> **Hoosier State College, Fall 20XX**
> **Student Characteristics**
>
> • 6,934 Total Enrollment
>   • 34% African American
>   • 48% Caucasian
>   • 18% Hispanic
> • Mean Age 26; Median Age 24
> • 60% Female; 40% Male

spanning from the impoverished community of Eastland (one of the poorest communities in the United States) to the fairly affluent communities of Hoosierville North, Hoosierville South, and Richton Fields. The college's primary purpose is to provide excellent educational opportunities for all students in occupational areas.

Problem/Need

The virtual explosion of information technology (IT) job opportunities, coupled with the dearth of students who are preparing for these jobs, provides a unique challenge for HSC. Many of the students who enroll at HSC are most likely to have graduated from under-funded, under-equipped, "property tax poor" high schools. Because of this situation, HSC has the difficult task of shaping these minimally prepared students into skilled workers for tomorrow.

According to the Information Technology Association of America (ITAA), more than a million new IT jobs have been created in the last decade with more than 840,000 IT jobs unfilled this year. Toby Richards, Educational Customer Programs Director at Microsoft Education Solutions Group, stated that IT represents some of the best paying jobs available—"the average high tech job pays 78 percent more than the average non-high tech job." He continues, "this will present a tremendous challenge and opportunity for schools to develop new curriculum and to prepare teachers to teach new subjects." According to a study conducted by ITAA and William M. Mercer (a leading human resources consulting firm), it takes 37 percent longer to fill IT jobs than non-IT jobs. All employers from large corporations to small retail stores require competent IT workers to maintain a smooth-running business.

Answers to Exercise 5-2 continue on the next page.

Exercise 5-2: Prepare a Grant Application (continued)

(Chapter 5, p. 134)

Richard Greenberg, in his article, "Filling the Gap" in the October 20XX issue of *Techniques*, claims that successful IT training programs are driven by industry needs. Hoosier State College's Computer Information Systems Program and its advisory board members have been discussing the rapid technological changes in the workplace with implications for curriculum for several years. In response to the changing technology and in an effort to prepare students for IT careers, Hoosier State College, in collaboration with four district high schools, has teamed up with 3Com Corporation (one of the world's preeminent suppliers of data, voice, and video communications technology) to train a generation of network workers. See the appendix for our NetPrep Regional Training Center Agreement. The Computer Information Systems–NetPrep Network Technology Program will lead to an industry-recognized certification, a Hoosier State College Certificate, or an Associate in Applied Science degree. The comprehensive curriculum will provide:

- an in-depth understanding of the theory, hardware, and software of computer networking,

- contemporary hands-on training,

- 80 percent of the coursework toward certification,

- a vendor-neutral program,

- a state-of-the-art curriculum developed and supported by 3Com Corporation,

- industry-recognized certifications by the National Association of Communication Systems Engineers (NACSE), and

- NetPrep Senior Network Specialist certificate completion in as few as two semesters.

HSC's NetPrep program will provide students with a vital connection to workplace experiences and internship opportunities. In fall 20XX, it is anticipated that 150 students will be enrolled in at least one of the sequenced courses in the networking program at HSC.

Answers to Exercise 5-2 continue on the next page.

Exercise 5-2: Prepare a Grant Application (continued)
(Chapter 5, p. 134)

Project Goals and Objectives

HSC's proposed project is in alignment with the primary goals presented in Indiana's "Excellence in Education" plan. The following project goals specifically address the State Community College Board's agenda for increasing higher education's partnership, opportunities, and excellence and at the same time preparing our district students to enter the IT profession.

Goal 1

Recruitment: Increase awareness of career opportunities among high school students and increase the number of high school graduates enrolling in Information Technology.

Objectives

- Develop brochures, press releases, and ads for use in local and district high school newspapers.

- Hold informational meetings and host visitation programs for prospective IT students.

Goal 2

High School/College Program Linkages: Develop a dual credit program that begins with the junior year in high school, continues through a certification program, and provides workplace experiences.

Objectives

- Students will complete the NetPrep sequence of courses in preparation for certification.

- Students will complete workplace experiences and internships in regional businesses.

Goal 3

Employer Linkages: Create additional partnerships with area business and industry and professional associations.

Objectives

- Add regional business and industry partners to our partnership pool.

- Form an IT student organization at HSC.

Answers to Exercise 5-2 continue on the next page.

Exercise 5-2: Prepare a Grant Application (continued)
(Chapter 5, p. 134)

Project Activities, Outcomes, and Timeline

ACTIVITIES	OUTCOMES	TIMELINE
Goal 1. Recruitment		
1.1a: Develop marketing program for high school students and parents.	1.1a: 500 brochures, 10 press releases, and four newspaper ads will be developed.	1.1a: August 20XX
1.1b: Host evening informational meetings for students and parents.	1.1b: Two informational meetings for students and parents will be held at HSC.	1.1b: August 20XX
1.1c: Host visitation programs at HSC for interested high school students.	1.1c: Two half-day visitation programs will be held at HSC.	1.1c: August 20XX
1.1d: Increase IT enrollment.	1.1d: 150 IT students will be enrolled in NetPrep.	1.1d: September 20XX
Goal 2. High School/College Program Linkages		
2.1a: Review and select IT curriculum materials.	2.1a: Text and lab manuals for high school and HSC IT courses will be purchased.	2.1a: August 20XX
2.1b: Develop two high school IT courses to articulate with existing HSC IT courses.	2.1b: Two dual IT courses will be established.	2.1b: August 20XX
2.1c: Develop two new IT courses for HSC.	2.1c: Two advanced IT courses will be developed.	2.1c: August 20XX
2.1d: Send one instructor from each high school and four teachers from HSC for training to teach IT curriculum.	2.1d: Nine IT instructors will complete training.	2.1d: August 20XX
2.1e: Develop two additional courses to articulate with the new courses at HSC and to complete a NetPrep secondary school certificate preparing students for employment as an entry level network technician.	2.1e: Four dual credit courses will be implemented.	2.1e: September 20XX
2.1f: Prepare students for industry standard certification and for advanced coursework leading to certification.	2.1f: 120 students will complete NetPrep sequence of courses in preparation for certification.	2.1f: May 20XX
2.2a: Schedule workplace visitations and job shadowing for high school students.	2.2a: Sixty high school students will be provided workplace experiences in regional businesses.	2.2a: May 20XX
2.2b: Expand existing internships in IT to include opportunities in computer networking for college students.	2.2b: Ten additional computer networking internship sites for college students will be established.	2.2b: May 20XX
Goal 3. Employer Linkages		
3.1a: Actively recruit business and industry partners.	3.1a: Six regional business and industry partners will be added to the existing pool.	3.1a: May 20XX
3.1b: Establish working relationships with IT professional associations.	3.1b: Student organization will be formed at HSC.	3.1b: May 20XX

Answers to Exercise 5-2 continue on the next page.

Exercise 5-2: Prepare a Grant Application (continued)

(Chapter 5, p. 134)

Project Leadership and Partners

Dr. Patrick Smith, the project director and associate vice president of academic affairs at HSC, will lead the project leadership team. David Johnson and Sue Gorbitz will serve as IT coordinators and create a close working relationship between the four district high schools, the Career Preparation Network, 3Com Corporation, and local district businesses. Résumés for key staff are located in the appendix. This fall, HSC's pilot project established links between partners by conducting several committees to develop the IT curriculum and establish internship sites with local businesses. Partners and their roles are described below.

Organization	Description	Role In Project
College Community	Hoosier State College	• Increase awareness among high school students of career opportunities and increase high school graduates enrolling in IT. • Develop a dual credit program that begins in the junior year of high school and continues through a degree or certificate program and provides workplace experiences. • Develop partnerships with technology business and industry and/or related professional associations.
High Schools	Eastland, Hoosierville North, Hoosierville South, Richton Fields	• Explore and develop dual credit courses. • Recruit potential students for IT programs. • Include IT courses in high school and college catalogues. • Identify teachers who require IT training. • Grant high school credit for completion of IT courses. • Provide guidance for student transition from secondary to postsecondary programs.
Education Support Organization	Career Preparation Network	• Develop and distribute recruitment materials to high school students and the public. • Serve as a liaison between high schools and HSC to develop IT programs and student transition. • Assist in expanding IT work-based learning experiences for high school students. • Provide professional development opportunities for IT instructors.
Businesses	3Com, Local Businesses	• Provide necessary materials and equipment for program curriculum. • Provide workplace experiences and internships for students.

Answers to Exercise 5-2 continue on the next page.

Exercise 5-2: Prepare a Grant Application (continued)
(Chapter 5, p. 134)

Appendix

A. Résumés for key staff members

- Patrick Smith, project director

- David Johnson, IT coordinator

- Sue Gorbitz, IT coordinator

B. Organizational charts

- HSC Organizational Structure (project location within the organization)

- IT Project Organizational Structure (staff and reporting duties)

C. Letters of support

- Local high schools

- Local business and industry

- Career Preparation Network

D. 3Com training curriculum

- Course syllabi

- Quizzes and tests

E. NetPrep Regional Training Center Agreement

- Hardware and software commitment

- Training

- Certification standards

Exercise 5-3: Edit the Narrative

(Chapter 5, pp. 135–136)

Sample Edited Responses

(Author's note: There are several possible edited responses.)

1. **Poor:** The proposed project will afford participants the opportunity to master contemporary computer skills.

   Better: Project participants will master contemporary computer skills.

2. **Poor:** Local colleges are producing highly skilled graduates in light of the fact that community businesses are requiring a stronger technical workforce.

   Better: Local colleges are producing highly skilled graduates to meet business demand.

3. **Poor:** Outside consultants will conduct an evaluation of the entire project.

   Better: Consultants will evaluate the project.

4. **Poor:** The end-of-the-year annual performance report will be submitted each program year.

   Better: A performance report will be submitted at the end of each program year.

5. **Poor:** Each and every report shall conform to the government agency's instructions.

   Better: All reports shall conform to the government agency's instructions.

6. **Poor:** The grantee is directed to submit project reports.

   Better: The grantee shall submit project reports.

7. **Poor:** It is the duty of the grantee to submit documented financial reports.

   Better: The grantee shall submit documented financial reports.

8. **Poor:** The grantee shall submit project reports for the reason that the government agency's approval is mandatory.

   Better: The grantee shall submit project reports for the government agency's approval.

9. **Poor:** Partners will make annual contributions of $1,000 a year.

   Better: Partners will make $1,000 annual contributions.

10. **Poor:** A comprehensive job description listing all duties connected with the proposal manager's position is included in the appendix.

    Better: A comprehensive job description for the proposal manager is in the appendix.

Exercise 6-1: Prepare a Proposal Budget (Information Technology)
(Chapter 6, p. 157)

Sample Budget

Name of College: Hoosier State College

CFO Name: Dr. Janet J. Passmore

CFO Signature:

Line Item and Description	Government Agency	Matching Funds	Total Amount
Personnel Salaries			
P. Smith (10% x $70,000)	0	7,000	7,000
D. Johnson (25% x 50,000)	12,500	0	12,500
S. Gorbitz (10% x 60,000)	6,000	0	6,000
	18,500	**7,000**	**25,500**
Fringe Benefits			
($18,500 x 35%)	6,475	0	6,475
($7,000 x 35%)	0	2,450	2,450
	6,475	**2,450**	**8,925**
Travel and Per Diem			
(4 instructors x 325 airfare)	1,300	0	1,300
(4 instructors x 152 per diem x 3 days)	1,824	0	1,824
	3,124	**0**	**3,124**
Equipment and Expendable Supplies			
Computers with printers (10 x $1,200)	12,000	0	12,000
Cabling for labs	0	1,000	1,000
3Com Workbooks (150 workbooks x $41)	6,150	0	6,150
3Com Lab Manuals (150 workbooks x $25)	3,750	0	3,750
500 brochures	0	625	625
	21,900	**1,625**	**23,525**
Contractual Services			
Curriculum Consultant 6 days x $250	0	1,500	1,500
	0	**1,500**	**1,500**
Other Direct Costs	0	0	0
	0	**0**	**0**
Total Project Costs*	**$49,999**	**$12,575**	**$62,574**

Note: No indirect (facilities and administrative) costs were allowed.

Exercise 6-2: Prepare a Proposal Budget (School-To-Work)
(Chapter 6, pages 158–162)

Proposed Budget

Personnel Salaries and Fringe Benefits		Agency	ASD	Total
Oversight Manager ($85,010 x 15%)	=	0	12,752	12,752
Project Administrator ($78,008 x 25%)	=	19,502	0	19,502
Project Specialist #1 ($40,996 x 100%)	=	40,996	0	40,996
Project Specialist #2 ($50,003 x 100%)	=	50,003	0	50,003
Financial Manager ($85,010 x 10%)	=	0	8,501	8,501
Document Specialist ($36,000 x 25%)	=	0	9,000	9,000
Personnel Total	=	110,501	30,253	140,754
Fringe Benefits (Personnel x 25%) Total	=	27,625	7,563	35,188
Personnel and Fringe Benefits Total	=	**$ 138,126**	**$ 37,816**	**$ 175,942**

Travel and Per Diem
S-T-W Conference

22 ASB members x $100 per person for travel	=	0	2,200	2,200
22 ASB members x $140 per diem x 2 days	=	0	6,160	6,160
22 teachers x $100 per person for travel	=	2,200	0	2,200
22 teachers x $140 per diem x 2 days	=	6,160	0	6,160
1 national speaker x $800 for travel	=	800	0	800
1 national speaker x $140 per diem x 2 days	=	280	0	280
2 state speakers x $400 per person for travel	=	800	0	800
2 state speakers x $140 per diem x 2 days	=	560	0	560
Subtotal	=	**$ 10,800**	**$ 8,360**	**$ 19,160**

Student Work Experience

20 students x $100 (each) for travel	=	2,000	0	2,000
20 students x $50 per diem x 14 days	=	14,000	0	14,000
Subtotal	=	**$ 16,000**	**$ 0**	**$ 16,000**

S-T-W Implementation Project in Schools

2 specialists x 22 sites x $100 for travel	=	4,400	0	4,400
2 specialists x 22 sites x $35 per diem x 3 days	=	4,620	0	4,620
Subtotal	=	**$ 9,020**	**$ 0**	**$ 9,020**
Travel and Per Diem Total	=	**$ 35,820**	**$ 8,360**	**$ 44,180**

Equipment and Expendable Supplies

Curriculum materials (22 x $1,000 per school)	=	22,000	0	22,000
Career and occupational information packets	=	0	1,000	1,000
Equipment and Expendable Supplies Total	=	**$ 22,000**	**$ 1,000**	**$ 23,000**

Contractual Services

Honorarium: 1 national speaker x $1,000	=	1,000	0	1,000
Honorarium: 2 state speakers x $500	=	1,000	0	1,000
Conference rental ($1,000 per day x 2 days)	=	2,000	0	2,000
Career center ($50 per sq ft x 400 sq ft)	=	0	20,000	20,000
Contractual Services Total	=	**$ 4,000**	**$ 20,000**	**$ 24,000**

Total Project Costs*	=	**$199,946**	**$67,176**	**$267,122**

*Note: No indirect (facilities and administrative) costs were allowed.

Exercise 7-1: Write a Cover Letter and Determine Proposal Delivery Method
(Chapter 7, pp. 179–180)

Sample Cover Letter

233 South Wacker ▪ Chicago, Illinois 60606   Sears Tower COLLEGE

February XX, 20XX

U.S. Department of Education
Application Control Center
1990 K Street, NW
Washington, D.C. 20202-4725
Attn: Ms. Pam Sarver, POC   **CFDA Number**

Re: Grant Application for CFDA #255G

Number of Proposals

Dear Ms. Sarver:

Sears Tower College (STC) is pleased to submit the enclosed grant application to the U.S. Department of Education in response to CFDA #255G. Enclosed are one original and eleven copies of our proposal, which includes the following sections:

- Problem/Need
- Goals/Objectives   **Proposal Contents**
- Project Activities
- Evaluation Plans
- Budget

If awarded, STC will commit high-level administrators to the successful completion of this project. If you have project oversight questions, please contact Dr. Gregory Maxwell, associate vice president of academic affairs. Dr. Maxwell has an extensive background in managing the successful completion of numerous large-scale grants and will serve as the administrative supervisor of the project. Dr. Maxwell can be reached at 312-555-1212 or gmaxwell@searstowercollege.edu.

If you have specific questions about the project, please contact Mr. Alex Robinson, project director, at 312-555-2123 or e-mail: arobinson@searstowercollege.edu.

Sincerely,   **Contact Person**

Dr. David Jackson

Dr. David Jackson, President
312-555-2120

c: Dr. Gregory Maxwell
        Mr. Alex Robinson

searstowercollege.edu ▪ stc@searstower.edu ▪ 800-555-1234

Answers to Exercise 7-1 continue on the next page.

Exercise 7-1: Write a Cover Letter and Determine Proposal Delivery Methods

(Chapter 7, pp. 179–180)

Possible Proposal Delivery Methods and Cost

Delivery Methods	Approximate Costs	Pros/Cons
Commercial Carrier www.fedex.com www.ups.com www.dhl.com	Prices will fluctuate. Check online or call commercial carrier for current rates.	Inexpensive compared to using personal automobile or airline. Commercial carrier is responsible for delivering the package. Commercial carrier flight may be cancelled due to bad weather.
Personal Automobile www.mapquest.com www.randmcnally.com maps.google.com	1,418 miles @ current government rate. See www.policyworks.gov. Must also consider costs for tolls, meals, and lost time.	You are responsible for delivering the package. Round trip is more than 24 hours. Must consider inclement weather.
Car Rental www.enterprise.com www.thrifty.com www.avis.com www.nationalcar.com www.hertz.com www.goalamo.com	Prices will fluctuate. Check online or call car rentals for current rates. Cost will also depend on size and model of car. Must also consider costs for tolls, meals, and lost time.	Same as personal automobile.
Airlines www.american.com www.delta.com www.nwa.com www.transworldairlines.com www.united.com www.usair.com	Prices will fluctuate. Check online or call airlines for current rates. Must also consider costs for Washington, D.C. ground transportation, meals, and lost time.	You are responsible for delivering the package. Airline flight may be cancelled due to bad weather.
Train www.amtrak.com	Prices will fluctuate. Check online or call Amtrak for current rates. Must also consider costs for Washington, D.C. ground transportation, meals, and lost time.	You are responsible for delivering the package. One-way travel time is approximately 18 hours.
Bus www.greyhound.com	Prices will fluctuate. Check online or call Greyhound for current rates. Must also consider costs for Washington, D.C. ground transportation, meals, and lost time.	You are responsible for delivering the package. One-way travel time is approximately 19 hours.
Kinko's www.kinkos.com	Prices will fluctuate. Check online or call Kinko's for current rates.	Kinko's is responsible for delivering the package. Entire grant application must be sent electronically to Kinko's for reproduction.

Exercise 8-1: Evaluate Proposals in Response to Criteria
(Chapter 8, pp. 202–212)

Sample Strengths/Weaknesses and Lessons Learned

Criterion #1: The proposal must clearly describe the need for supervisory training for small business owners.

Strengths/Weaknesses

Lincoln Department of Development provided a needs statement concerning supervisory training from a survey of small business owners. Jefferson Chamber of Commerce stated, "education is the key element to continually improve economic development," but did not provide feedback regarding the need for training small-business owners.

Lessons Learned

Always provide data-based statements to support the grant project need.

Criterion #2: The proposal must clearly describe a schedule for analyzing, designing, developing, implementing, and evaluating supervisory training.

Strengths/Weaknesses

Lincoln Department of Development provided a schedule for analyzing, designing, developing, implementing, and evaluating supervisory training tasks. The schedule showed a logical progression and overlap of activities across time. Jefferson Chamber of Commerce said it recognized the importance of having a detailed project schedule but failed to provide one.

Lessons Learned

Always provide exactly what is requested in the solicitation. Whenever possible provide a graphic presentation of activities with a time schedule. Include additional narrative to supplement the proposal schedule.

Criterion #3: The proposal must clearly describe time commitments of key personnel who will be responsible for completing the proposed activities.

Strengths/Weaknesses

Lincoln Department of Development provided a table that identified the names of key personnel, their positions, and time commitments allocated for completing the proposed project activities. Jefferson Chamber of Commerce provided narrative that did not indicate the names of key personnel.

Lessons Learned

Identify key personnel by name as well as their role in the proposed project. Do not bury key information in narrative. Use tables, charts, and figures to provide a summary of important information. Note: This is a quality issue rather than a compliance issue.

Answers to Exercise 8-1 continue on the next page.

Exercise 8-1: Evaluating Proposals in Response to Criteria (continued)
(Chapter 8, pp. 202–212)

Criterion #4: The proposal must clearly describe the involvement that stakeholder groups (administration, board members, small business owners, and the educational community) will have in training.

Strengths/Weaknesses

Lincoln Department of Development used the active voice, while Jefferson Chamber of Commerce used the passive voice in presenting information about stakeholders' roles.

Lessons Learned

Always use the active voice in presenting information in grant proposals.

Criterion #5: The proposal must clearly describe the project director's experience and training in strategic planning.

Strengths/Weaknesses

Lincoln Department of Development provided specific information about the executive director's experience and training, while Jefferson Chamber of Commerce presented vague information about the executive director's experience and training.

Lessons Learned

Always provide quantitative information about key grant personnel.

Criterion #6: The proposal must provide evidence of commitment to the project that indicates that the training program will be successful.

Strengths/Weaknesses

Lincoln Department of Development provided specific information about financial support and time commitments for this project. Jefferson Chamber of Commerce did not provide financial and time commitments for this project.

Lessons Learned

Indicate dedication for the proposed project by providing specific financial support and time commitments.

Criterion #7: In a single sentence, the proposal must clearly describe the project mission.

Strengths/Weaknesses

Lincoln Department of Development provided a one-sentence description of the project mission. Jefferson Chamber of Commerce used three sentences and did not describe the project mission.

Lessons Learned

Always provide exactly what is requested in the RFP/RFA, no more and no less.

Answers to Exercise 8-1 continue on the next page.

Exercise 8-1: Evaluating Proposals in Response to Criteria (continued)
(Chapter 8, pp. 202–212)

Criterion #8: In 30 pages or less, the proposal must address the following: (1) problem/need, (2) proposed activities, (3) key personnel, (4) commitment to broad-based participation, (5) evaluation plans, and (6) budget.

Strengths/Weaknesses

Lincoln Department of Development provided a table of contents that followed the order of required factors. Jefferson Chamber of Commerce provided a table of contents that did not follow the required factors and was more than 30 pages.

Lessons Learned

Always present information in the order requested in the grant criteria. Use the exact headings and subheadings identified in the RFP/RFA. Never provide more pages than requested.

Criterion #9: The proposal must clearly describe what materials will be produced during the development phase of the project.

Strengths/Weaknesses

Lincoln Department of Development presented a bulleted list of specific materials to be produced during the development phase of the project. Jefferson Chamber of Commerce provided narrative concerning the project materials to be produced.

Lessons Learned

Provide bulleted lists to highlight important proposal requirements. Always include the specific number of items to be produced.

Criterion #10: The proposal must clearly describe what performance indicators will be used to monitor the effectiveness of the program.

Strengths/Weaknesses

Lincoln Department of Development provided a bulleted list of performance indicators to monitor the effectiveness of the program. Jefferson Chamber of Commerce provided performance indicators in the narrative.

Lessons Learned

Do not bury important responses to grant criteria in the proposal narrative. Use a list of items to highlight important information.

Exercise 8-2: Evaluate Two Proposals

(Chapter 8, pp. 213–240)

Sample Strengths/Weaknesses and Lessons Learned

Author's note: Both proposals have strengths and weaknesses. Funding seekers should incorporate the strengths and avoid the weaknesses identified in these two proposals when preparing grant applications.

Instructors, Inc.

Strengths

- Philosophy was tailored for EagleEye Analysts
- Presents strategy to analyze needs before training
- Clear timeframe of tasks to be completed for each project phase
- Clear project management structure with lines of authority
- Clear presentation of personnel duties and responsibilities
- Strong evaluation plans (use of pretest/training/posttest to arrive at results)
- Clear identification of deliverables
- Attractive two-column proposal format (some agencies will not allow)
- Good use of textboxes to highlight key messages
- Good use of comparative figures with captions

Weaknesses

- Lacks evidence to support expertise in the aerial/satellite photograph analysis
- Lacks specific detail about teaching methods
- Repetitive use of the term "hands on"
- Some graphics provide limited information
- No discussion of post-evaluation activities (project sustainability)

Technical Trainers, Inc.

Strengths

- Provides evidence of expertise in aerial/satellite photograph analysis
- Thorough description of teaching philosophy
- Clear goals and objectives
- Detailed agenda
- Clear project steps
- Good match between objectives and methods
- Detailed narrative with organizational headings and subheadings
- Good use of bullet points

Weaknesses

- Boilerplate narrative is nonspecific—must customize for EagleEye Analysts
- Lack of information about the expertise of proposed personnel
- Lack of citations to support philosophy
- Lack of integrated graphics—figures lose impact in back of proposal
- Wordy "textbook" sentences and paragraphs
- Reference to exhibits are placed at the end of the proposal
- No discussion of post-evaluation activities (project sustainability)

Answers to Exercise 8-2 continue on the next page.

Exercise 8-2: Evaluating Two Proposals (continued)
(Chapter 8, pp. 213–240)

Sample Strengths/Weaknesses and Lessons Learned

- Include easy-to-understand proposal narrative that is well documented to support specific claims and demonstrate expertise in the field. Use short sentences and paragraphs to reduce reader fatigue. Use graphics and textboxes to support central messages, especially when the RFP/RFA limits the number of proposal pages.

- Avoid using generic boilerplate and "textbook" narrative. Know your audience and adapt your message to meet the government agency's wants and needs.

- Include clear and understandable project methods and procedures. Use a timeline that describes when activities will be accomplished. Use the active voice to describe activities and procedures.

- Include well-documented narrative that discusses the strength and expertise of key personnel who will manage the proposed project. Use an organizational chart to show lines of authority. Include résumés of key personnel in the appendix.

- Include strong evaluation plans that describe formative and summative methods to assess project outcomes. Include a discussion about how quantitative and qualitative data will be collected, analyzed, and reported to the government agency.

- Provide a proposal that is organized according to the RFP/RFA specifications. Provide only what is required.

- Include support material in a well-organized appendix. Include a table of contents with page numbers prior to appendix materials to help agency reviewers locate specific documents.

Appendix C

Answers to Comprehensive Review Questions
(Comprehensive Review Questions, pp. 261–268)

1. What are the primary sources for government (public) and non-government (private) funding? See Chapter 1, p. 1.

   - *Government funding* comes from federal and state agencies.
   - *Non-government funding* comes from individuals, corporations or philanthropic foundations.

2. What are three types of government funding?
   See Chapter 1, p. 1.

   - Grants
   - Cooperative agreements
   - Procurement contracts

3. What is the purpose of a government grant? See Chapter 1, p. 1.

   Government grants transfer money, property, or services to eligible recipients in order to accomplish a public purpose where no substantial involvement is anticipated between the funding agency and recipient during the performance period.

4. What is the difference between a discretionary grant and a mandatory grant?
   See Chapter 1, pp.1–2.

   - *Discretionary grants* are competitive grant opportunities in which the government agency has the authority to determine the award amount and recipients.
   - *Mandatory grants* are federal pass-through funds allocated by state agencies to institutions and organizations based on predetermined formulas.

5. What is the purpose of a cooperative agreement? See Chapter 1, p. 2.

   Cooperative agreements transfer money, property, or services to recipients to accomplish a public purpose where substantial involvement is anticipated between the funding agency and recipient during the performance period.

Answers to Comprehensive Review Questions continue on the next page.

6. What is meant by substantial involvement? See Chapter 1, p. 3.

   Substantial involvement is when government agency staff members provide assistance, guidance, or participation in the management of the project.

7. What is the purpose of a procurement contract? See Chapter 1, p. 3.

   Procurement contracts acquire property or services for the direct benefit of or use by the federal government.

8. What are two broad groupings of procurement contracts? See Chapter 1, p. 4.

   • Fixed-price contracts

   • Cost-reimbursement contracts

9. What is the primary search engine used by funding seekers to locate procurement contract solicitations over $25,000? See Chapter 1, p. 4.

   • FedBizOpps (www.fedbizopps.gov)

10. What are the major differences between assistance agreements (grants and cooperative agreements) and procurement contracts? See Chapter 1, p. 5.

Assistance Agreements (Grants and Cooperative Agreements)	Procurement Contracts
Information listed in the *Federal Register*	Information listed at *FedBizOpps.gov*
Project announcements	Competitive bidding announcements
Provides assistance	Procures property or services
Multiple awards	One award
Idea conceived/initiated by the funding seeker	Idea conceived/initiated by the agency
Funding seeker determines direction	Agency determines direction
Grant recipient may keep equipment	Government may keep equipment
Cost sharing may be required	Cost sharing is not required
Award contains general conditions	Award contains detailed specifications
Payments made upfront	Payments made after expenditures

Answers to Comprehensive Review Questions continue on the next page.

11. What are the differences between a restricted and an unrestricted gift?
See Chapter 1, p. 6.

  • An unrestricted gift is donated to an organization without contingencies.

  • A restricted gift is donated to an organization for a particular use.

12. What are the differences between government and non-government funding? See
Chapter 1, p. 7.

In general, government proposals are lengthy and require specific narrative and
budget components, while non-government proposals are usually brief and may
not require specific components. Peer reviewers evaluate government proposals,
while a board of directors reviews non-government proposals. Progress reports are
usually required by both funding sources.

13. What are the six distinct proposal development phases that funding seekers must
go through to prepare a winning grant application? See Chapter 2, p. 11.

  • Complete work before the RFP/RFA is released.

  • Conduct prewriting activities after the RFP/RFA is released.

  • Write, review, rewrite, and edit the proposal narrative.

  • Prepare, review, and revise the proposal budget.

  • Produce, assemble, and submit the grant application.

  • Perform postsubmission activities.

14. What are the steps involved in the grant process from legislation and acquisition to
award? See Chapter 2, p. 12.

  • Government legislation appropriates funding for a specific purpose.

  • The appropriate government agency disseminates the solicitation to the general
    public via the *Federal Register*.

  • Funding seekers develop grant applications in response to solicitation
    guidelines/criteria.

  • Funding seekers submit grant applications to the government agency before the
    deadline.

  • Reviewers read grant applications and make recommendations to the
    government agency.

  • Government agency awards financial assistance to organizations that submitted
    the best grant applications.

  • Winning grant organizations complete project activities within a time frame.

Answers to Comprehensive Review Questions continue on the next page.

15. What five activities should funding seekers complete before making a *preliminary* bid/no-bid decision? See Chapter 3, p. 23.

  • Identify a "good" project idea that addresses a problem/need.

  • Develop a proposal prospectus.

  • Search for funding opportunities.

  • Review potential solicitations.

  • Gather intelligence about solicitations.

16. If the *preliminary* decision is to bid, what activities should funding seekers complete prior to release of a government solicitation? See Chapter 3, p. 23.

  • Develop a "model" solicitation.

  • Identify a proposal director and key team members.

  • Determine needed partners, subcontractors, and consultants.

  • Write the preliminary proposal narrative.

  • Prepare the preliminary proposal budget.

17. What is a proposal prospectus? See Chapter 3, p. 26.

A proposal prospectus is a 1–2-page concept paper that provides details about the proposed project. The prospectus is used to communicate the project idea to upper management, proposal staff members, and potential government agency representatives.

18. What sources are used to locate grant opportunities? See Chapter 3, p. 29.

  • *Catalog of Federal Domestic Assistance*

  • *Federal Register*

  • Grants.gov

  • Community of Science

  • Grant-funding newsletters

  • Federal agency websites

  • Office of sponsored programs

  • Other sources

Answers to Comprehensive Review Questions continue on the next page.

19. What six components should funding seekers consider when reviewing a potential solicitation? See Chapter 3, p. 35.

    - Eligibility
    - Program purpose
    - Selection criteria
    - Funds available
    - Deadline date
    - Contact person

20. Who should funding seekers contact before making a preliminary bid/no-bid decision to submit a grant application? See Chapter 3, p. 37.

    - Point of contact
    - Past award winners
    - Government agency reviewers

21. What questions should funding seekers ask a Point of Contact before the RFP/RFA is released to the general public? See Chapter 3, p. 38.

    - Does the proposed project fall within the agency's funding priorities?
    - What is the total funding available? What is the average award?
    - Will awards be made on the basis of special criteria?
    - What is the anticipated application/award ratio?
    - What common mistakes have prevented funding seekers from winning?
    - What should be in a proposal that other applicants may have overlooked?
    - Should the proposal be written for reviewers with non-technical backgrounds?
    - How are proposals reviewed? How many grant applications are reviewers expected to read? How long do reviewers have to read the applications?
    - Would you send me the evaluation form used by reviewers to assess proposals?
    - Would you review a two- to three-page prospectus and/or proposal draft?

22. What questions should funding seekers ask past award winners? See Chapter 3, p. 41.

    - Did you contact the POC before writing the proposal?
    - Whom did you find most helpful on the government agency's staff?
    - Did the POC review a proposal draft prior to final submission?

Answers to Comprehensive Review Questions continue on the next page.

- What materials did you find most helpful in developing your grant proposal?
- *What was your problem/need statement and what approach did you use to improve the situation?*
- How close was your initial budget to the awarded amount? What budget items, if any, were cut?
- What would you do differently next time?
- Would you be willing to send us a copy of your winning grant application?

23. What is a "model" solicitation? See Chapter 3, p. 44.

A "model" solicitation is a "mock-up" RFP/RFA that funding seekers develop from information obtained from an analysis of similar solicitations from the same government agency.

24. Who are the key staff members of a proposal development team? See Chapter 3, p. 45.
    - Upper administration/management
    - Proposal director
    - Writer(s)
    - Financial/budget staff members
    - Reviewer(s)
    - Editor(s)
    - Graphic designer(s)
    - Partners, subcontractors, and consultants
    - Staff members from the office of sponsored programs

25. What are the pros and cons of using external grant writers to develop a grant application? See Chapter 3, p. 47.

    Pros
    - External grant writers bring a fresh perspective to the proposed project and usually have a thorough understanding of the grant development process and what it takes to win.
    - External grant writers develop proposals without interrupting the daily duties of staff members.

    Cons
    - External grant writers are usually expensive. Some grant writers charge a flat fee while others charge a percentage of the total award.
    - External grant writers will not be responsible for completing the daily activities identified in the proposed project if the grant is awarded.

Answers to Comprehensive Review Questions continue on the next page.

26. What major activities should grant seekers complete the first day after the release of a government solicitation? See Chapter 4, p. 73.

    - Analyze the RFP/RFA contents.
    - Identify ambiguities and request clarification.
    - Adjust/reevaluate estimated probability of winning.
    - Make formal bid/no-bid decision.

27. What questions should funding seekers answer before making a *formal* bid/no-bid decision about developing a grant application? See Chapter 4, p. 74.

    - Is this project consistent with the organization's mission and goals?
    - Is the organization qualified to complete the project in a timely manner?
    - Are organizational cost-sharing funds available to support this project?
    - Is there commitment by the organization beyond the funding period?

28. What proposal planning tools should funding seekers develop prior to holding a proposal strategy meeting? See Chapter 4, p. 76.

    - Compliance checklist
    - Proposal schedule
    - Proposal outline
    - Proposal style sheet

29. What major topics should be discussed at a grant proposal strategy meeting? See Chapter 4, p. 81.

    - Strategies/themes to be used in the proposal narrative
    - Key project cost items
    - Proposal writing assignments
    - Due dates for proposal drafts

30. What four skills should proposal writers possess? See Chapter 5, p. 97.

    - Subject-matter knowledge
    - Writing skills
    - Analytical and creative expertise
    - Marketing savvy

Answers to Comprehensive Review Questions continue on the next page.

31. What are the five "C's" of good proposal writing? See Chapter 5, p. 99.

    - Thorough understanding of the proposed project *content*
    - *Communicate* information to the reading audience
    - Seek *clarity* in proposal narrative
    - *Commit* to completing the grant writing tasks within a specified time
    - Be *consistent* with format and presentation of information

32. What major narrative sections are contained in most grant applications?
    See Chapter 5, p. 101.

    - Cover sheet   - Goals/Objectives
    - Table of Contents*   - Methods/Activities
    - Abstract   - Evaluation Plans
    - Introduction*   - References/Bibliography*
    - Problem/Need   - Appendix*

    Note: *Indicates an optional proposal narrative component.

33. What are the guidelines for writing a good problem/need statement?
    See Chapter 5, p. 106.

    - Document a problem/need that relates directly to the government agency's
      interest. Be succinct, yet use sufficient evidence to provide a convincing
      argument.
    - Identify a problem/need of reasonable size that is manageable.
    - Describe a problem/need within a context. Use comparison data to show how
      your problem/need compares to others.
    - Provide an original and innovative project idea, approach, or vision to solve,
      reduce, or improve a problem. Avoid painting a hopeless situation.

34. What are the guidelines for developing good goals/objectives?
    See Chapter 5, p. 109.

    - Listed in chronological order of achievement
    - Measurable in quantitative terms
    - Ambitious, but attainable
    - Practical and cost effective

Answers to Comprehensive Review Questions continue on the next page.

35. What major topics are discussed in a good methods/activities section of a grant application? See Chapter 5, pp. 111–114.

   - Plan of work that identifies specific tasks designed to meet project goals/objectives within the government agency's performance period
   - Management plans identify the names and titles of key personnel to be used in the project as well as indicating the lines of authority within the organization
   - Key personnel qualifications and time commitments

36. What are two forms of evaluation used in grant applications? See Chapter 5, p. 117.

   - Formative evaluation is used to monitor the initial and ongoing progress of a grant project.
   - Summative evaluation is used to judge the overall quality or worth of a grant at the end of the project.

37. What documents are commonly found in a grant application appendix? See Chapter 5, p. 120.

   - Organizational mission statements
   - Résumés of key project members or job descriptions of personnel to be hired
   - Letters of support and letters of commitment
   - Evaluation instruments (tests, questionnaires, etc.)
   - Annual reports and other supplemental documentation

38. What is the difference between a "letter of support" and a "letter of commitment?" See Chapter 5, pp. 120–122.

   - *Letters of support* come from individuals within or outside the institution applying for the grant (e.g., politicians, community leaders, and local business and industry representatives) who endorse of the merit of the proposal but will not have an active role in the project.
   - *Letters of commitment* come from individuals or organizations that will be actively involved in your proposed project. These letters should document specific financial and non-financial commitments (personnel time, office equipment, materials, supplies, building space, etc.) to the project.

Answers to Comprehensive Review Questions continue on the next page.

39. What is the purpose of an Institutional Review Board (IRB)? See Chapter 5, p. 123.

An IRB consists of selected members of an institution who review and approve research to ensure that the rights and welfare of human subjects are protected. The IRB does not judge the science or worth of the research effort, but rather serves as an ethical reviewer of the proposed research.

40. What government agency certifications or assurances are often included in a grant application? See Chapter 5, pp. 124–125.

- Antidiscrimination
- Drug-free workplace
- Lobbing restrictions
- Sex and age discrimination
- Health, safety, and welfare of human subjects
- Public employee standards

41. What are two types of proposal editing? See Chapter 5, p. 126.

- Content editing focuses on accuracy and completeness of proposal ideas.
- Style editing focuses on clarity and readability of proposal ideas.

42. What "boilerplate" documents are often used to prepare a grant proposal? See Chapter 5, p. 129.

- Institutional mission statements/strategic plans
- Reports from studies, community forums, and case studies that document current problems that will be addressed as a result of grant funding
- Goals/objectives from approved proposals completed by your organization
- Various time/task and project organizational charts
- Successful evaluation strategies used in similar winning grant proposals
- List of components included in your institution's fringe benefits package

43. What five *direct* cost items are used in grant budgets? See Chapter 6, p. 137.

- Personnel salaries and fringe benefits
- Travel and per diem
- Equipment and expendable supplies
- Contractual services
- Other direct costs

Answers to Comprehensive Review Questions continue on the next page.

44. According to Office of Management and Budget Circular A-21, what four criteria are used to judge "allowable" costs for sponsored projects? See Chapter 6, p. 139.

   - Reasonable
   - Allocable
   - Consistent treatment
   - Conform to limitations

45. What six *indirect* (facilities and administrative) cost items are used in grant budgets? See Chapter 6, pp. 140–141.

   - Facility operation and maintenance expenses (e.g., utility costs, custodial service costs, non-capital improvements, and insurance premiums)
   - Library charges (books, library facilities, and library administration)
   - General administrative expenses (e.g., accounting, payroll, and purchasing)
   - Departmental administrative expenses
   - Office of sponsored programs administrative expenses
   - Student services

46. What is an indirect cost-rate agreement? See Chapter 6, p. 141.

   Organizations that develop grant proposals on a regular basis will often negotiate an indirect cost-rate agreement with a cognizant agency that is honored by other government agencies when applying for grants. Indirect cost-rate agreements establish a specific indirect cost percentage of the total direct costs or modified total direct costs. Indirect cost-rate agreements are negotiated with a federal agency every three years.

47. What are total direct costs and modified total direct costs? See Chapter 6, pp. 141–142.

   Total direct costs are all direct costs charged to a project.

   Modified total direct costs are total direct costs excluding equipment and capital expenditures, patient care, tuition remission, rental costs, scholarships and fellowships, and subawards in excess of $25,000.

Answers to Comprehensive Review Questions continue on the next page.

48. What are two cost-sharing categories used in grant proposals?
    See Chapter 6, pp. 143–144.

    - *In-kind* contributions are non-financial donations to the proposed project from the grant-seeking institution, partners, and local business and industry.

    - *Matching funds* are cash that comes from the institution's general operating funds, private donations, foundation funds, or other sources.

49. What are budget detail and budget narrative? See Chapter 6, pp. 146–147.

    - *Budget detail* is a brief description of how project expenditures were determined (e.g., three computers @$1,500 = $4,500). These parenthetical statements must explain each line item so information is clear to reviewers.

    - *Budget narrative* provides a written explanation of complex or unusual expenditures. Narrative is not necessary when costs are straightforward.

50. What are three common budget problems with grant applications?
    See Chapter 6, p. 153.

    - Arithmetic errors in subtotals and totals
    - Lack of budget detail
    - Unrealistic costs for budget items
    - Budget items are inconsistent with proposal narrative
    - Little or no budget narrative
    - Vague and unexplained source(s) for cost-sharing dollars
    - Indirect costs are missing from budgets

51. What four steps should funding seekers follow when submitting grant applications electronically through the Grants.gov portal? See Chapter 7, pp. 168–169.

    - Download the appropriate grant application package and instructions.
    - Complete the necessary grant application documents and forms offline.
    - Upload all documents and forms and submit the application online.
    - Track the status of the completed grant application.

52. What three components are found in a good proposal transmittal (cover) letter?
    See Chapter 7, pp. 171–173.

    - RFP/RFA or *CFDA* number
    - Number of proposals in package as well as contents of each proposal
    - Address, telephone number, and e-mail address of contact person

Answers to Comprehensive Review Questions continue on the next page.

53. What are two reasons to hold a debriefing meeting with writers and reviewers after the grant application has been submitted? See Chapter 8, p. 181.

   • Discuss proposal strengths and weaknesses

   • Prepare to answer government agency questions about the grant application

54. What questions should proposal team members attempt to answer at the debriefing meeting? See Chapter 8, p. 181.

   • Is the proposal compliant?

   • Are project claims substantiated?

   • Are project benefits emphasized?

   • Are costs appropriate?

55. When are government agencies not obligated to review grant applications? See Chapter 8, p. 183.

   • Eligibility requirements were not met

   • Review criteria were not addressed

   • Proposal preparation guidelines were not followed

   • Proposal funding exceeds the agency's limits

   • Proposal was submitted after the deadline

56. What basic questions do agency reviewers answer when evaluating grant applications? See Chapter 8, p. 185.

   • Is the proposed project consistent with the agency's funding priorities?

   • Were proposal guidelines followed?

   • Is there a compelling problem/need statement for this project, and is it well documented?

   • Is the project's purpose (goals and objectives) clearly identified?

   • Do the methods/activities describe specific tasks to meet the project's goals/objectives? Do project personnel have the knowledge, skills, and commitment to carry out the project tasks within the period of performance?

   • Will the proposed evaluation plans determine project effectiveness?

   • Is the budget within the agency's funding range, well justified, and accurate?

   • Is the grant proposal well written, logical, reasonable, and free from errors?

Answers to Comprehensive Review Questions continue on the next page.

57. What are three reasons why grant proposals are not funded? See Chapter 8, p. 189.

   • Lack of a good idea that addresses a problem/need

   • Superficial, unfocused, or unrealistic project methods

   • Poor evaluation plans

58. What three activities should be completed if your grant proposal is not funded? See Chapter 8, pp. 189–191.

   • Request a debriefing meeting with the Point of Contact

   • Request a copy of reviewers' comments (if none were received)

   • Request copies of several winning grant applications

59. What information is included in most grant award documents? See Chapter 8, p. 193.

   Most grant award documents contain information regarding the following:

   • Amount of funds awarded,

   • Period of performance,

   • Work to be done,

   • Financial and performance reports and deadlines,

   • Contractual conditions, and

   • Other documents incorporated by reference.

60. What are three characteristics of successful grant projects? See Chapter 8, p. 195.

   Successful grant projects:

   • Begin the project on time,

   • Complete all activities within the budget period and the funds authorized,

   • Schedule regular meetings with key project personnel to keep them informed,

   • Keep in-house administration informed about the project,

   • Complete the evaluation plan as specified in the proposal,

   • Recognize project problems and develop solutions,

   • Prepare and submit timely project reports, and

   • Prepare and submit accurate and timely financial reports.

Appendix D

Evaluation Rubric for Comprehensive Review Exercise
(Comprehensive Review Exercise, pp. 269–272)

Name: _____	Date: _____	
Evaluation Criteria	**Value**	**Score**
Transmittal (Cover) Letter • Organizational letterhead • RFP number • Proposal contents • Contact person, phone number, and e-mail address • Appropriate signature	5%	
Grant Application Cover Sheet and Project Abstract • Comprehensive project description • 200 words or less	10%	

Project Narrative (maximum five pages)
• Problem/Need with recent and relevant citations (15 points)
• Goals/Objectives that identify measurable project outcomes (10 points)
• Methods/Activities (25 points)
    • Plan of work—logical and detailed description of project activities
    • Key personnel—qualifications, responsibilities, and time commitments
    • Management plan—organizational structure of project
    • Timeline—reasonable time to complete major project activities
• Evaluation plan (10 points)
    • Formative and summative assessment strategies
    • Staff member responsible for evaluation
    • Activity reports—information to be sent to agency
	60%	

Budget • Direct cost for project with detail and narrative, where appropriate (15 points) • Matching funds represent 25% of total costs (5 points)	20%	
References • Citations—recent and relevant documents • Format, style, and consistency—follows an acceptable writing manual	2%	
Appendix • Relevant materials—includes important materials that support the project • Organization—neatly organized so agency reviewers can find documents	3%	
Total	100%	

Index

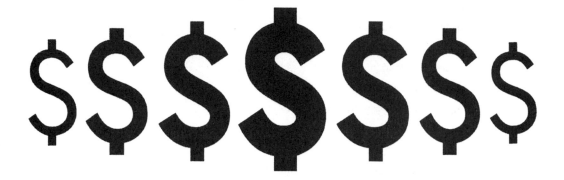

Still need help?

Our customized grant workshops are designed to walk funding seekers through the major phases of the grant development process.

Professor and author Patrick W. Miller, Ph.D. shares the tips and tricks of grant writing in one- or two-day workshops.

To schedule a workshop, go to

www.grantwritingpro.com